The Principal's Guide to Improving Reading Instruction

Robert L. Hillerich

Bowling Green State University

Allyn and Bacon, Inc.
Boston   London   Sydney   Toronto

Copyright © 1983 by Allyn and Bacon, Inc.
7 Wells Avenue, Newton, Massachusetts 02159

Library of Congress Cataloging in Publication Data

Hillerich, Robert L., 1927–
    The principal's guide to improving reading instruction.

    Includes bibliographical references and index.
    1. Reading.   2. School superintendents and principals.   I. Title.
LB1050.H54   1983   372.4'1   82-18447
ISBN 0-205-07820-6

10 9 8 7 6 5 4 3 2 1 88 87 86 85 84 83

Printed in the United States of America.

To Dottie

Contents

Preface

This book is intended for the principal's individual reference and guidance, both for personal growth and as a handbook for leadership among the staff in reading instruction. It may also be used as inservice material for principals as a group, as well as by them to inservice their staffs. With a slight shift in point of view, it can be a valuable guide for general supervisors or consultants, and may be used by them as a guide for the inservice of teachers. The topics and suggestions provide an outline for extensive inservice.

The purpose of this book is to help you, as a busy principal or consultant, to become aware of your role in reading instruction and to help you establish some priorities in the teaching of reading by examining some of the important issues that you can lead your staff to investigate.

This book has been many years in developing. It began with ideas accumulated in the days when I was a young principal interested in—but knowing little about—the teaching of reading. Ultimately, it is a composite of those ideas found workable from experience, along with evidence from research and authoritative opinion, as well as the good practices observed—and stolen from—the many dedicated principals with whom I have worked.

Administrators' workshops in a number of states have helped to smooth off the rough edges. I am particularly grateful to many principals and consultants in Iowa and Ohio for their practical reactions to a series of principals' workshops and for their input of concerns and problems.

It is not the intent of this volume to imply that the principal must become a "reading expert." While this certainly would not be objectionable, few principals have the time or the inclination to become that specialized. On the other hand, any principal who hopes to be effective must be, among the many other things, the educational leader in the school. Hence, the principal must be a model and must know enough about the teaching of reading to assess its effectiveness, to set priorities, to ask the right questions, and to know where to turn for answers. And what area of the elementary school curriculum is more important than the teaching of reading?

I have made no attempt to include or to duplicate content of Administration 101 or Community Relations 102. We assume basic knowledge of administration and techniques of communicating. Now we deal with *what* should be done and communicated about the reading program.

While the text is documented adequately if you want to follow-up on any remarks, it has been kept free of the usual footnotes. Annotated reference lists at the end of each chapter may be pursued, but are offered with the intent that many such items, relating to a topic to be explored with staff, will be delegated. After all, the leader who gets too far ahead of the staff is no longer leading anyone.

Finally, Chapters 1 through 3 are a foundation and, therefore, ought to be read first. After that, you may dip into the remaining chapters in any sequence, choosing items that may already be a high priority with you and your staff. Chapters 4 through 8 do follow a sequence that is somewhat logical, but not necessary.

Note: Type had already been set for this book when "Title 1" was changed to "Chapter 1." Since the change in nomenclature resulted in no substantive change in program or in identification of pupils, use of the original term should present no problems.

CHAPTER 1

You Are Important!

Much has been said about the importance of the teacher to the success of any reading program. In fact, one of the primary conclusions of the National First Grade Studies (1966) was that there is more difference between two teachers using the same reading program than there is between different reading programs. From this came the conventional wisdom that the teacher makes all the difference.

Of course, those studies only investigated teacher and reading program variables, with their effect on the reading achievement of children. Naturally, given a choice between a good teacher or a good program, you and I would agree that the teacher is more important. Now, however, I would like to go a step further to insist that it is the principal who makes even more difference!

One of the major studies supporting the importance of the principal's role in improving reading instruction was a report from the New York State Office of Education (1974) on two inner-city schools. These schools were matched, with half the population of each on welfare. One was a high-achieving and one a low-achieving school. This study indicated that the major differences between the two schools were factors that were under school control; the outstanding finding was that the behavior of administrators was most influential. The administrators in the high-achieving school had a "plan" for reading. This does not mean, necessarily, that they were reading specialists; it does mean that they supported and provided time for planning the reading program.

1

Related to this kind of finding is the Cane and Smithers study (1971) from London, England. They included twelve infant schools in deprived areas, half of which were high-achieving and half low-achieving schools. One of the major differences between the two kinds of schools was the lack of systematic instruction in the low-achieving schools. Of course, this is a factor that is—or certainly should be—under the control of the principal.

A three-year study by the Philadelphia Public Schools (1979) indicated that principals who had a background in reading instruction had students who made greater gains. Another finding indicated that the more time principals observed teachers in reading classes, the higher the children achieved. While this particular study may have some flaws in design, it certainly falls in line with other studies, as well as with common sense.

Miller (1976) also supported the importance of the role of the principal in improving pupil achievement. On the other hand, Miller pointed out that merely having good organizational skills—skills that result in cooperation and efficiency—can help to implement bad programs as well. Hence, the principal must have some knowledge and understanding of what reading is all about if he or she is to lead in positive directions.

If any doubt remains about the importance of the principal's role and the need for the principal to be knowledgable about reading instruction, examine Laffey's (1980) summary of research on this topic. He concluded: "Among other things, the principal needs to establish reading as a priority in the academic curriculum; to act as the key change agent in adopting new programs (insuring adequate resources and materials, providing inservice training, and judiciously supporting experimentation); to act as a constructive evaluator; and to present the reading program in a favorable light to the community at large" (p. 634).

WHAT IS THE ROLE OF THE PRINCIPAL?

Essentially, you, as principal, must serve three functions if you are to improve the instructional program in reading in your school. In plain English, you must:

1. Grease the skids.
2. Pay attention.
3. Use a compass.

The first point refers to the principal's role as a manager or facilitator. It includes not only provision of the basic physical materials and equipment, but also includes establishment of a climate for good interpersonal relationships—

that group cohesiveness and harmony that lead to higher productivity. It also, of course, encompasses the proper scheduling of time and the elimination of unnecessary interruptions. While incidental comments are scattered throughout this book relating to this area of administration, our emphasis is really on the other two functions of the principal.

The second point—paying attention—means that the principal must monitor the program. This is the area of supervision, and it requires not only that the principal be present but that the principal *value* reading improvement.

Doesn't every principal value reading? I am certain any principal who is asked would assure us that reading is the most important area taught in the elementary school. On the other hand, how many principals demonstrate their value of reading through their actions? And actions demonstrate values far more clearly to teachers and children than do words.

Do you work with your staff to see that they have adequate time for reading instruction? Do you establish schedules that provide for a minimum of interference with the teaching of reading? Do you work with your staff to plan for reading? Do you participate in staff inservice meetings about reading, or do you merely introduce the speaker and then go out to take care of the latest report that is due in the central office?

Logan and Erickson (1979) presented some telling evidence on this latter point. They surveyed 204 elementary teachers about their inservice programs. Among the responses they sought were teacher ratings of the principals' involvement in inservice programs. There were two ratings, one in terms of quantity and one in terms of the quality of principals' participation. On a scale of one to five, the largest percentage of ratings, on both quantity and quality, fell at the lowest point. Most teachers saw the quantity of principals' participation as "very limited" and the quality as "not helpful."

The third function—using a compass—is to assure that changes in instruction are in the right direction. After all, we could facilitate and value so well that we move very rapidly and efficiently in the *wrong* direction. The principal must work with staff to clarify goals and philosophy. The principal must get help on the details, either from print or through specialists who have expert knowledge of the field. Such help may be from teachers on the staff who have advanced knowledge or specialization in reading, local reading consultants, or outside professionals.

Sound guidance is essential. Stoll (1977) reported, on the basis of 114 schools in Florida, that "overachieving" schools were those in which the reading program was more like exemplary programs in that they followed expert opinion. She suggested that educational decision makers ought to make use of research and informed professional opinion in guiding their reading programs.

Finally, on this point, you must be certain that any special staff you select is the most qualified. For example, the outstanding first-grade teacher is not necessarily the best qualified to be a reading teacher or consultant. Sometimes such a person is an excellent first-grade teacher as a result of personality or understanding of children, but that person may not necessarily have the professional background or the interpersonal skills and understandings to be successful in relating to adults.

WHAT'S YOUR EXCUSE?

We have all seen the teacher poster that says, "Nobody said teaching was going to be easy." We might replace those words with even larger print saying, "Nobody said principaling was going to be easy!"

For one thing, in contrast to principals, teachers are at least somewhat trained for their jobs. As Damon (1978) said, " . . . people with degrees in educational administration are no better qualified for the principalship than they would be if they had received a degree in another field or had none at all." You got your training, as any principal does, *after* you took your first principalship.

While there has been an ebb and flow in terms of emphasis—and there certainly has been an increase in pressures—there has been no dramatic change in the role of the principal in the past few decades. The expansion of materials and specialists in the 1960s often led to relinquishment of the leadership role of principals in curriculum. Now, with a reduction in support staff, combined with citizen demands for increased emphasis on "the basics," some principals have found themselves out of touch with curricular detail.

The increase in bureaucracy and central office demands have also reduced some principals to the role of middle-management in the sense that they have become little more than extended paper-shufflers for the central office. Yet, in a report of the Belmont Conference, Houts (1975) indicated that the principals participating in that conference found no task that could not be delegated—*except that of leadership!*

Houts also reported little change in the problems of the principal. Added to the already existing multitude have been the issues of collective bargaining and minority groups. The former has helped to shape the role of the principal in decision-making, whereby that function is now a shared or group process. And that's not all bad! Shared decision-making does not remove the principal from the role of leadership or decision-making; the principal is still as influential as he or she is informed. In other words, shared decision-making puts the true leadership in the hands of those who deserve it in terms of their understanding rather than in terms of their position.

In travels about the country, I have observed that every school building has an educational leader, and that leader is not always the building principal. If the principal becomes occupied with papers and telephone, someone else fills the vacuum. In some cases, the gap is filled with the overt help of the principal who is busy or uninformed and suggests that the teacher "Go see

Miss Taylor." After enough teachers have been told to see Miss Taylor, they don't even bother the principal; they automatically go to Miss Taylor.

The "Miss Taylor" who replaces the principal has various official titles, but clearly she has the leadership in the building. Leadership in different schools has been assumed by—or given away to—the reading teacher, the LD teacher, the psychologist, or even the school clerk. Who is the educational leader in your building?

SOME FIRST STEPS

Listed here are just a few basics of organization that might be considered. They are some easy first steps toward involvement in the improvement of reading instruction, and they announce that you *do* value reading. Any of these steps ought to be taken right along with your staff, since no one can be a leader unless there are followers.

Professional Reading

In addition to your own reading of such journals as *Principal, Educational Leadership,* and *Phi Delta Kappan,* you should have in your school, for yourself and teachers, the two main journals of language arts teachers: *The Reading Teacher* and *Language Arts.* If you are responsible for middle school or secondary, you would also want *The Journal of Reading* and *English Journal.* Furthermore, it is wise to keep abreast of articles that might appear in some of the popular "supermarket" variety of magazines.

Periodically, call attention to a professional article that is especially pertinent to concerns in your school. Provide time for discussion of such at a regular faculty meeting. In fact, the agenda for *every* staff meeting ought to include some element of reading instruction. The time is there if more of the administrative details are relegated to bulletins.

Time to Teach

Of all the things a principal can do to improve reading instruction, nothing is more simple, more obvious, or more effective than merely seeing to it that teachers have time to teach and that they are aware of the importance of this factor. Sit down with your staff to discuss what you and they can do to assure this vital element.

And vital it is! Wiley and Harnischfeger (1974) reported that mere "exposure to schooling" (including such factors as attendance, length of school day, and length of school year) was a significant contributor to achievement. Gettinger and White (1979) supported this strongly when they reported that "time to learn" is a more significant factor in achievement than is IQ. Yap (1977) indicated that 60 to 70 percent of the variance in reading achievement related to the amount of reading done; only 22 to 25 percent related to IQ.

Despite such findings, how much time is lost in a school day? I observed a first-grade class where the teacher was about to begin instruction with a reading group. A knock at the door signaled a parent collecting raffle tickets. As soon as the teacher settled with the parent and started to sit with her group, there was another knock at the door. This time it was a sixth-grade girl collecting the milk money. That settled, the teacher was once more about to begin the reading lesson when the loudspeaker went on. Now it was the principal with some momentous decision about whether there would be indoor or outdoor recess. In that one day, with that one reading group, the teacher lost exactly fourteen minutes of instructional time. For what they were getting in reading, those children might as well have been absent for three months of the year.

Once the obvious eaters of time have been eliminated with your staff, take the next step. *Time* for reading instruction is not going to do the job if that time is spent by children coloring workbook pictures while the teacher corrects other pages. How much time is spent *on task?* This question is not to quarrel with independent reading (see Chapter 6), since children also learn to read by reading; however, instruction in basic skills is also important. In her observations of reading comprehension instruction, Durkin (1978–1979) found that less than 1 percent of the time was actually devoted to instruction.

Visit and Observe

Too often "Teacher Evaluation" is nothing more than a "pass/fail" grade on a report card for the teacher. Classroom observations ought to go beyond this perfunctory level. They ought to be springboards for improving the instructional program. As such, they must be done by a principal who knows something about the reading program—who knows what to look for—and who then sits down with the teacher to discuss their mutual goals and assessment.

Before we can get to this, however, let's remove one hurdle. The immediate response to the suggestion for visitation is, "I'd really like to, but I just can't find the time."

We all make time for what we *value!* Yes, it is easier to sit in the office and get that next report done, and be interrupted in that task by all of those phone calls. Keep a record for just one week of exactly how you spend your time. Then analyze that record and see what can be combined, what delegated, and what forgotten. You will find, for example, that the fifteen phone calls scattered through your day can be taken as messages. Half will not require your attention; the other half can be handled collectively in one-fourth the time they would have taken separately.

Find any open time you have on your calendar, whether it be the day after tomorrow or next week. Schedule yourself to visit a classroom. Let nothing change your schedule any more than you would cancel a scheduled conference that you were to have with the superintendent or with the board president.

What do you look for during the visit to the classroom? Once you get beyond evaluating interpersonal relationships, organization, time on task, and so on (all of which are important in their own right), you will want to observe the effectiveness of reading instruction. That is what most of the balance of this book is about: the identification of priorities, things to look for in your reading program.

A very simple, albeit important, preparation for your observations is to read the introduction in the teacher's guide (or course of study) of whatever reading program you are using. In most reading programs, that introduction is a whole course in the teaching of reading. It establishes philosophy, methods, skill emphases, and will give you some important clues to look for.

Unless your staff is very different from most, they have not read that introduction either. It can become an excellent topic for a "bootstrap" inservice program in your building meetings. Have each teacher bring a manual and walk them through, discussing important points. It does not matter that each has a different level of the program, since the introductory portion is usually the same in all levels.

Add Spice to the Year

Possibly one of the most important contributions for children from the "innovative '60s" was recognition of the Hawthorne Effect. People involved in an experiment tend to perform better, regardless of the experimental variable imposed. In other words, if you put an armband on every other child (or teacher, for that matter) and said, "You are our experimental group," in all likelihood they would perform better than the others. Why don't you use this phenomenon to perk up those January to March doldrums?

Teachers usually have, or can be helped to identify, some question about instruction or about their children. Help them to verbalize this and to engage in a little action research to investigate it. While they may not revolutionize the teaching of reading, they may renew or enliven their interest and may be helped to take a closer look at their children and their teaching.

Topics for such investigations can be pulled from ideas presented in the balance of this book. They may include everything from assessing the oral language development of entering kindergarten children to the effectiveness of a particular technique in developing a critical reading skill.

SUMMARY

Even in these days of negotiating and bargaining, the principal is a model for teachers. Whether you are a leader for better or for worse, teachers are susceptible to your priorities. They react to your body language in much the same way that children react to theirs. What you do is often more important than what you say.

Evidence has been cited that shows the importance of the principal in improving reading instruction. That influence has been discussed in terms of three areas of expertise: the principal as a facilitator of reading instruction, as a monitor of its implementation, and as a beacon for its direction.

There has been no intent to suggest that the principal must become an expert in the teaching of reading. It is, however, imperative that the effective principal know some of the highlights and establish with the staff the priorities for reading instruction within the school. A few simple techniques were outlined that will aid the principal in participating in the improvement of reading instruction and in demonstrating to the staff that reading is "valued" in the school.

References

Cane, Brian, and Smithers, Jane. *The Roots of Reading: A Study of 12 Infant Schools in Deprived Areas.* London: National Foundation for Educational Research in England and Wales, 1971. Investigated factors that distinguished high- and low-ranking schools. Major positive factors were systematic instruction and teacher direction of learning.

Damon, Parker. "Inservice Blues." *Principal* 57 (March 1978): 45–51. Discusses the need for inservice of principals.

Durkin, Dolores. "What Classroom Observations Reveal about Reading Comprehension Instruction." *Reading Research Quarterly* 14 (1978–1979): 481–533. Based on observations of twenty-four fourth-grade reading classes and social studies classes in grades 3–6, Durkin found practically no comprehension instruction in the latter and only 1 percent in the former. Largest proportion of time was spent in assessment or help with assignments.

Gettinger, Maribeth, and White, Mary Alice. "Which Is the Stronger Correlate of School Learning? Time to Learn or Measured Intelligence?" *Journal of Educational Psychology* 71 (August 1979): 405–412. Based on two studies in grades 4–6, the authors reported that time to learn had a higher correlation with achievement than did IQ (.88 and .86 vs. .67 and .68).

Houts, Paul L. "The Changing Role of the Elementary School Principal: Report of a Conference." *Principal* 55 (November/December 1975): 62–73. Extensive report on the Belmont Conference, with a final recommendation that principals need "more extensive and improved inservice education." This one is worth reading in its entirety.

Laffey, James L. "The Role of the Elementary Principal in the School Reading Program." *The Reading Teacher* 33 (February 1980): 632–634. Summarizes ERIC research on the importance of the principal in improving reading instruction.

Logan, John W., and Erickson, Lawrence. "Elementary Teachers' Reading Inservice Preferences." *The Reading Teacher* 33 (December 1979): 330–334. Based on a survey of 204 elementary teachers. Reports their preferences and their rating of principals' participation.

Miller, William C. "Can a Principal's Improved Behavior Result in Higher Pupil Achievement?" *Educational Leadership* 33 (February 1976): 336–338. Supports the principal's role, but indicates that good organizational skills may enhance implementation of poor programs as well as good ones.

National First Grade Studies. *The Reading Teacher* 19 (May 1966). The entire issue is devoted to an overview and reports of the individual studies making up the collection.

New York Office of Education. "School Factors Influencing Reading Achievement: A Case Study of Two Inner City Schools." New York State Office of Education, 1974 (ERIC ED 089-211). Investigated two matched schools, one high-achieving and one low-achieving. Major differences were related to factors under school control.

Philadelphia Public Schools. *What Works in Reading?* Philadelphia: Office of Research and Evaluation, School District of Philadelphia, 1979. A three-year study of fourth graders' gains in reading scores, supporting the importance of the principal as a contributor.

Stoll, Lynn J. "Teacher Perceptions of Reading Practices in Overachieving and Underachieving Florida Elementary Schools." Doctoral dissertation, University of Miami, 1977 (ERIC ED 158-233). Data from 753 primary teachers in 114 schools indicated that "overachieving" schools had programs in line with expert opinion in reading.

Wiley, David, and Harnischfeger, Annegret. "Explosion of a Myth: Quantity of Schooling and Exposure to Instruction, Major Educational Vehicles." *Educational Researcher* 3 (April 1974): 7–12. Significant variables on achievement were found to be "prior pupil characteristics" and "exposure to schooling." The latter was analyzed to include attendance, length of school day, and length of school year.

Yap, Kim Onn. "Relationships between Amount of Reading Activity and Reading Achievement." *Reading World* 17 (October 1977): 23–29. Based on 202 second-grade pupils, Yap concluded that number of books read had a greater influence on achievement than did IQ.

Professional Journals

Educational Leadership. Association for Supervision and Curriculum Development, 225 North Washington Street, Alexandria, VA 22314.

Elementary School Journal. University of Chicago Press, 5801 Ellis Avenue, Chicago, IL 60637.

Language Arts and/or *English Journal.* National Council of Teachers of English, 1111 Kenyon Road, Urbana, IL 61801.

Phi Delta Kappan. Phi Delta Kappa, Eighth and Union, Box 789, Bloomington, IN 47402.

Principal. National Association of Elementary School Principals, 1801 North Moore Street, Arlington, VA 22209.

The Reading Teacher and/or *Journal of Reading.* International Reading Association, 800 Barksdale Road, Box 8139, Newark, DE 19711.

CHAPTER 2

Speak Up for Reading!

Do you feel buffeted about? Perhaps that is partly because you are a buffer in many ways. You are a buffer between child and teacher, sometimes between teacher and teacher, between teacher and parent, and between staff and community, to mention just a few. This chapter deals with the latter—your readiness to discuss your school's reading program, and to interpret the reading skills data to the community.

OPEN SEASON ON READING

It is always open season on reading, partly because nothing else in the schools attracts as much public interest as the teaching of reading and the reading achievement of students. Periodically, individuals use popular journals or the press to lash out at the status of reading instruction in this country. At times the attacks are by vested interest groups with their own axes to grind.

"Back to basics" is the current clarion call of those who would criticize the teaching of reading. These are the people who say reading isn't taught as well as it was in "the good old days." Roger Farr, past president of the International Reading Association, likes to point out that, when asked to define "the good old days," individuals define them as "when I was in school," regardless of whether the person speaking is forty, fifty, sixty, or ninety years of age.

A roll call of individual critics in the past three decades would include such people as Richover, Hersey, Walcutt, Trace, and Flesch. Interestingly, they have in common a lack of background in elementary education, not to mention the teaching of reading. While these are past history, new names will arise in the future, just as certainly as the popular press benefits more from controversy than it does from praise of existing institutions.

Unfortunately—although perhaps *fortunately* for the busy principal—most parents are too apathetic to be bothered by such general criticisms. Another large portion of the parents may nod their collective heads about the sad state of affairs in the country at large, but may have enough confidence in their local school to know "it isn't happening here." The size of this group will depend upon the extent to which you and your staff have kept parents informed about reading instruction in your school.

Finally, a few people will become upset enough about the article to contact school officials. When they do, are you prepared to give a sound educational answer, and one that is not just a shaky defensive mechanism? Your answer to parents may well be in two major parts: (1) tell them the status of reading instruction as it really is, and (2) describe your own school's reading program in relation to the criticisms made in the article or book they read.

In taking your position, do not immediately assume that every critic of reading instruction is wrong, or that any single one is wrong on all points. Many critics have made unfounded emotional appeals and some have attacked straw men, but some have hit upon true weaknesses in our programs. After all, we have not yet reached the epitome of perfection in the teaching of reading.

HOW ARE WE DOING IN READING?

The first initiative is to provide the facts on the status of reading instruction. It is most unusual for any critic to bring in facts to support allegations about the downfall of reading.

To begin with, let's recognize that "facts" in such a broad area as the status of reading instruction are very difficult to isolate. Even where records exist on large populations over comparatively long periods of time, consideration must be given to the age of the children in the two periods, the differing retention policies, the drop-out rates, and so on. As Gates (1961) pointed out in his comparison of reading achievement in 1937 and 1957, by upper-elementary levels the populations were quite different in the two periods as a result of changes in school policies.

A further tempering effect in the post-Sputnik era was the amount of time taken from the language arts and devoted to other subjects such as science and math. As pointed out earlier, the more time devoted to an area, the higher the achievement is likely to be in that area.

Finally, we must also remember that results of testing do not always reflect the influence of *current* methods and materials. For example, an eighth-grade student tested in 1983 actually reflects the methods and materials used in 1975, as much as eight years earlier when that student was in first grade.

Historical Perspective

Let's begin with some earlier studies and work our way to the present. In 1961, Gates compared reading achievement in grades two through six from 1937 to 1957. He tested the standardization sample of 31,000 pupils with the 1937 and 1957 forms of the Gates Reading Test. He concluded: " . . . a very conservative estimate is that today's children achieve, after about five years of attendance in the elementary school, a level of reading ability that is at the very least better than a half year in advance of the attainment of pupils of equivalent intelligence, age, and other related factors of twenty years ago."

Another way to look at achievement is to examine major standardized tests when they are renormed without any change in content. Such a procedure was followed by the California Test Bureau when they produced 1964 norms for the 1957 California Achievement Test in Reading. Conversion tables for this test indicated that a given raw score in 1964 resulted in a grade equivalent about five months lower than that same score on the 1957 norms, suggesting that the reading level of students in 1964 was about five months higher than in 1957.

Isolated examples in various communities also suggest gains over the years. Based on a Lincoln, Nebraska, study comparing students in 1921 and 1937 who were administered both versions of a reading test, Gates reported an increase in reading achievement in the later period. In fact, the average raw score for fifth-grade students in 1937 was higher than the average for the seventh-grade children in 1921. On this point, Gates further suggested that this finding possibly reflected what a number of reading authorities had suspected: The period from 1920 to about 1935 was the one in which the greatest advancements were made in the teaching of reading.

Still another move forward was reported by Globe Book Company (1966–1967). The 1932 and 1962 versions of the same reading test were administered to seventh- and eighth-grade students in a Brooklyn junior high school. Investigators found a considerable gain in reading achievement for the later group; in fact, 73 percent of the 1962 students scored higher on the 1932 test. Many who were considered below-grade-level readers in 1962 would have been above grade if judged by the 1932 version.

Blake (1964) reported an interesting sidelight: One of the concerns of public librarians, leading to a major study, was the problem created by the fact that Johnny *was* reading! The picture drawn by this study indicated that the average secondary student devoted eleven to twelve hours a month to school-related reading outside the classroom; read almost four nontext books per month; and spent an additional six to seven hours a month reading for personal interest or amusement.

More Recent Studies

Probably the most ambitious attempt to evaluate the status of reading instruction was the study reported by Tuinman, Rowls, and Farr (1976). These researchers examined a span of about one hundred years and attempted to draw conclusions from a variety of sources. In terms of existing research literature, they found that reading achievement was generally reported as improving—certainly not as declining—from year to year, through the last such study reported in 1952.

From data accumulated by large public school systems, these researchers concluded that between 1960–1965 there "may have been a slight rise" in reading achievement, but the 1970 level was slightly lower than 1960 and 1965. Independent school data also indicated that between 1940 and 1965, "there was a steady improvement in reading achievement" and "a slightly negative trend" after 1965. In summary, these researchers concluded: " . . . children of the present are reading better (or at least scoring higher on tests) than children of twenty or more years ago."

Another recent attempt at evaluating the status of reading instruction nationwide was reported by the Education Commission of the States (1981). This report compared levels of achievement on the third national assessment in reading (1979–1980) with results of the second (1974–1975) and the first assessments (1970–1971). Two very positive findings stand out: Nine-year-olds in the latest assessment were significantly higher in all three areas tested (literal and inferential comprehension and study skills), and black students improved even more dramatically than did the total sample. At the thirteen- and seventeen-year-old levels, there was little change over the three assessments; in fact, in most of the comparisons there was a slight decline in inferential comprehension and study skills. Both nine- and thirteen-year-olds showed a significant gain in literal comprehension.

Farr, Fay, and Negley (1978) compared the reading achievement in the state of Indiana between 1944–1945 and 1976. They replicated, in grades 6 and 10, a statewide testing that was done in 1944–1945, using the same test that was used in the earlier period. In grade 6, they found achievement about the same by grade, but the 1944 groups were ten months older. Comparison by age indicated that the 1976 groups were significantly higher on every subskill. In grade 10, they reported the 1976 groups were "dramatically" ahead.

Dubbs (1979) completed a study in Wood County, Ohio, that replicated two studies from the turn of the century. One was a study of the comprehension ability of sixth graders, using a paragraph in the antiquated language of the school law on attendance at that time. The second was a study of vocabulary, where eighth graders were to define five words. Of the five words, two were so exotic that they were not even included in the two most recent studies of adult English vocabulary.

Despite the outdated nature of the tests, Dubbs found that sixth graders in 1978 were significantly better in reading comprehension than were students in 1917. In terms of vocabulary, she found no significant difference in the eighth graders in 1978 as compared with those in 1919.

Munday (1979a) used norming data from a variety of sources. Consistently he reported that the peak in reading achievement at any grade level was about 1965. Using 200,000 students per year, he compared 1956, 1964, and 1971 reading achievement in grades 3 through 8. In grade 3, reading achievement continued to climb through 1971. There was a slight decline (less than one month) from 1964 to 1971 in the other grades; however, only in grade 6 did the 1971 achievement drop to the level of 1956.

Munday's overall conclusion was that the mid-1960s saw an all-time high in reading achievement and that we are maintaining that high. In fact, he also pointed out that the peak in ACT scores was also in the 1965–1966 period, and that the decline we are experiencing is only 2 to 3 percent of a standard deviation per year.

In a follow-up study, Munday (1979b) compared grades 4 and 8 between 1970 and 1977. He did the comparisons for students scoring at the 10th, 50th, and 90th percentiles. In this extension from the previous study, Munday found that achievement maintained consistently over the years at all three percentile rankings, with the possible exception of the 90th percentile in grade 8, which may have dropped slightly in 1977.

Overall, from this brief summary, it can be seen that teachers are certainly not doing a poorer job in the teaching of reading than was done in "the good old days." On the other hand, we are not doing—and probably never will do—as well as we would like to do, since improvement is always possible.

Especially in light of the latest national assessment, we must concentrate on the more sophisticated skills of inference, critical reading, and study skills, while not letting up on our attention to the beginning areas. Proponents of "back to basics" are clearly answered in that the basics of literal comprehension and simple decoding are already handled as well as, if not better than, ever. We need to get to the advanced levels of reading skill, beginning in the primary grades and continuing through all levels of schooling.

"How are we doing in reading?" The best answer to that quesiton is the summary statement of Tuinman, Rowls, and Farr: "We are convinced that anyone who says that he *knows* that literacy is decreasing is ignoring the data. Such a person is at best unscholarly and at worst dishonest."

HOW IS YOUR SCHOOL DOING IN READING?

The second part of your reply to parents deals with the major thrust of their concern: "What's happening in my own children's school?" The reply should deal with levels of achievement in the school and with methods of instruction, since the latter are most often included in criticisms under the cry for "phonics."

Most school districts administer standardized tests for the major academic areas, and principals are well aware of what these are and when they are administered in the district. The further use of tests is discussed in Chapter 9, but for now let's clarify a few points about the interpretation of tests to parents.

If you are reporting in terms of national norms (the norms accompanying the test), be certain to look at and interpret to the interested parties the total picture. The emphasis in a nationally normed test does not always coincide at each grade level with the local emphasis in curriculum. For example, if you teach certain basic skills later in your school than is done nationally, or later than is assumed by the test you use, your students might score lower at the grade level where the skill is usually taught nationally. The important question is, do your students then make a better showing at later grades because of the more delayed introduction? If so, be certain to make this point clear to parents.

You must also be careful about making judgments between grade levels where different levels of a test are used. With few exceptions, the growth of one year produced from two different levels of a test is not the same amount of growth as is indicated when children make that progress within the same level of a test. For example, a middle-grade child may have been making a year's growth each year in grades 4, 5, and 6 on the intermediate level of the test battery. That child takes the advanced level of the battery in grade 7 and may show only six months gain. This may indicate a difference in levels of that test rather than a weakness in the child or in the sixth-grade program.

In other words, articulation between levels of a test is not always smooth, and it is up to the test publisher to prove otherwise to you. Look for unusual gains or drops between the grades where children receive different levels of a test.

Many school districts develop and use their own local norms, while still keeping in touch with national norms. This is a good practice in that you develop a backlog of experience on how your own students are doing from year to year. However, anytime a test is renormed or revised, you must be able to convert from one version to the other or your backlog of information is lost.

As demonstrated in the previous section of this chapter, even with national norms you can be misled when a publisher renorms a test. A "renorming" is nothing more than using the same test with a new sample population in order to update the norm tables; that is, to get them more in line with what typical children of the present can do.

When the California Test Bureau did this in 1964, the same score that earned a child a grade placement of 5.5 in reading in 1957 would result in a grade placement of 5.0 in 1964. Anyone not aware of the conversion factor would think the teaching of reading had disintegrated in a year!

In talking with parents about testing on a general basis, this point needs to be made constantly: No matter how much we improve the teaching of reading, every time tests are renormed, that increase or improvement is brought back to zero. In other words, your average achievement in reading may show a growth of a full year above national norms. Yet, if this is a nationwide trend and the test is renormed, the average that was a year above grade level is brought right back to grade level.

There is another very basic fact about test scores that the general public, as well as boards of education and some educators, fail to understand. In fact, even newspapers have carried headlines decrying the fact that "46 percent of our fourth graders are reading below grade level!" Such people do not understand that the norm for a grade is an average. They tend to look at the norm for any grade level as a floor or a minimum level for that grade. They fail to understand that, as an average, the norm really means that, in a typical school, 50 percent of the pupils will be at or below that level.

If you think these statements of misunderstanding are a fiction, look at the Silberbergs' report (1977). They asked 200 *educators* what percent of children they thought were reading at or below grade level. Only 22 percent answered this question correctly on a five-item multiple choice test. (On a five-choice test, one would expect 20 percent to answer correctly by chance!)

Your second area of clarification of your school's position in reading has to do with the particular charges in the critical article as they relate to your own reading program. Since reading programs vary, it is difficult to be as specific here as we would like. You will find additional help in the chapters dealing with skills (Chapters 4 through 8).

Most critics will include strong comments about the need to teach phonics. I believe I am familiar with just about every reading program on the market; yet, I have to say that I know of *not one* that does not include some provision for the teaching of phonics! In fact, have you ever heard of anyone in the field of reading who was opposed to the teaching of phonics?

Arguments in the field of reading do not deal with whether or not we should teach phonics in beginning reading. The arguments deal with the *kind* of phonics that should be taught, *how soon* phonics instruction should begin, and what *method* should be used. (See Chapter 4.)

For the purpose of clarifying with a parent, take out the teacher's guides or the scope and sequence chart for the program you use and show the parent where and how phonics is taught. Also clarify the other important skills that are taught in the program, as well as the quality literature your children are reading. In other words, you will want to point out that, indeed, phonics is taught, but it is a *tool* for improved reading, not a goal in itself.

Usually a positive approach, such as has been described in this chapter, is the most helpful. One could, of course, do a blow by blow analysis of the critical article, but that usually leads only to debate about trivia. For example, one of the latest criticisms of reading instruction was Flesch's short article (1979). Any reader with a modicum of critical reading skill could decimate the logic; any educator who knows anything about reading programs could even point out misclassifications of programs as "look-and-say" and "phonics-first." As previously stated, it is usually better to answer criticisms by taking a positive stand, using the facts about reading instruction and about your own reading program.

SUMMARY

Critics of education and reading instruction are always with us. It is up to the effective educator to take the initiative in answering charges, both general and specific.

In terms of general charges, evidence indicates that the teaching of reading is still in its "golden age." A composite of studies indicated that reading instruction, as measured by test scores, continued an upward climb until about 1965. After that, there seemed to be a plateau, but none of the evidence suggests a drop below 1955 highs.

The principal must also be able to interpret local test results in terms of the meanings of scores, at individual grade levels and over all the grades. This requires understanding of the nature of local and national norms, as well as how the test relates to the local curriculum plan.

Finally, the principal must have access to and be able to interpret the scope and sequence for the reading program used in the school. It is at this point that the principal can take the initiative and show parents what is being done for their children.

References

Blake, Joseph. "The Student Problem: Johnny Is Reading." *Delaware Valley Reading Bulletin* (April 1964). Reported on a study of the reading habits of over 100,000 individuals. Indicated that one problem is how to handle the demand for reading materials.

Dubbs, Mary Wray. "How Good Were Readers in the Good Old Days? Replication of Two Studies." *The Reading Teacher* 32 (May 1979): 933–939. Replicated two studies of sixth and eighth graders done at the turn of the century. Reported that sixth graders today were significantly better in comprehension; there was no significant difference in the vocabulary ability of eighth graders.

Education Commission of the States. *Three National Assessments of Reading: Changes in Performance, 1970–80* (Report 11-R-01). Denver: Education Commission of the States, 1981. Compared the 1979–1980 assessment in reading with those done in 1974–1975 and 1970–1971. The more recent assessment indicated improvement in reading in some areas, especially in the "basics."

Farr, Roger; Fay, Leo; and Negley, Harold. *Then and Now: Reading Achievement in Indiana (1944–45 and 1976).* Bloomington: Indiana University, 1978. Replicated the same tests in grades 6 and 10. Revealed higher achievement at both age levels for the more recent group.

Flesch, Rudolph. "Why Johnny Still Can't Read." *Family Circle* (November 1, 1979): 26, 43–44. Classified seventeen reading programs as "phonics-first" or "look-and-say." Appealed to parents to force their school to teach phonics.

Gates, Arthur. *Reading Attainment in Elementary Schools: 1957 and 1937.* New York: Teachers College, Columbia, 1961. Tested 31,000 pupils in grades 2 through 6. Concluded that 1957 pupils were about 0.6 years ahead in reading attainment.

Globe Book Company. "Find Students Reading Better Than They Did Generation Ago." *Globe Language Arts Bulletin* 11, no. 1 (1966–1967). Compared reading achievement of seventh- and eighth-grade students in 1962 with those in 1932 edition of a test. Some 73 percent of 1962 students scored higher than their counterparts.

Munday, Leo A. "Changing Test Scores, Especially since 1970." *Phi Delta Kappan* 60 (March 1979a): 496–499. Numerous comparisons on several tests, from 1956 to 1974, indicated a peak in reading achievement about 1964–1965, with a general plateau effect thereafter.

Munday, Leo A. "Changing Test Scores: Basic Skills Development in 1977 Compared with 1970." *Phi Delta Kappan* 60 (May 1979b): 670–671. Comparisons in grades 4 and 8 for students at the 10th, 50th, and 90th percentiles indicated consistent performance over the seven-year period, with the possible loss for 90th-percentile students in grade 8.

Silberberg, Norman E., and Silberberg, Margaret C. "The Great Reading Score Deception." *Principal* 57 (October 1977): 70–71. When 200 educators were asked what percent of children read at grade level or below, only 22 percent answered correctly out of five choices.

Tuinman, Jaap; Rowls, Michael; and Farr, Roger. "Reading Achievement in the United States: Then and Now." *Journal of Reading* 19 (March 1976): 455–463. Based on a variety of sources, reading achievement showed a steady improvement through 1965, with a leveling off after that point.

CHAPTER 3

An Overview of Reading

Everyone knows what "reading" is—at least until asked to define it. Yet, with vague and often diverse beliefs about what reading is, school staffs adopt and use reading programs. Any reading program at least implies a particular definition or philosophy of reading, and school staffs ought to match their own philosophy with that of a reading program or approach they want to use.

What is your definition of reading? How do your teachers view this thing called "reading"? What definition or philosophy of reading has been implied, at least, by the way reading is taught in your school?

If you want the most honest answer to this last question, you might ask the children. Depending on the approach your school takes to beginning reading, young children might answer that reading is "sounding out words," "learning words," or "using our readers." More positively, your children might reply that reading is "having fun," "reading stories," or "learning things."

I suggest that "reading" is the act of approximately reproducing, mentally or orally, the ideas a writer has represented in print. We must say *approximately* because seldom does a reader reproduce *exactly* the ideas a writer had in mind.

To this definition we need to add a definition of "good reading." Good reading is the act of approximately reproducing *and reacting to* the ideas a writer has represented in print. This kind of reading is often referred to by reading teachers as *critical reading*.

Chapter 3

APPROACHES TO BEGINNING READING

The approaches to beginning reading are many and varied. Aukerman (1971) listed one hundred different ones. While we certainly do not intend to repeat his efforts, we should look at the types and their underlying premises about reading.

The different kinds of reading programs can be laid out on a continuum from the extreme of an early, intensive emphasis on phonics to the other extreme of a delayed emphasis on phonics with meaning stressed from the beginning. Other terms professionals use for the two extremes are "synthetic phonics" and "analytic phonics." As stated in Chapter 2, I know of no reading program that does not include phonics at some point.

Synthetic phonics programs begin with phonics before children learn to read any words. Pupils learn the sounds for the letters and they *synthesize* those sounds together in order to "sound out" words. Other terms used for such programs are "phonics-first," "phonics," or "deductive approach." Analytic phonics programs usually begin by having pupils learn some words in context. Then pupils *analyze* the words in order to develop phonic generalizations. Other terms for these programs are "meaning emphasis," "sight," "look-and-say," or "inductive approach."

Major reading programs might be classified on a continuum between synthetic and analytic emphases, as shown in Table 3–1. The two programs in the middle column, "Linguistic" and Houghton Mifflin, are difficult to classify on this continuum. "Linguistic" programs are unlike the analytic approaches because their initial emphasis is not on semantic meaning or context; it is on learning the phonic skills through word patterns, such as "Can Nan fan Dan?"

Table 3–1   Classification of Major Reading Programs

SYNTHETIC PHONICS		ANALYTIC PHONICS
Distar	"Linguistic"	Allyn & Bacon
Economy	Houghton Mifflin	American Book
Lippincott		Ginn
Open Court		Harcourt
i/t/a, Unifon, etc.		Harper
		Holt
		Laidlaw
		Macmillan
		Random House
		Riverside
		Scott Foresman
		"Language Experience"
		"Individualized Reading"

However, they are also unlike synthetic phonics programs because they usually do not teach phonic rules, nor do they have pupils pronounce consonant sounds in isolation.

Houghton Mifflin could be classified as a meaning emphasis program because it emphasizes the use of context from the very beginning. However, it has also been classed as a phonics-first program because it introduces the letter-sound associations for consonants (phonics) before it introduces any words. In this latter respect, it is more like the synthetic programs, but the consonant sounds are not pronounced in isolation.

Synthetic Phonics—Decoding Emphasis

Most synthetic phonics programs teach the sounds for the letters through a stimulus-response method. Children learn that *b* stands for "buh," *d* for "duh," and *w* for "wuh." On the other hand, some students are taught the letter-sound associations through rules. For example, children might learn that when they see the letter *a* between two consonants that letter has its "short" sound, as in *hat*.

One of the challenges faced in any approach to phonics has to do with the nature of the English language. There are only twenty-six letters to represent the twenty-five consonant sounds and the fifteen vowel sounds of English. The fifteen vowel sounds alone are represented by at least sixty-nine different letter combinations.

In an effort to circumvent the problem of these different representations of the sounds of English, we have seen programs that manipulate the symbols of English. Programs such as i/t/a and Unifon invented additional symbols in order to create beginning reading materials where each symbol represented only one sound and every sound was represented fairly consistently by the same symbol.

"Words in Color" presents the same kind of philosophy, except that this program uses a different color for each sound represented.

Whether new symbols or colors are used, or whether the vocabulary is controlled to a fixed word pattern as in "linguistic" programs, the emphasis in these approaches is *decoding*. Decoding is the process of converting or translating the printed word to its spoken form, whether mentally or actually.

Analytic Phonics—Meaning Emphasis

At the other end of the continuum, meaning emphasis programs usually begin by teaching children some words in meaningful story context before they begin with phonics; hence, the term "sight" or "look-and-say."

In contrast to "linguistic" programs that control vocabulary in terms of word patterns, these programs tend to select vocabulary in terms of frequency of use and familiarity, and to control the rate of introduction and repetition of new words. Usually, at the beginning levels, the most frequently used words of English are introduced first, and additional words are gradually added.

Even with the first word or two that children read, the teacher provides story background orally. Then children read the words as a natural follow-up to what the teacher said. For example, a great deal of newspaper coverage was given to the old Scott Foresman "Dick and Jane" because it began in the first book with "Look, look, look." This was not very exciting as the popular press presented it, but children first heard the background as story context and then read what Dick said. To children this could be exciting.

After children learn to recognize some words "at sight," the teacher helps them analyze the words for specific phonic generalizations. For example, if children can recognize *hat*, *her*, and *him*, the teacher can then develop a generalization for the letter *h* through the "See, Hear, Associate" method commonly used. First, the teacher has the children *see* how all three words are alike (letter *h*); next he or she has them *hear*, by saying the words, how the words sound alike (at the beginning); then he or she has them *associate* letter and sound by telling them that whenever they see that letter at the beginning of a word it will usually represent the sound they hear at the beginning of *hat*, *her*, and *him*.

Among meaning-emphasis approaches, the two at the most extreme end of the meaning continuum are "language experience" and "individualized reading." The former capitalizes on the oral language of the pupil, using pupil-dictated stories as the material for reading instruction. The latter, recognizing the danger of a lockstep in basal readers, uses library books on a pupil-selected basis as the vehicle for learning to read.

What Does Research Say?

Anyone looking to research for a clear and definitive answer to the question of the best reading program for beginning readers is going to be disappointed. A massive, federally funded effort was launched in the mid-1960s to get an answer to this question. Twenty-seven research studies were sponsored in various parts of the country, comparing many different approaches to beginning reading. Out of this effort, we learned that there was more difference between two teachers using the same program than there was between any two programs (Bond and Dykstra, 1967).

If you, as principal, have observed reading instruction in your school, you are not surprised at this finding. You know that a teacher and pupils may be holding a meaning-emphasis program in their hands, but that teacher may be teaching it as if it were a synthetic phonics program. Teachers are not always teaching the program that the school district has adopted. Reasons vary from lack of acceptance of the program, lack of understanding the program, or just falling back on some of the methods by which the teachers themselves were taught.

In any event, research fails us partly because this teacher variable is so great. It undoubtedly fails us as well because most children will learn to read, no matter how they are taught, if only they are exposed to print—and fortunately, all reading programs do that. Research will probably continue to fail us if we are trying to discover "Is this particular reading program better than that one?"

In contrast, if we look at the accumulated mass of research in order to seek direction, there are some signs that seem to point out strengths and weaknesses in both extremes. Research may not solve any philosophical question, but it can provide evidence on which to make decisions.

Strengths and Weaknesses

First of all, common sense ought to tell us that the extremes represented by reading programs today could not have existed over the years unless there was some truth on both sides. This observation does not excuse us from the responsibility of trying to find the best program we can for children today. This same common sense, combined with the failure of some of the "novel" programs of the 1960s, should also suggest that we are unlikely to suddenly find the panacea for problems of teaching reading.

The combined body of research does suggest that there are both strengths and weaknesses in either extreme of teaching reading. For the phonics extreme, the strength seems to be in the early start in reading. Children in such programs tend to score higher on reading achievement tests at the end of first grade.

A quick look at first-grade achievement tests will explain this advantage. The "comprehension" sections of such tests are limited in terms of measuring understanding. They consist of paragraphs of two or three very short sentences, so there is little to comprehend. Hence, any child who can say all of the words can usually do well on a first-grade reading achievement test.

This early strength has a potential weakness. Because most children in a phonics emphasis program can learn to say all the words, they are presumed to be reading. Without the use of context and stress on meaning, however, some tend to suffer in terms of comprehension—a factor that often does not show up until third or fourth grade.

Meaning emphasis programs seem to have just the reverse strengths and weaknesses. Children tend to get a slow start in reading, but their attention is on meaning from the beginning. This tends to pay dividends later in terms of better comprehension of what is read, which results in higher achievement in later grades.

Trends in recent years, as reflected in the 1981–1982 revisions of programs, also support these statements. For example, a number of meaning-emphasis programs have introduced more phonics earlier, while at least one of the synthetic programs has incorporated comprehension from the very first level.

Naturally, any school staff aware of the potential weakness of a given approach can help to counterbalance that weakness. We have all seen teachers who focus on context and do a lot of discussing of stories, even though they may be using an extreme phonics program, just as we have seen teachers in a delayed phonics program who "smuggle in" some early phonics to help their children. However, if you are trying to implement an agreed-upon reading program in your school, it is doubtful that you would want to rely on the incidental modifications of your teachers to make it work to best advantage. Your responsibility includes organizing the staff for a concerted effort to capitalize on existing strengths and to overcome inherent weaknesses.

APPROACHES TO READING IN MIDDLE GRADES

By the middle grades the divergence of approaches to skills is not so apparent. The degree of agreement on approaches does not mean that research has answered all of the questions. In fact, it more likely means that there is too little definitive research to argue about.

Depending on the program used in the primary grades, the assumption is that by either second or third grade most children will have mastered the basic decoding skills: They will have learned *how* to read and will be able to read any material that they would understand if it were read to them. By the middle grades, reading programs focus primarily on comprehension—with some work on literary skills—and study skills.

This is not to say that all reading programs are the same at this level. By the middle grades, in this area of comprehension and study skills, there are so many things that could be taught that the skills content of reading programs differs mostly in terms of the choices in emphasis that they make. One reading program may be particularly strong in the study skills, with lesser emphasis on certain comprehension skills. Another may select, even within the comprehension skills, particular ones that will be stressed. Inferential and critical reading skills will be the battleground between reading programs of the 1980s.

A WORD ABOUT MANAGEMENT SYSTEMS

Management systems, a product of the 1970s, were a natural outgrowth of interest in behavioral objectives. They are, as the name implies, a means of organizing or managing the skills sequence in reading. They are not reading programs, but serve as the means for diagnosing, evaluating, and recording pupil progress within the skills sequence of any reading program. In addition to those that accompany most basal reading series, management systems are also available separately. Wisconsin Design or Fountain Valley are examples of such separate management systems, which then refer the user to appropriate practice sections in basal readers for needed skill development.

Management systems break the reading act down into a multitude of specific skills. Teachers may then pretest individual children for each of the specific skills to determine if that child does or does not have the skill. If not, the program includes or suggests practice material for the skill and follows with a posttest to determine if mastery is attained. Finally, a pupil record card or "profile" of the skills is punched or marked by the teacher to show mastery of the skill by that pupil.

Management systems have made a contribution to the teaching of reading in that they have made teachers more aware of specific skills for instruction. They have also provided a means of keeping track of pupils' skill development.

These very strengths are also potential weaknesses. When the management system serves the teacher, it is positive; when the teacher becomes a bookkeeping slave to the management system, the principal had better step in.

Management systems have so fragmented the reading process that teachers may not allow time for pupils to read because they are so busy testing and giving practice in the myriad of "skills" included in the management system. Many of these so-called "skills" are little more than busywork, and it is on this point that the principal can step in with a staff to do some cooperative "housecleaning" of the management system.

Most of the time-wasting "skills" in management systems deal with decoding skills. Specific suggestions about which skills are important and which are not are given in Chapters 4 and 5.

THE TOTAL READING PROGRAM

In Chapters 4 through 8 we will discuss specifics of skill instruction that you, as principal, ought to be concerned about with your staff. Before we do that, however, let's look at the big picture—the major components that make up a total reading program.

While the following brief discussion provides a capsulated summary of what reading is all about, it is no substitute for knowledge about your own reading program. Examine the introduction in a teacher edition of your reading program. You might even want to compare the following table with the "Scope and Sequence" chart that is available with your reading program.

Table 3–2 provides an overview of reading, unbiased by any specific phi-

Table 3–2   Overview of the Four Components of a Total Reading
Program

BASIC SKILLS	COMPREHENSION SKILLS
	(Preschool–adult)
Decoding Skills	*Aids*
(Preschool–Grade 2 or 3)	Oral Thinking Skills
Readiness in Oral Language	Decoding Skills
Context (Recognition Vocabulary)	Punctuation
Phonics: Consonants/Vowels	Special Type
Structural Analysis:	*Skill Categories*
Syllables	Literal Comprehension
Base	Inferential Comprehension
Prefixes/Suffixes	Critical Reading
Compounds	*Literary Skills*
Contractions	Plot
Dictionary Skills	Characterization
(Grade 2 or 3–Adult)	Theme
Context + Dictionary for:	Genres
Location	Mood
Meaning	Style
Pronunciation	
Spelling	
Study Skills	
(Grade 3 or 4–Adult)	
Locating Information	
Reading for Various Purposes	
Evaluating Information	
Organizing/Retaining Information	

INDEPENDENT READING	ORAL READING
(Preschool–Adult)	(Grade 1–Adult)
Purposes	*Purposes*
Application and Practice	To Relate Print to Talk
of Skills	To Entertain
Interest	To Provide Information
Appreciation	To Prove a Point
Vocabulary Development	To Diagnose or Evaluate
Means	*Skills*
Availability of Books	Basic Silent Reading Skills
Accessibility of Books	plus
Awareness of Books	Oral Reading Skills
Motivation to Read	Pronunciation
Sharing about Reading	Enunciation
Implementation	Phrasing
Being Read to	Breath Control
Using Reading	Emphasis
	Eye Contact

losophy. Regardless of their particular philosophies of reading, teachers would not disagree with the topics included. The only exception might be a person at the extreme of decoding emphasis who could quarrel with inclusion of "context" in the decoding section. Otherwise, disagreements with the topics will usually be confined to word choice—and later, to method and degree of emphasis. A complete reading program ought to have the major components listed as headings in the four columns: basic skills, comprehension skills, independent reading, and oral reading. As you see, decoding, dictionary, and study skills follow a sequence of development, while the other components run concurrently from the beginning of reading instruction.

With each component, we have identified approximate levels at which teachers or readers typically work with those skills. With the exception of basic phonic skills, development should continue throughout life, since it is doubtful that anyone ever completely "masters" the art of reading.

Decoding Skills

These skills are discussed in detail in Chapters 4 and 5. As stated in Chapter 2, reading professionals have not argued about whether or not to teach phonics; their debates have been about when, how much, and with what methods.

Readiness actually begins before a child starts school. It is rooted in familiarity with and control of the oral language, and it is the essential starting point for any instruction in reading. An individual must speak and understand the language before that person can be taught to read in that language.

The sequence of skills for the remainder of the Decoding section may vary according to the particular philosophy of reading. Some would begin with a recognition vocabulary, some with vowel generalizations, and some with consonants. Regardless of their differing views on the other points, most reading professionals would agree that Structural Analysis belongs last in that sequence.

Use of context can begin at the oral level, where the teacher says a sentence but leaves out a word for pupils to decide upon. Such an approach can be a "readiness" for using printed context.

Recognition Vocabulary—or "Sight Vocabulary"—refers to those words an individual can say without any assist from context or phonics. The amount of emphasis on a recognition vocabulary depends on the degree to which a program is teaching children to "sound out" words letter by letter, or the degree to which it is suggesting that learning to read is a matter of "building a word bank" (memorizing words). Even the most extreme decoding emphasis recognizes that there are some words that do not fit phonic generalizations and must be learned at sight. I believe that anyone who hopes to be a fluent reader must develop some automatic vocabulary, so those words can serve as the context for identifying other words.

Phonics refers to whatever method is used to develop understanding of the sounds letters represent in print. As stated earlier, the method may use a stimulus-response training, it may use rules, or it may limit vocabulary to word patterns as in "linguistic" approaches. Although most programs begin with phonics for consonants, some begin with vowels.

While phonics deals with individual letters and sounds, Structural Analysis deals with larger segments of print, pronounceable or meaningful units of words. Most programs provide for teaching children how to divide words into syllables. Even before this, they teach suffixes such as the plural (-s) and past marker (-ed) as meaning units. Since teachers will be teaching some of the common prefixes and suffixes for meaning, they must also teach children to identify the base word to which the prefix or suffix has been added. Related instruction includes work with compound words and contractions.

Skill in decoding is often referred to as "word identification skill." It is a skill readers use in order to figure out what a strange word is. Most programs suggest that the progression for use is context plus phonics and, if more help is needed, structural analysis.

We must recognize the limitation of phonics. It is a valuable tool at the beginning stages of reading, where the content being read is made up of words already in the listening-speaking vocabulary of the reader. At this level of reading, children would know the meaning of every word if you said those words to them; the words are strange only in their printed form.

If a word is outside the listening-speaking vocabulary, all of the phonics in the world will not help the reader decide on the meaning of that word. In fact, phonics will not even assure the correct pronunciation. For example, suppose you were reading about a *cicisbeo*. You probably have never met this word before, although it is in the dictionary. Analysis by phonics may lead you to think the *c*'s are pronounced /s/ and the *i*'s pronounced /i/, as in *city*, and that the word is accented on the first or second syllable. The fact is, the word is pronounced /chē chəz bā' ō/.

Once learners reach this stage, where they meet words outside their listening-speaking vocabularies, they need another tool besides phonics. This brings us to the next skill section of a reading program, the development of dictionary skills.

Dictionary Skills

No later than second- or third-grade reading level, children begin to meet words that are outside their listening-speaking vocabularies. If they have been taught to use context, they will sometimes get the meaning of a word from that. Most often, however, they need more help, and that help is the dictionary. (Dictionary skills are presented in more detail in Chapter 8.)

Obviously, before anyone can use a dictionary for pronunciation or meaning, that person must know how to find words in a dictionary. The locational skills of alphabetical order and guide words are usually taught in grade two, although readiness is developed in the kindergarten with picture dictionaries.

Children learn to use a dictionary for meaning before they learn to use it for pronunciation. The former is easier, and it is in keeping with priorities in reading: We are more concerned about the meaning of a word than about its pronunciation. Even in initial practice with using a dictionary for meaning, the words children look up should always be in context, since there are few words in English that have only one meaning. Teachers sometimes forget this point in their own preparation of practice materials.

Learning to use a dictionary for pronunciation is a difficult task. Besides, most reading programs do a poor job of teaching this skill because they attempt to provide *independent* practice materials. This is an oral-aural skill, therefore worthwhile practice must be oral, with teacher participation. You might want to work with your teachers on this point, as discussed in Chapter 8.

Children must also learn how to use a dictionary for spelling. This is another essential and even more neglected skill, and one that is also discussed in Chapter 8.

Study Skills

According to the last national assessment of reading (Education Commission of the States, 1981), we do not do as well as we need to do in the area of study skills. Possibly one reason for our failure lies in the fact that, even when the skills are taught in the reading class, if they are not followed with *application* in content reading they are lost. Too often, the application is neglected.

Table 3–2 contains four major categories of study skills. Subsumed under these four categories are a great number of specific skills that are discussed in detail in Chapter 8.

The ability to *locate information* requires skill in the use of many aids, from the card catalog to time tables, from biographical dictionaries to encyclopedias. Locational skills also include the ability to use various parts of a book, such as a table of contents or an index.

Reading for various purposes includes development of flexibility of rate of reading; that is, adjusting the rate of reading according to the purpose. We do not read a science text or technical article at the same rate we read a novel. While flexibility of rate is an important skill to develop, speed reading—the effort to increase rate for its own sake—has no place in the elementary curriculum.

Other purposes for reading include the ability to skim and to scan. We scan material in order to find a specific—a word, date, name, and so on. We skim in order to get a general idea of what the material is about without reading the entire selection.

The skill of *evaluating information* overlaps with critical reading. It concerns the ability to determine if the information is pertinent to the topic, complete, accurate, and so forth. Specific skills are outlined and discussed in Chapter 7.

Comprehension Skills

As listed in Table 3–2, the reading comprehension skills require use of the basic "aids" to reading: oral thinking skills, decoding skills, and understanding of punctuation and special type. Then the major skills to be developed are in three categories: literal comprehension, inferential comprehension, and critical reading. Finally, some of the major "literary skills" are listed: plot, characterization, mood, style.

Reading comprehension skills actually begin in the preschool years. What we call "reading comprehension skills" are really thinking skills applied in reading. Hence, they begin in oral language development. These skills—the heart of reading—are discussed in Chapter 7.

The "aids" listed in the table are prerequisites to the comprehension of material being read. The reader must be able to think in the language, must have the basic decoding skills, and must be able to use the signals of punctuation and special type appropriate to the reading level.

The "literary skills" listed are usually developed somewhat lightly at the elementary level. Teachers and children do discuss plot and characterization, and they do usually discuss genres in the sense that pupils ought to be able to distinguish biography from fiction. The major thrust, however, is in the three skill categories of literal, inferential, and critical reading. Unfortunately, too many teachers limit this thrust to the first category—literal comprehension.

Most reading professionals refer to these three items as "levels" instead of "categories." I much prefer the latter term because too many teachers interpret level to mean degree of difficulty. This notion is certainly not true. We can ask a difficult literal question or an easy-to-answer inferential or critical question. Do your teachers have a misunderstanding about "level"?

Literal comprehension has to do with recognizing and recalling what an author said. Inferential comprehension requires reading "between the lines" to determine what the author meant by what was stated. Critical reading includes the ability to bring other experience and knowledge to bear in evaluating the worth, accuracy, and completeness of what an author said and meant. Most often these skills are practiced through teacher-questioning techniques. Not only do the questions most often asked leave a lot to be desired, but mere practice of a skill is not enough. The skill ought to be taught as well.

Independent Reading

Suggestions for the Independent Reading component are provided in Chapter 6. In too many schools this portion of the reading program is sadly neglected if not entirely lacking. Teachers are too busy *teaching* instead of *using* reading.

Yet, accumulated evidence from studies of "individualized reading," where basal readers were thrown out in favor of library books, suggests very clearly that children also learn to read by reading.

The purposes and activities listed in Table 3–2 for independent reading should be evident enough at this point. However, the portion of the total reading program to be devoted to this aspect of reading probably is not. I feel that 50 percent of the time called "reading" in the classroom ought to be devoted to the enjoyable application and practice of the skills in library books.

Teachers should not look upon this component of the reading program as a reward for getting work done, nor should they fear that the principal will think they are loafing merely because everyone is sitting around having fun reading. Properly conducted, independent reading requires more than merely providing time to read. To make it worthwhile, teachers must also plan and motivate opportunities and means for sharing about the reading done. This sharing, in turn, becomes a motivating factor for other children to read the books shared.

A part of every day, at every grade level, ought to be allotted for reading to children. At all levels, this is an important motivating factor for reading. At lower grades, it also acquaints children with the language of print, a language pattern that differs from the patterns of oral English.

Oral Reading Skills

As indicated in Table 3–2, oral reading has a number of worthwhile purposes: to relate print to oral language, to entertain, to provide information, to prove a point, or to evaluate. The skills require use of the basic silent reading skills, but go beyond them to include skills peculiar to oral reading: pronunciation, enunciation, phrasing, breath control, emphasis, and eye contact.

This component of the total reading program is not discussed beyond this chapter because what needs to be said about it can be stated here. First, it should be clear from the skill list in Table 3–2 that oral reading is more than silent reading out loud. Good oral reading must include the basic silent reading skills, but it should exceed them to require the additional oral reading skills listed.

Second, all oral reading should be purposeful. In your school, how often is it no more than just taking turns reading aloud? In fact, unless the teacher wants specifically to teach and practice oral reading skills and have pupils check on that oral reading, there is no excuse for everyone to have a book open while one of the class reads what the others have in front of them. An exception may be during a discussion of a story, when there is a disagreement about a point and the teacher has the first pupil to find the point in question read it out loud to the group as a time-saver.

At times, as discussed in Chapter 9, individual oral reading may be requested by a teacher in order to evaluate the reading level or skill needs of a student. In such instances, the focus is not on the oral reading skills, but rather it is on the reading behavior, miscues, and comprehension of the student.

Too much oral reading in the "round robin" variety also develops slow and plodding readers. It develops readers who are more concerned about saying all the words than they are about the meaning of what they are reading. As Frank Smith (1978) has stated so well, we ought to be less interested in developing word-perfect readers; we ought to be helping children become "risk-takers" in reading if we are to develop fluent, mature readers.

All this is not to suggest that we go back in history to an all-silent approach with first graders. The first purpose listed in Table 3–2 is that of relating print to talk. First graders need to *hear* what they are reading in order to associate those squiggles on the page with the language they have been speaking and understanding for four or five years.

Even with first graders, however, the oral reading should be purposeful. The first-grade teacher can get about a dozen purposeful oral readings out of the three words on the page merely by asking different pupils to read it "the way you think ___ said it." And the principal should not be surprised or concerned when he or she enters a first-grade class in Spring where pupils are reading library books "silently," to observe that they are reading "silently out loud." There is a constant buzz and mumble as these beginners still need to relate print to the spoken language.

Finally, silent reading should *always* precede oral reading, unless the reading is being done as an oral reading test. Once more, even in first grade where there might be only three or four words on the page, children should have the opportunity to read those words silently before they are asked to read them orally for a purpose.

Teachers usually justify the great amount of oral reading with two excuses. First, they say that is the only way they know if the children are learning the skills and reading all of the material. On the latter, there are some stories where no sane person would read every word. And the teacher should know about skill development if that teacher is observing children's understanding as the skill is being taught, if the children are moving forward in terms of the level of difficulty they can read, and if that teacher sees that the pupils are enjoying stories and really reading.

The second excuse is usually, "My children like to read orally." True. I have seen classes of third and fourth graders who do not think they have "had reading" unless they take turns reading orally. Children were not born with this understanding of what reading is; they have been brainwashed by class after class of oral reading. Once again, such a practice will lead to unnecessarily slow and plodding reading.

Of course, oral reading skills should not be ignored. On the contrary, while "taking turns reading" is counterproductive, instruction in oral reading skills is an integral part of the total reading program.

The *teaching* of oral reading *skills* is usually done through demonstration and practice. In other words, by third or fourth grade, we would expect teachers to work with their children on the specific skills. The teacher might select the skill of reading with proper emphasis. After examples from the teacher of different ways a sentence might be read, pupils will read orally with their interpretation of the appropriate emphasis and the class will discuss the various interpretations.

Since oral reading is not discussed again in any detail, let's review the possible direction a principal might take in improving this component of the reading program. Essentially, there are three points that might be checked in the school:

1. Is oral reading done for a purpose, such as to entertain, to inform, or, in the case of an oral test, to evaluate?
2. When children read orally, are they given time to read silently first?
3. In middle grades, is there some *teaching* of the specific oral reading skills?

SUMMARY

This chapter began with a discussion of the meaning of reading. It presented an examination of approaches to beginning reading, an area about which there is still much debate. Philosophies of beginning reading range from an extreme emphasis on phonics to the other extreme of an emphasis on meaning with a delay in phonics instruction. Strength of the former lies in an early start in reading, while the latter encourages comprehension from the very start.

Differences among programs in middle grades lie not so much in philosophy of method as they do in degree of emphasis on different skills. The skills themselves are primarily the comprehension and study skills.

A brief explanation of management systems suggested their strengths and potential dangers. These systems, whether as part of a basal reading program or independent of it, have helped to make teachers more aware of specific skills. Their potential dangers are in their proliferation of "skills" and in their excessive demands on teacher time for bookkeeping.

Finally, an overview of a total reading program suggested four major components: basic skills, including decoding, dictionary, and study skills; comprehension skills; independent reading; and oral reading. Each of the components should run concurrently, with the independent reading encompassing about 50 percent of the total reading time.

Suggestions for Action

If you have not already done so, examine the introduction in a teacher edition of the reading program you use. What philosophy of beginning reading is espoused there? In middle grades, what skills are emphasized? Now pick an area from the overview in Table 3–2 to discuss with your staff. You might pick one of the following topics for that discussion:

1. *Philosophy:* What is our philosophy of beginning reading? What are its strengths and weaknesses? What can we do about the weaknesses?

2. *Comprehension:* How well do we develop comprehension skills? To what extent do we develop them as thinking skills through listening and discussion from kindergarten on? What proportion of our instructional effort is devoted to inferential and critical reading as opposed to literal comprehension?

3. *Study Skills:* What study skills are taught in middle grades? Which ones are neglected? How are they practiced *in application* in the content areas?

4. *Independent Reading:* To what extent is independent reading recognized and practiced as an integral part of the total program? How and when is it developed?

5. *Oral Reading:* In what ways do we provide for *purposeful* oral reading? Is there too much oral reading? What oral reading skills are actually *taught?* When?

References

Aukerman, Robert. *Approaches to Beginning Reading.* New York: John Wiley and Sons, 1971. Summarizes about one hundred approaches to beginning reading. The objective descriptions of the programs can be helpful. The subjective evaluations are most generous.

Aukerman, Robert. *The Basal Reader Approach to Reading.* New York: John Wiley and Sons, 1981. Includes objective descriptions of fifteen major basal reading programs. While this book can serve as a helpful reference, the evaluations of each program should be approached cautiously.

Bond, Guy, and Dykstra, Robert. "The Cooperative Research Program in First Grade Reading Instruction." *Reading Research Quarterly* 2 (1967): 5–142. Reports results on the collected data from twenty-seven comparative studies of beginning reading programs.

Education Commission of the States. *Three National Assessments of Reading: Changes in Performance, 1970–80* (Report 11-R-01). Denver: Education Commission of the States, 1981. Presents a comparison of the results of the national assessments in reading in 1970–1971, 1974–1975, and 1979–1980. Suggests improvement in the latest assessment with minority groups and in decoding and literal comprehension.

Smith, Frank. *Understanding Reading.* New York: Holt, Rinehart and Winston, 1978. An excellent presentation of what the act of reading is all about. You might want to read this one in its entirety.

CHAPTER 4

What Are Your Priorities: Readiness and Beginning Reading

This area of readiness and beginning reading is the very foundation of education, regardless of the age of the person working at this level. If an individual is given the proper start here, almost nothing or no one will prevent that person from becoming a successful reader. And a poor start here can present a lifetime handicap.

Most educators agree that reading instruction for children should begin with something called "reading readiness." Once that point is made, agreement ends, and various educators and programs go down different avenues to accomplish this "readiness."

Perhaps it would be better just to call this chapter "Beginnings," since its purpose is to deal with the kinds of experiences appropriate for children in the first year or two of their school life. In administrative terms, this may be called Headstart, Nursery School, Kindergarten, or First Grade. The purpose of this chapter is to identify concerns and possible solutions in this area in the hope that you, as an educational leader, will work with your teachers to arrive at an agreed-upon philosophy and goals—your own "answers," based on research, logic, and a consensus of the total staff.

Some of the questions to be explored are: What is readiness? What form should "early identification" or "kindergarten screening" take? Is there a place where or when "readiness" should begin? What should be its content? When should "reading" begin? Should kindergarten programs be "formal" or "informal"?

37

READING READINESS

Over the years, much of the debate about readiness has centered on differences between professionals with a developmental view and those with a cognitive view. At one extreme, developmentalists would wait for maturity with a warning of "Don't dare touch the little children." At the other extreme, the cognitive emphasis would encourage teaching, in some cases making kindergarten over into a "little first grade."

Fortunately, progress is being made. The debates of the 1960s are being resolved between the two extremes. In fact, even back then the "solution" was voiced beautifully by Carpenter (1961) when she said that readiness is "somewhere between wanting to and having to." Most educators today recognize that we should not just twiddle our thumbs and wait for readiness to happen, nor can we force it upon children. Without getting into a semantic debate, perhaps we cannot even "teach" readiness, but we can provide experiences that will help to develop it.

Most formal definitions of readiness offer little help in identifying just what it is that must be done. For example, Tinker and McCullough (1975) indicated, "Reading readiness means attainment of the level of development that enables a child to learn to read in regular classroom instruction by a competent teacher" (p. 79). Durkin (1978) quoted Ausubel's general definition of readiness as "the adequacy of existing capacity in relation to the demands of a given learning task" (p. 161). Lapp and Flood (1978) say that reading readiness is "a term used to refer to the necessary level of preparation a person should attain before formal reading instruction is begun" (p. 767).

Perhaps we should recognize that reading readiness is a multifaceted continuum of physical, cognitive, and affective elements developed from birth to that *stage* where an individual has the skills, understandings, and attitudes necessary for reading.

Implied in this last definition is the view that there is not, nor should there be, any fine demarcation between "reading readiness" and "reading." In fact, any positive new experience must be looked upon as an "achievement" at that stage and another step toward "readiness" for the next stage, whether that experience results in the addition of a new word to the two-year-old's oral vocabulary or in the understanding that *s* represents the sound heard at the beginning of *sun* and *sock*, in the case of the four- or five-year-old.

This "reading-readiness/reading" is best clarified by a consideration of the elements of concern to educators. First, however, before we go off in the moderate "cognitive" direction, let's provide for consideration of the developmental view.

Those who take such a view will point to comparative studies, where children in different cultures begin school at different ages. Regardless of the age of beginning reading instruction, those studies reveal not much difference in reading achievement in later years. You and your staff might want to consider this point. In contrast, I feel that the sooner children get started reading *enjoyably*, the more and varied experiences they will have. On the other hand, given only the choice between an early unpleasant beginning or a later more pleasant beginning, we obviously must choose the latter. But do we have to make such a choice?

Elements Considered in "Reading Readiness"

In considering or evaluating your beginning program, you and your staff need to discuss the contribution of the many elements usually discussed under the heading of reading readiness. Some are important and some are truly irrelevant.[1]

Chronological Age	Visual Motor Skill
Mental Age	Experience
Visual Development	Language Development
Socio-Economic Status	Auditory Discrimination
Emotional Development	Rhyming Words
Neurological Problems	Visual Discrimination
Social Development	Letter Form Discrimination

We will examine each of these factors for your consideration and that of your staff. Many myths have developed over the years in reference to a number of them. Such myths need to be identified and dismissed so that time-wasting activities are eliminated in favor of experiences that contribute positively to the development of children.

Chronological Age

Kindergarten teachers seem convinced that they can identify the youngest child in class because of immaturity, lack of skill development, and so on. Work in a number of states has led me to an interesting discovery: In Illinois a child must be five on or before December 1 in order to enter kindergarten. There, teachers insist that they can "spot that November birthdate the minute he walks into the room." In Ohio the cut-off is September, and kindergarten teachers insist that they can "spot that August birthdate the minute he walks into the

---

[1]In keeping with our original promise not to clutter the book with a proliferation of citations, positions indicated in this section are not documented in the present volume. If you want detailed research evidence on any of these points, see either or both of the following summaries for specific research studies: Robert L. Hillerich, *Reading Fundamentals for Preschool and Primary Children* (Columbus: Charles Merrill, 1977); Jeannette Jansky and Katrina de Hirsch, *Preventing Reading Failure* (New York: Harper and Row, 1972).

room." No doubt, if the date were moved back to April, they would think they could identify the "March birthdate."

This conviction of kindergarten teachers is just not true. Chronological age is not an important factor in reading success or failure. In fact, one study reported that the relationship between the chronological age of *four*-year-olds and their achievement on specific skills was less than 10 percent better than chance, and certainly six months represents a larger chunk of a four-year-old's life than it does of a five-year-old's.

With some of your teachers, you might want to take a look at children's records in your school. Compare achievement and chronological ages at the end of first grade, or third grade for that matter. You will undoubtedly find that this is one topic that can be removed from your concerns about "readiness." Besides, if chronological age were a factor, what could you do about it except to sit by and wait?

Mental Age/IQ

Most people in the field of reading instruction have heard the statement that a mental age of six or six-and-a-half years is necessary for success in beginning reading. That myth originated in 1928, and too many educators have lived with it ever since. The fact is that no one can identify a mental age that is necessary for beginning reading. The level of intellectual development necessary for success is going to depend on the background of pupils, as well as on the methods and materials used for instruction. With some instructional materials I have seen, children would require much more than a mental age of six in order to be successful!

We know, today, that even the relationship between IQ and success in reading is not terribly high at the beginning levels. In fact, at these beginning levels of reading, correlations indicate that IQ can predict only about 10 to 15 percent better than chance. As indicated in Chapter 1, the simple factor of time devoted to reading is about twice as important as IQ. In other words, given the normal range of intelligence, mental age or IQ are not important considerations in beginning reading.

Visual Development

This consideration refers to the caution that children's eyes need to have matured physically before we expose them to print. In response, reports from ophthalmologists indicate that children's eyes are physically mature enough at age one to handle normal print. By age five, the eye is more accommodative than at any other age. In other words, there is no danger of harming the eye of a four- or five-year-old by exposing that child to *normal* size print.

Some primary teachers have formed mistaken impressions that large type is used in primary materials because children cannot "see" smaller type. This is not so. Large type is used in order to "blow up" or enlarge the print, since beginners cannot have too many words on a page at once or they would require a month to read that page. Conversely, if regular size newsprint were used with only three words on a page, the words would get lost in all the white space.

Socio-Economic Status (SES)

There are some who say that low socio-economic status is a "cause" of reading failure, or that instruction should be delayed for children from such situations. Research is clearly mixed in reports on this point. If you work in a school where children come from low SES families, this is a most important point for discussion with your staff, and one for which they should not merely accept the conventional wisdom.

I would resist the implication that low SES is a significant factor in reading failure or that instruction should be delayed for such youngsters. This "blaming" of low SES is an unhealthy attitude from at least three vantage points: First, there is not much that can be done about a family's SES. Second, it is most probably not the low SES that is a factor. It is usually the other elements associated with the low SES; namely, poor nutrition, lack of being read to, low priority on educational achievement, and so on. Third, and most important in my view, in too many inner-city schools low SES is used as an excuse for not teaching. It is too easy to say, "How can I teach him to read? Look at the home he comes from. . . ."

In other words, do your teachers concern themselves about such things over which they have no control, or do they practice that most ancient slogan of education: "It is our job to take each child where he or she is and move from there." If the child has gaps in language development, we will develop language; if the child has no experience with books, we will provide that experience. In fact, the more limited the background of a child, the *more* urgent the need to provide instruction, and the more urgent it is that such instruction be appropriate to the level of development identified.

Emotional Development

Discussion on this topic is usually related to the influence of emotional problems on reading success. Here, too, the research findings are mixed, but they are fairly clear in indicating that we don't know which came first, the chicken or the egg. From studies of children who were evaluated for emotional problems before they entered school, we learn that emotional problems have little relationship to success or failure. Conversely, studies of older pupils who have difficulty in reading usually indicate that such pupils also have emotional problems. Naturally, we might expect the latter finding, since you or I would have emotional problems, too, if we failed day after day in something as important as reading is in the school—and worse, were repeatedly told we were wrong!

For practical purposes, a common-sense approach seems best here. Failure in reading can be a cause of emotional problems. The secret then is to help children avoid failure by advancing them in steps appropriate to them. For children already identified as having such problems, let's get the help indicated, but even for them we should not *withdraw* instruction. While failure can aggravate an emotional problem, success certainly will not.

Neurological Problems

Most research indicates that severe neurological problems are *not* a significant cause of reading failure. Before we jump to a broad conclusion here, however, let's clarify the point: Neurological problems are not a significant factor merely because the incidence of such problems is not that great. This lack of significance does not mean that *some* child might not have a severe neurological problem that must be considered before he or she will learn to read.

To put this on a practical level, if my kindergarten teacher came to me and said that she believes her student Johnny has some neurological problem, I'd say we'd better take a look at Johnny. On the other hand, if that teacher came to me and said that she had six youngsters in her class with neurological problems, I'd say we'd better take a look at the kindergarten teacher! What is 2 percent of thirty? It's half a child, not six out of thirty!

Social Development

This topic is often used by those who espouse a traditional, informal, or developmental kindergarten program. There is no denying that provision needs to be made for social development. In fact, individuals should continue to develop socially at any age. This development is particularly needed at ages four and five, where children tend to be egocentric, personally involved, and very "I"- and "me"-centered.

The need for social development, however, does not prescribe or describe any particular type of program other than one that allows and encourages interpersonal relationships. In other words, children should have many opportunities to relate to each other and to the adult(s) around them, and these experiences should be as varied as possible. Young people can develop socially in all kinds of situations, not merely in play situations. In fact, most likely whatever social development they have had up to this point has been in the context of play.

Visual Motor Skill

Visual motor skill relates to eye-hand coordination and is often included with general coordination. This is a skill tested for in many "kindergarten screening" or "early identification" programs. Despite these tests and programs to the contrary, it is also clearly an area that has no place in a discussion of reading readiness—or reading, for that matter. Visual motor skill, or the lack of it, has nothing to do with success or failure in reading.

Discussion of this skill is so often included in talks about reading readiness because research consistently reports a good correlation between tests such as the Bender-Gestalt and future reading success or failure. However, as you know from your first course in statistics, "correlation" does not necessarily imply a cause-effect relationship. It merely means that two factors vary together, either directly (positive correlation) or inversely (negative correlation). Perhaps this will clarify the point: There is a high correlation between the height of elementary school children and their reading ability—sixth graders are taller than kindergarteners and they read better, but we do not suggest stretching kids to make them better readers. The two factors are independent of each other and are both dependent on other factors, such as age and experience.

We can dismiss visual motor skill as a factor in determining readiness because we know that merely increasing visual motor skill will not make anyone more ready or more successful in reading. Merely because a child learns to walk a balance beam does not mean that that youngster will be a better reader.

On the other hand, you and your teachers are concerned with more than the reading ability of your pupils. What about coordination as it relates to using scissors, holding a pencil or crayon, and so on? We must all have some faith that experience with these tools will increase skill in using them. However, research summarized by Hammill, Goodman, and Wiederholt (1974) indicates that existing programs designed to develop visual motor skill even fail to do that.

The practical point here is that they have nothing to do with *reading* readiness. If you and your staff feel that walking balance beams or other kinds of physical coordination activities are important—and they certainly are appropriate physical activities for this age child—then use them, but do not consider them as part of "reading readiness."

Experience

Kindergarten teachers have long recognized the need to provide five-year-olds with a variety of experiences. Besides the fact that experience, in and of itself, is a growth process, the intent in reading readiness was to provide experience with the real world so children would have referents for the words they were about to read. The young reader needs to have experience with apples, horses, buses, and fire engines before the words *apple, horse, bus,* or *fire engine* have any meaning.

There can be little argument with this point of view. It seems that the area for discussion with your staff might deal with the question "What kinds of experiences have our children had and what additional experiences do they need?" Do you provide the same kinds of experiences year after year, whether the youngsters need them or not? Are other experiences needed? Perhaps even more important, do your kindergarten teachers realize the necessity of constant verbal mediation? An individual might see that "thing" over there fifteen times or more, and still be unaware of what it is until someone supplies the word "disc" in connection with the thing. This gets us to one of the most important elements of any reading readiness program: language development.

Language Development

It is an axiom in the teaching of reading that no person can learn to read successfully in a language that he or she does not speak and understand. Some children enter kindergarten with minimal skills in English and need intensive language development. Conversely, the "average" child comes to kindergarten having mastered all the sentence patterns of the language and having a vocabulary of thousands of words. Many of these latter children are "ready" for the next step in their reading development.

There are many facets to language development. It is here that teachers may need some time and assistance in breaking down the instructional tasks into their specific elements. For example, even youngsters who are very facile in the oral language, if they have not been read to at home, may be lost when it comes to facing or even hearing the more linear or organized patterns of printed language.

While oral language development is certainly one of the most important parts of a "readiness" program, the specific elements that need to be taught will be discussed later in connection with kindergarten diagnosis. This is where it belongs, so we identify what each child has and what each needs in terms of specific language elements.

Auditory Discrimination

Auditory discrimination has traditionally been considered one of the major elements in reading readiness. Unfortunately, it is probably also one of the most misunderstood elements we will discuss. Too many teachers, from nursery school through first or second grade, seem to think that the job here is to teach children to hear sounds or to hear differences in sounds. Activities to accomplish this have included everything from "hearing" the difference between the roaring of a jet and the clanging of a bell, to "hearing" the difference between the slamming of a door and the dropping of a pin.

These strange practices grow out of the idea that we must begin with gross differences and gradually narrow down until we are working with fine differences, such as the difference between "pin" and "tin." Yet, you might discuss with your staff why they believe children do not already hear the latter difference. Any child who speaks English already hears the difference of one phoneme in a word. Ask teachers to check for themselves. They can hold up a picture of a house and ask the child if this is "mouse." That child, if he or she speaks English, will invariably correct them by saying, "No. It's a house."

I've found that even four-year-old Headstart children could "hear" the difference of one phoneme in a word. When asked his name, a child might respond "Johnny." "Oh, Connie?" "No, Johnny!" "Oh, Bonnie?" "NO. JOHNNY!" In twenty-two centers, not one child was found who had a problem distinguishing this difference of one phoneme.

Why do teachers think children have a problem hearing differences in sounds? Probably partly because commercial programs provide these kinds of practice material in gross discrimination. Also, teachers may create a problem because of their own faulty instructional language. A first-grade teacher once told me that many of her children could not "hear sounds." Yes, they did speak English. "Well, then," I asked, "how do you know they can't hear sounds? What did you ask them?" This teacher had asked children "How does *box* begin?" My first reaction was that she was asking for the spelling of the first sound, and spelling ought to follow learning how to read. "No, I just wanted them to tell me how *box* begins." It turned out, she was asking her children to respond with "buh."

Even the teacher who is more straightforward in his or her question will find a problem if that question deals with comparisons of beginning sounds. The teacher who asks young children if *fish* and *fan* begin with the same sound is likely to get answers ranging from "yes" to "no," with a lot of "I don't know" responses between. However, this kind of response does not necessarily mean that those children do not "hear" the difference. It most often means that they do not know what the teacher is talking about when she talks about *beginning* sounds.

Discuss this point with any teachers who are doubtful about it. The non-reading child usually has no conception of what a "word" is, much less what the "beginning" of a word is. All this is not to minimize the difficulty of teaching about "beginning sound." However, anything we want to teach is made easier if we understand where the child's problem lies. The problem is not in the inability to hear differences in sounds; it is in the lack of understanding of what we are talking about when we ask about the "beginning" of a spoken word.

Your staff discussion might clarify the teaching point in connection with this skill. The skill itself will be discussed later in this chapter, along with other more formalized "readiness" (or "reading"?) skills. Of course, for the child who comes from a different language background, there may be a problem in "hearing" differences between some of the sounds of English if those sounds were not part of that child's native language. This particular difficulty will be discussed in a following section entitled Diagnostic Procedures.

Rhyming Words

Activities dealing with the identification of rhyming words are a part of many commercial reading readiness programs. Yet, a thorough search of the research literature revealed no evidence that work with rhyming words contributes anything at all to reading success. Have you and your teachers discussed the role of rhyming words in beginning reading? Are we starting children to read in a language that they are to read from left to right or from right to left?

In the absence of any definitive research for or against the teaching of rhyming words, I can only suggest some serious discussion based on my own experience and common sense. Nothing is more difficult than trying to clarify what we mean by the "beginning" of a spoken word with kindergarteners who have been in a program stressing rhyming words. Such youngsters are quick to tell us that "rock" and "sock" begin with the "same sound."

Calling attention to the endings of words before children have started to read seems to be a good way to set them up for reversals, or at least to encourage confusion about where to begin in their identification of a printed word. As you discuss this concern with staff, you should point out that such criticism has nothing to do with reading and enjoying poems and jingles. In such cases, pupils are merely listening to and enjoying the sounds of language; their attention is not being called to the particular point—beginning or end—where the sound is heard.

Visual Discrimination

Many injustices are committed against young children in the name of visual discrimination. We have all seen worksheets with a mug, followed by four mugs turned different ways. Pupils are to find one that looks like the first one. Whoever makes such worksheets ought to know that a mug is a mug is a mug. It is a mug no matter which way it is turned. Some teachers even do the same thing with triangles. In the following example, children are to find the one that is "different":

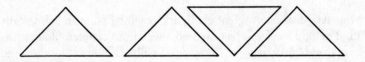

Such an exercise is teaching children a *misconception* in math: A triangle remains a triangle, no matter which way it is turned. Besides the misconception, what do these things have to do with reading? No one is going to read pages of mugs and triangles, not to mention pages of one-eared and two-eared rabbits.

Once more, as in auditory discrimination exercises, the thought that we must move from gross to fine differences is the culprit. Yet, all the experience in the world with one-eared and two-eared rabbits will not help youngsters distinguish *b* from *d*, and that is what they must do if they are going to learn to read.

Letter Form Discrimination

Experience in visual discrimination needs to be related to letter forms if a child is to learn to read. The letters A and *a* are the "same" letters, while *b*, *d*, *p*, and *q* are "different." Yet, the latter are much more "the same" than are A and *a*. The letters *m* and *n* are really the "same," in that they are both humpbacked letters. Yet, when we deal with them as representations of speech sounds, they are quite different.

Your discussion with teachers should lead them to discard some of these time-wasting activities in order to provide for those activities in letter-form discrimination that will help children learn to read. If your teachers do this, they will also find that they have more time to devote to other worthwhile activities, such as rhythms, art activities, and field trips, as well as more time to read to children.

"Early Identification" ("Kindergarten Screening")

"Early identification" or "kindergarten screening" programs have existed in many schools since the late 1960s. They grew primarily out of special education and were originally designed to identify and place "high risk" children; that is, those children who could be predicted as likely to have difficulty in school.

Most instruments or research in this area reveal their purpose through their titles or subtitles: "Predicting Reading Failure." Most often, this "predicting" is done by first assembling a group of tests that have been demonstrated to correlate with reading success or failure. These tests are then administered to kindergarten children at the beginning of the year. When those youngsters finish first grade, they are tested for reading achievement, and a correlation is done between the original tests and the reading achievement scores. Usually the examiners can say, "Great! Our tests are good: Children we said were going to fail did fail!"

The first task any principal and staff have in this area of "early identification" is to decide on their purposes. Is the purpose to *predict* failure or to *prevent* it? If the purpose is to predict or to sort youngsters, certain kinds of tests are appropriate—tests that show a high correlation with reading test scores. If the purpose is to diagnose in order to prevent failure, other kinds of tests will be needed—tests related to the skills needed for success in reading.

Predictive Measures

Probably the most commonly used predictive measures are commercial reading readiness tests. These contain items that have been demonstrated to correlate with future reading success or failure, including subtests such as letter names, copying geometric forms, and so on. Such tests are administered at the end of kindergarten or the beginning of first grade, and are used to determine which children are "ready" and which are not.

Unfortunately, the predictive accuracy of even the best of these tests is not very good; for groups, it is only about 15 percent better than chance. For an individual child within the group, the predictive value has been found to be only 4 percent better than chance. Worse, if you use such tests in your school, you might discuss with the appropriate teachers just how much *we have caused* what little predictive value such tests have. We usually use them to determine who is "ready" and who is not. Then what do we do? We begin *teaching* some skills to those identified as "ready," and we provide more general "readiness" for those who are not. Which children are going to be better readers at the end of first grade—those who received more instruction and experience with reading, or those who had more "readiness"?

If your goal is to do this kind of prediction, you might save both time and expense by merely making up a simple test of letter names. Randomly put four letters in a row, and continue doing this until you have twenty-six rows, so that each letter can be named once in the total test. Then simply ask the child to mark (or point to) the letter ___ in this row. The youngster who can correctly identify all the letters named can be expected to be more successful in reading; the child who cannot name most of the letters is to be considered "not ready."

Do not, however, consider such a test to be diagnostic. It does not indicate the kind of instruction the less able child needs, since no one needs to know the names of the letters in order to be able to read. Knowledge of letter names is just another example of a test using items that correlate with, but do not cause, reading success.

On this point of letter names, there are still a few teachers who believe such knowledge is essential if children are to learn to read. Both research and logic refute this belief. Half the consonant letters have names that do not begin with the sound the letter represents; for example, *h* ("aitch") and *w* ("double you") are about the worst. What do "aitch" and "double you" have to do with *horse* or *water*?

Second, too much drill on letter names leads children to go through an intermediate step of naming a first letter before beginning to pronounce a printed word. What pupils *do* need to know in order to learn to read is the sounds the letters usually represent, a point that will be discussed later.

Some of the items previously discussed as correlates of reading success are used for this kind of prediction. These include visual motor tests, such as the Bender-Gestalt or Frostig, various kinds of gross visual or auditory discrimination activities, and even skill in coordination, such as walking a balance beam.

Diagnostic Procedures

If the goal identified by you and your staff is not merely to predict but, rather, to diagnose and teach, the kinds of procedures you use will be different. Once such a purpose has been agreed upon, you will want to analyze your kindergarten program (or preschool program, if you have one) in both directions from where you have usually begun. On the one hand, what background experiences and skills have we presumed all children have when they enter our school? Do they *all* have these experiences? On the other hand, what background experiences and skills have we presumed every child lacks upon entrance to our school? Do they *all* need these experiences? In other words, any preconceived program may be too advanced for some and not advanced enough for others.

Of course, one might object to a formal diagnostic procedure with the thought that kindergarten teachers are quite capable of identifying the needs of their children. Research would bear out this conclusion in the sense that very early the kindergarten teacher is accurate in her or his assessment of the group. On the other hand, kindergarten teachers tend to be global in their assessments and can use some direction—their own or someone else's—to set down the specifics that must go into that global judgment if they are to identify what to teach each child.

The following specifics are the kinds of things you and your staff might want to consider as part of the initial assessment of four- or five-year-olds entering your school for the first time. The items are arranged in somewhat of an ascending order, from the most basic to more sophisticated. (For additional detail on testing and instruction, see Hillerich (1981).) Furthermore, the suggestions indicate that this kind of testing is criterion-referenced; that is, there need be no concern about norms. The assumption is that the teacher should be interested in whether or not a child can perform the task, and not how that child ranks with others on the task. Methods for quickly and easily checking on each item are discussed following the list:

Auditory Discrimination
Ability to Understand Instructional Language
Ability to Follow Oral Directions
Listening Comprehension
Ability to Identify Sequence

Expressive Language Development
Vocabulary
Ability to Categorize or Classify
Ability to Use Oral Context
Ability to Discriminate Letter Forms

Once more we are faced with an arbitrary division. In order to keep the list manageable, I have stopped with letter form discrimination as the division between "readiness" and "reading." While we will pick up the continuum in the discussion of beginning reading skills, you might see the division just as properly as being before or after this point.

Auditory discrimination. After the earlier discussion of auditory discrimination, inclusion of this topic in this list might come as a surprise. It is included here as a "basement" level because, in a research study involving 916 entering kindergarten pupils, we did find a few who had problems in this area. They were youngsters who came from non-English speaking homes and did not have some of the sounds of English in their native language backgrounds. Such pupils would not be expected to "hear" differences that were not significant in their own language, just as most English speakers do not hear a difference between the three *different* sounds of *p* in *pin*, *spin*, and *stop*. Since the differences in those three sounds for *p* do not distinguish words in our language, that difference is not significant in the language and we do not "hear" it.

In order to identify youngsters who do not "hear" some of the sounds of English, we have to be careful how we test. Some auditory discrimination tests present a problem if they are used with young children. It is confusing to them if they are asked to tell us whether *man* and *pan* are the same or different. They usually do not understand what we are talking about any more than they know what we mean by "the beginning" of a spoken word. To avoid this communication problem, you might test by using pairs of pictures whose names differ by only one phoneme. For example, use pictures of man/pan, rock/sock, and even ring/wing. Tell the child the names of two pictures and then ask that youngster to point to one of them. If the youngster consistently points to the requested picture, he or she obviously understands the difference of one phoneme.

Since reading instruction is usually going to begin with beginning sounds and beginnings of words, testing need only include initial consonant sounds. Very few children will be identified as having a problem in this area, but if only one needs help, it is important to identify that child and to provide follow-up instruction.

Instructional language. A teacher's instructional language is crucial to children's understanding. What special vocabulary do your kindergarten teachers use? Teachers usually use instructional words such as *in, on, under,* and so on. Pick the ten or so words that are most important and check children's understanding of them. The "testing" may consist of pictures where a child is to point to the object "in" the box, "under" the box, and so on. Youngsters might even be asked to put a block "in," "on," or "under" a box.

Oral directions. Since pupils are given oral directions from the moment they enter school, it is important to see if they understand how to follow them. Straightforward one-step, two-step, and three-step oral directions can be given as a diagnostic test. A three-step oral direction might be to close the door, put this book on the table, and touch the window.

While most children can follow three-step oral directions, our study identified some who could not follow a one-step direction. In fact, your kindergarten teacher may have a child who needs to be given a one-step direction and then to be taken by the hand and shown how to carry it out. Is this latter "basement" level kind of teaching provided in your school, as well as the more advanced practice that comes from activities such as "Simon Says"?

Listening comprehension. Crucial to any success in reading is children's ability to understand a story when it is read to them. Anyone who cannot listen to a story and comprehend it is unlikely to be able to learn to read a story and understand it. Part of the diagnosis, then, ought to include a simple one-paragraph story to be read to the youngster with the request that he or she tell what it was about.

In the research with 916 children, this is the first of the areas discussed where a good number of children had difficulty. Most of those with difficulty came from a school community where parents admitted doing very little reading to them in the preschool years. Certainly the importance of reading to children is a topic worth intensified discussion with parents in your school, since your teachers are already aware of the importance of reading to their pupils.

At the risk of a serious digression, this seems the appropriate place to comment on another aspect of your discussion of purpose with staff. Implied in the foregoing presentation of items for discussion was the thought that the purpose of this kind of diagnosis is to individualize in the kindergarten. We all recognize that kindergarteners are not noted for their independent work habits. However, individualized instruction in these skill areas is not a highly technical job. While *all* children need to be read to, this kind of diagnosis will identify some who need two or three times as much of this experience in order to make up for the years they have missed it. Such reading can be done by a parent volunteer, a senior citizen who would love such an opportunity, or by an older student who also needs more experience in reading easy material.

If your school already welcomes parent volunteers, their use in this area can also strengthen the volunteer program. Too often these parents mean well and want to help, but they come to school and find themselves feeling a little like fifth wheels. Here is an opportunity to be specific in identifying a definite and justified job for that parent to take over.

A final point about reading to children, whether done by teacher, parent, or older student: Too often we forget the purpose of the follow-up discussion; it is to be a "discussion" *for fun*, not a quiz. If youngsters get involved in the discussion, the development of comprehension skills will follow.

Sequence. The ability to identify or recall sequence is another important reading comprehension skill that begins at the listening level. The recall of sequence can be checked in connection with the previous story read to pupils. When the youngster retells the story, is the retelling in sequence? If not, can the child tell what happened first, next, and so on?

Another way to check on the identification of sequence is to use sequence cards: a set of three or four picture cards that can be put in order to tell a story. If such are used, teachers should realize that almost any set of such cards can be placed in more than one logical sequence. They should accept *any* sequence that the child can explain or justify.

Expressive language. Do your teachers have an organized or conscious method of evaluating the expressive language of their pupils? Is their attention on the sophistication of language used, or is it only on "correcting" inappropriate usage such as "ain't" or "feets"?

A quick and effective method for identifying the child who is weak in expressive language is to use the sequence cards previously mentioned. After the child has identified a sequence, flip on a tape recorder and ask that youngster to tell the story about the pictures. Later, the language sample can be analyzed. The easiest and most objective method for analyzing the oral language sample is by counting the number of words used per T-unit.

"Words per T-unit" is a way of getting around "words per sentence." This is necessary because the average kindergartener uses about 376 words per sentence. The child says, "We went to dinner and then we went to a show and then . . . and then . . ." A T-unit is any independent clause with all of its subordinate clauses and modifiers. More simply put, any simple or complex sentence is a T-unit; a compound sentence is more than one T-unit.

The typical kindergartener speaks in five to five-and-a-half words per T-unit. Again, this is not to suggest that you should develop or be impressed with norms, since the task is to identify those children who need help and to provide that help. However, this average figure is provided as a guide, with the added thought that any child below about 4.0 words per T-unit is in serious difficulty in terms of oral language development.

Vocabulary. Basic oral vocabulary is another area to be checked with entering kindergarteners. While no one has identified the precise words or exact number of words a child must understand in order to be successful in reading, it is obvious that anyone who has no understanding of words used every day for articles of clothing, foods, furniture, animals, and so on, is going to have problems in learning to read.

To test this area, your kindergarten teacher can collect a group of pictures of common objects and ask children to identify what they are. Concern need not be expressed for a particular word, so long as the child has an appropriate term to use for each picture. For example, a picture of a jet may be called "jet," "airplane," or even "DC-10."

Categorizing. If teachers put related pictures together on cards for the vocabulary test, they can also use the cards to discover if youngsters have learned to categorize. For example, in our study, we put six pictures of animals together on one card, six pictures of foods on another, and so on. After youngsters named as many of the pictures on a card as they could, they were asked how all the pictures were alike. The child who could abstract the idea that they were all animals, all foods, and so on, certainly had learned about classification.

Based on the study of 916 entering kindergarteners, we found categorizing to be an area where a great number had difficulty. While this finding was not surprising, it certainly indicated a need for some instruction if pupils are going to be asked to classify words according to beginning sounds or in any other way.

Oral context. Your teachers will probably also want to check children's ability to use oral context in predicting a missing word. Such a skill in oral language is basic to using printed context as an aid to reading. Very few children will have a problem in applying a missing word for a statement, since even a four-year-old who speaks English thinks along with the speaker and expects words said to make sense.

Letter forms. Finally, a simple test of letter form discrimination—"visual discrimination" as it specifically relates to reading—gets us right up to the point of reading instruction. Your testing here might begin with capital letters, since they are easiest to discriminate, and conclude with lower-case letters, even with a final set having the child find the letter that looks like this (*b*) in the set of *d, b, p, q.*

Using the Diagnosis

Several points need to be made about such a diagnosis. If it is going to be used by a teacher, that teacher ought to be the one to do the testing. A collection of numbers on a test record are not very meaningful when they are merely handed to a teacher.

Second, for the benefit of the child and the teacher, the diagnostic procedure should be brief. The entire series of items just described can be administered in fifteen to twenty minutes.

Finally, testing should immediately precede use. It is not advisable to test at kindergarten roundup in May if results are not going to be used until September. (Children grow and change in four months.) On the other hand, some schools have had excellent results with testing in May and then scheduling individual parent conferences. At the conference, results of the testing are shared, and the parents are given a brief set of specific activities related to their child's own weaknesses, so they can follow-up during the summer months. Then the teacher needs only recheck on the weak areas in September when the child enters kindergarten.

Of course, all of this discussion and all of the testing your teachers may do along this line will be a waste of time if that testing is not followed with the appropriate instruction as indicated by the test. However, if instruction follows, you will see definite growth in children, not only in the prerequisites to reading but in later reading success as well. In fact, in the study of 916 entering kindergarten children, as compared with 881 in a control group, Hillerich (1978) found a significant difference in reading achievement by the end of first grade. Not only that, but the lower end of the curve of achievement scores was moved up sixteen points in the experimental group as compared with the controls. It is this lower end that is really the target group for such a program.

Some Administrative Concerns

What happens within the kindergarten classroom—the curriculum, if you prefer—is a matter for discussion between you and your teachers. There are other organizational concerns that ought to be discussed as well.

Early/Delayed Admission to Kindergarten

Part of your discussion with staff will undoubtedly get into the topic of decisions about admission of children to kindergarten. First, of course, you will want to check your state guidelines to assure compliance. Further policy ought to be based on a clearly thought-out view of what a kindergarten group is. If the policy represents consistent thinking, it will also relate to the position you took in the preceding discussion of prediction vs. diagnosis. On the one hand, you may believe in prediction and therefore cull out "high-risk" five-year-olds from kindergarten entrance for another year. On the other hand, if you believe in diagnosis, you will more likely accept all youngsters of kindergarten age and adjust instruction according to their identified needs.

In any school we can identify some children at age five who are much below the typical in their preschool experiences and language development. It is the practice in some schools for the teacher or principal to ask parents to keep that child home for another year. Such a practice deserves a hard look.

In effect, the school staff is implying that the parent can do a better job at home in a year than the school can do. If the home has done such a poor job in the preceding five years, why should the next year be any better? In fact, if you are going to make distinctions regarding kindergarten entrance on the basis of knowledge and skill, the least prepared should not be kept out of kindergarten; they should be admitted earlier. After all, who needs the most help?

This policy of delaying entrance for some also implies that we believe children should enter kindergarten at a certain level of development. Such a view belies the facts, since the usual kindergarten group is made up of youngsters ranging in development from a typical two-year-old in terms of oral language to a typical seven- or eight-year-old in terms of reading ability. What is a "normal" kindergartener? The best answer to that was stated by Jansky and deHirsch (1972) when they said that with kindergarteners "variation is the norm."

"Early admission" is another facet of the question. Here the answer is not as clear cut, but it too will depend partly on your view of delayed admission. Granting that "variation is the norm" in kindergarten achievement, we are faced with the fact that the only remaining common denominator to describe a group of kindergarteners is that they are "five-year-olds."

Chronological age has been criticized as an insignificant factor in achievement. However, given a group of twenty-five five-year-olds, that factor probably results in more commonality in terms of interests and experience than any other factor would offer with the same size group. In other words, if you view any "grade" in school as nothing more than an age grouping, you have established a position on "early" or "delayed" admission: You will accept youngsters of varied levels of development and will adjust instruction according to their needs. This point will be taken up in more detail in the discussion of promotion and retention in Chapter 9.

The Kindergarten "Day"

Fortunately, in our times, we do have public supported kindergartens. Unfortunately, kindergartens are still little more than "tacked on" to the rest of the school. First grade is seen as the beginning or *first* year of real school. Also, most kindergarten days are only about two and a half hours, and the kindergarten teacher works with two sections of children a day.

The principal is in no position to wave a magic wand and significantly change the length of the kindergarten day or provide each teacher with only one section of youngsters. However, as the educational leader, the principal is in a position to begin discussions and to plant seeds for change—change in thinking among staff, board of education, and community. Actually, while half-day kindergarten is typical, there are schools with alternate full-day, extended-day, and full-day programs for five-year-olds.

The alternate full-day program is nothing more than a response to financial and energy concerns, where busing is reduced. While the evidence is somewhat mixed, it is safe to say that present knowledge indicates this organizational pattern does not make much difference as compared with the half-day program. Instructional time works out to be about the same.

Extended-day programs are offered in some schools. In addition· to the regular half-day, children who are identified as "high risk" come to school for the regular morning session and remain at school for continued instruction in the afternoon. In one situation, this approach, combined with a diagnostic/instructional program, has resulted in having those "high-risk" children test right out of the top of the achievement test. Based on our discussion of the importance of *time*, we ought not be too surprised that doubling the amount of instructional time results in increased learning.

One step further than the extended-day program, which is usually for selected children only, is the full-day (every day) kindergarten for all. In these days, an increased number of children come to kindergarten having had nursery school experience, some for two or three years. Most youngsters come to kindergarten with a great deal more language and life experience than was true when kindergartens were first established in this country as a transitional phase from home to school. While not the most significant educational factor, there are also many families now with both parents working. Such facts combine to suggest that serious consideration ought to be given to establishing full-day kindergartens.

One of the more recent studies of the effectiveness of full-day kindergarten was completed by Humphrey (1980). In a carefully designed experimental study, he found significant academic and affective gains resulting from the full-day kindergarten. Parent reaction was interesting: 92 percent of parents of full-day kindergarteners preferred the full-day, while only 53 percent of half-day parents *thought* they would prefer full-day.

Articulation

As stated, kindergarten is too often seen as merely "tacked on" to the rest of the school. In fact, in some schools there is more of a curricular gap between kindergarten and first grade than there is between the elementary and the junior high or middle school.

Part of this problem undoubtedly is historical. First grade already provided for reading readiness and beginning reading, so kindergarten became a socialization kind of program, designed to serve as a transition from home to school. Furthermore, kindergarten teachers have usually been left to design their own programs; in fact, in many schools there is a curriculum guide for kindergarten, and then there are guides for the academic areas in the grades.

How well is the kindergarten program articulated with the other grades in your school? Have kindergarten and first-grade teachers met together and been willing to compromise with each other? After all, if we recognize that children grow on a continuum, there should be no division between kindergarten and first grade, and there certainly is no arbitrary point, such as October of first grade, when they are suddenly all "ready" for reading. Some were ready when they entered kindergarten, and some probably will not be ready by the *end* of first grade.

When Should Reading Instruction Begin?

Considerable debate—if not outright argument—has focused on the questions of whether the kindergarten program should be formal or informal, whether or not skills should be taught, and whether or not workbooks should be used in teaching skills. Underlying such concerns is the basic question: When should reading begin?

Obviously, because of the range of backgrounds in any school and the many differences among schools, there will be no absolute answer to the question of when to begin skill instruction. Let's start by discussing the "typical" school. We must also qualify remarks about youngsters in this "typical" school by using "some," "many," or "most," rather than "all" or "none."

In other words, it is not enough to know "the odds." It is not enough to know that the "average" child comes to kindergarten ready for beginning reading skill instruction; that in one school 80 percent of children were more advanced than the readiness skills previously discussed; or that in another school most children were not to the point of those skills by the beginning of first grade. The task is to know where each of your children is and then to take each one to the next step.

When should reading begin? It should be clear that this ultimate question cannot be answered in the abstract. It will begin for this child at age three and for that one at age eight, while most will probably begin somewhere between ages four and six. As indicated earlier in this chapter, there has been a definite shift in most schools in reference to how early they teach skills. Before the 1960s, most kindergarten programs avoided teaching any formal reading skills; since the 1970s, about three-fourths of kindergartens provide for such teaching.

Times change. This is a danger that principals and kindergarten teachers need to be aware of. With "Back to Basics," will the educational pendulum in kindergarten swing from its "nonteaching" extreme of the 1960s to an overly structured skills extreme in the 1980s? Let's remember that it is just as unfair to children to ignore their developmental needs for human interaction and movement in the 1980s as it was to ignore their cognitive needs in the 1960s.

Anyone seeking an answer to this basic question of *when* skill instruction should begin is asking a philosophical as well as a research question. Research can only answer questions such as "*Can* children learn this?" and "*How best* can they learn it?" Research cannot answer whether or not they *should* learn it.

With these understandings clearly in mind, we can say that research shows that "most" kindergarten children "can" learn basic reading skills such as will be discussed in the next section. Furthermore, most youngsters so taught will be better readers at later grades, as compared with those who are not taught the skills until first grade. Finally, while it is difficult to prove interest in reading is increased among the early readers, it certainly is not hampered.

The research-based answer that kindergarteners *can* learn basic reading skills does not answer the philosophical question "Should they?" If the teaching of these skills will remove other instruction that is more crucial, then let's not teach the skills. If we believe reading is a worthwhile activity that enlarges experience, that belief might add more weight to instruction as soon as children can benefit from it.

This question of when to begin instruction in reading skills is often confused with the "formal/informal kindergarten" debate. Actually, this latter debate should be irrelevant to the basic question. The degree of formality with which a kindergarten is conducted is a matter of the teacher's method and procedures. Some teachers can make skill instruction an exciting game with the informality of a party, while others, unfortunately, can turn a party into a fearsome formidable affair.

In other words, the good kindergarten teacher has always had some structure, but it is often hidden beneath flexibility. That teacher has had a plan, but has been willing to shift as the occasion dictated. Furthermore, skill instruction does not, and should not, preclude movement and activity, as well as games and fun.

Should workbooks be used for readiness/reading instruction in the kindergarten? On this point, research appears about evenly divided if you merely count the studies and separate them into reports that indicate superior achievement with use of workbooks and those reports that indicate no superiority for the workbook approach. There is an explanation for the difference in research findings if we look beneath the surface. The studies that favor use of the workbook were studies where specific skills were taught; those not favoring the workbook were studies where only generalized "readiness" was taught.

To put this plainly, once you have made the philosophical decision as to whether or not skills should be taught in the kindergarten, the research answer is clear: If you are going to teach skills, the workbook will help to do this more effectively; if you are not going to teach skills, you can "not teach skills" just as effectively without a workbook as you can with one.

The danger of a workbook in kindergarten—or at any level, for that matter—is not in its existence, but in its misuse. A workbook is a *practice* book, and *practice* presumes that some *teaching* has gone before. Therefore, if a workbook is used as a culminating practice *after* instruction and practice through games and movement, there is little danger that the kindergarten will become "a little first grade" or that the workbook will become the program.

BEGINNING READING

This division between readiness and reading is a completely arbitrary one, created only as a means of dividing the discussion. While the preceding discussion of skills will fit just about any subsequent reading program, the continuum should now proceed in different manners, depending on your philosophy of reading itself.

It is at this point, if we are to be specific, that my own philosophy and convictions about skills are interjected. It would be of little benefit to you and your staff for me merely to say: "Children learn to read in many different ways, so just teach any way you want." The following thoughts on what beginning reading is about and what sequence of skills should be taught does represent my philosophy, based on research and experience. Let's also recognize that there are certainly other successful approaches to beginning reading.

What Is Reading?

As indicated in Chapter 3, there are various approaches to beginning reading. The approach you and your staff take ought to be based on your understanding of what this act called "reading" is all about. A large part of that decision is a logical and philosophical one, so research will not provide all of the answers. Appendix C contains an instrument ("Clarifying a Philosophy of Reading") that may be of some help in establishing thinking on what reading is all about.

Basic to your consideration of what "reading" is, you may want to consider two principles to guide your decision making: We ought to seek an approach to beginning reading that (1) will get children started in reading as quickly and as efficiently as possible, but (2) will be an approach that does not become a handicap at more mature levels of reading.

The discussion of approaches to reading in Chapter 3 suggested that the extremes of phonics and of meaning emphasis programs both have strengths and weaknesses. In terms of the two criteria just mentioned, perhaps we and our children can have the best of both worlds of reading programs. Let's consider what we, as mature readers, do when we read. No doubt you can read this sentence:

L-t's h-lp ch-ldr-n f-nd th-t r--d-ng c-n b- f-n.

Now, can you read this sentence?

-e-'- -e-- --i---e- -i-- --a- -ea-i-- -a- -e -u-.

These two sentences demonstrate the advantages of consonant sound associations as opposed to vowel sound associations. For one thing, there are twice as many consonants on a page of English as there are vowels, hence, twice as many clues. Probably more important, consonants tend to be fairly constant in the sounds they represent. For example, seeing *f* at the beginning of a word is a good indication that word is going to begin like *fish* or *fan*; seeing *a* at the beginning of a word is no assurance of anything except its name, since such words might begin like *at, ate, all,* or *about*.

You did, however, use more than your knowledge of the sounds the consonants stand for. You had to use context as well. If not, you would not have known if the fourth word was *find, fund,* or *fend*; you could not have decided if the last word was *fin, fan,* or *fun*.

This ability to use context and the sounds consonants stand for combines to a skill that gets children started early in reading, and it is a skill still used by adult readers. Emphasis on context along with the consonant sounds can also help children avoid the unnecessary, and often distracting, processing of words letter-by-letter. For example, you can read the last word in this sentence, even though only the first letter is there:

I'd like a cold drink of w___.

And you would not confuse it with a similar sentence:

I'd like a cold drink of m____.

If a person knows what a word is, just from the use of context and the first letter, why analyze further? And why teach children to analyze letter by letter?

Of course, if reading is saying words from a list, there is no context. Then we must either recognize the word instantly or try to sound it out. However, in the "real world"—the world outside of school—we are seldom expected to read random words in isolation. Even a shopping list represents some kind of context, since we do not expect to find words such as *fly, train,* or *sky* on the grocery list. Perhaps street names are about the only example where we have no context at all. Incidentally, do these facts about the "real world" also have some implications for how we should expose children to printed words in school?

With your staff, you might discuss what the act of reading is. Then apply your understanding of reading to the impression your pupils receive about what reading is. Is it a matter of *learning words*? Is it a matter of *making sounds for letters*? Is it a matter of *saying words*? Is it a matter of *interpreting ideas represented in print*?

Language Experience and Reading

While the great majority of schools in this country use a commercial basal reading program, many also supplement reading instruction with a language experience approach (LEA), and some use language experience to the exclusion of a basal reading series.

Fundamental to LEA is the thought that beginners in reading need to relate print to the oral language they already know, and that they should learn to read from material in their own language style and vocabulary. In other words, any individual should be able to learn better if the words are already familiar and if the style of sentences is the same as that used by the learner. Furthermore, familiarity with the topic will provide stronger context as an aid to the reading.

Even kindergarten teachers who do not follow the LEA will often have children dictate experiences that the teacher copies down for them and then reads back to them. Such an activity is a very important device in helping children understand that print represents the spoken language they already know and use. This kind of activity is also important to the basic oral language and vocabulary development, previously discussed, that should grow out of shared experiences as part of the kindergarten program.

The approach in using LEA consists of steps such as the following:

1. Youngsters, individually or in a group, dictate an experience to the teacher.
2. The teacher writes on the board or chart paper what is dictated.
3. The teacher reads the "story" back to get suggestions for additions or revisions.
4. The experience story is then used as material for further skill instruction.

LEA has some great strengths to recommend it, and it also has some potential weaknesses. Its major strengths seem to be in capitalizing on and further expanding oral language development, as well as in helping children relate print to the spoken language.

This relationship between oral language and print also presents some problems in beginning reading. Children speak in more involved sentences and they use a greater variety of words than are usually deemed appropriate for beginning reading material. The teacher may then paraphrase the sentences or substitute words to make that story "easier" to read. If these adjustments are made, that material is no longer in the style and vocabulary used by the child.

Possibly more serious, unless a teacher is well trained in the teaching of reading, is that the teacher may neglect specific skill instruction and merely use the experience stories over and over until the children have memorized them. Such an approach will contribute little, if anything, to reading skill.

Properly used, especially as an adjunct to an organized skill program, LEA can be an asset. You and your staff will have to decide on the extent and ways in which it can be most helpful to your teaching of reading. One method has been to demonstrate the relationship between speech and print by having the teacher read back the dictated stories. Then the stories are saved until "we have learned to read and might want to look back and read about what we did earlier in the year." Regardless of the extent of use of LEA, your teachers will want to continue on to teach some specific skills, such as those outlined next.

Specific Beginning Reading Skills

Whether LEA or a basal reading program is used, once a clear definition of reading has been agreed upon, you and your staff will want to analyze the sequence of skills required. Your continuum may begin with the facets of oral language development discussed earlier, and then might continue in one of the three directions shown in Table 4–1. This table presents three sequences of skills—three approaches—in the same order as presented in Table 3–1. From left to right, they represent the extremes of phonic emphasis to meaning emphasis approaches.

While the specific may vary somewhat, most programs will provide for instruction in discriminating letter forms, listening for beginning sounds, associating letters and sounds, using the letter-sound associations to read printed words, recognizing high-frequency (or "irregular") words, and then reading book material. Along with all of these skills, if reading has to do with meaning, your teachers will be working with their youngsters to continue development of listening comprehension skills, as discussed in Chapter 7.

Table 4–1   Three Alternative Sequences to Beginning Reading

Developing Oral Language	Developing Oral Language Using Oral Context	Developing Oral Language
Distinguishing Letter Forms	Distinguishing Letter Forms	Distinguishing Letter Forms
		Recognizing Selected Words
Associating Vowel and Consonant Letter-Sounds	Associating Consonant Letter-Sounds	Associating Consonant Letter-Sounds
Blending Sounds into Words	Using Oral Context + Consonants to Read Printed Words	Using Context
Recognizing Irregular Words	Recognizing High-Frequency Words	Enlarging the "Sight" Vocabulary
Reading at Various Levels	Reading at Various Levels	Reading at Various Levels

Using Context

If you and your staff believe in one of the synthetic or "linguistic" approaches to beginning reading, this section on context is irrelevant to your interests. Otherwise, most reading programs would teach pupils to make use of context in order to help them figure out a new word. How much actual instruction do your teachers provide on this skill?

The four-year-old English-speaking child already uses oral context intuitively. Why not capitalize on this knowledge by making children consciously aware of what they are doing? Let them know that they are using the sense of other words in order to anticipate a word that makes sense. It might also be worth considering where the missing word (or later, the unknown word) occurs in the sentence. If teachers always have the missing word at the end of the sentence, are they "setting children up" to stop cold when they come to a word they do not know? The missing word ought to be in places other than at the end of a sentence so youngsters will begin to realize there is often more context *after* that missing or unknown word for them to use in determining the missing or unknown word.

If a major goal in the reading program is to teach children to use context as part of their skill in identifying an unknown word, what is the role of flash cards and word lists to be memorized? With such, there is no context and therefore there is no practice of this skill. Further, you might observe whether children are being *taught* how to use context or whether they are merely being given *practice* in using it. After an exercise, does the teacher merely correct and therefore merely give practice, or does that teacher ask the child to justify the particular word chosen by pointing out clues from the rest of the context? The identification of the clue words by the teacher or child is part of the act of teaching children how to use context.

Distinguishing Letter Forms

This has been discussed in connection with the readiness portion of the program. The point here is that pupils do need experience with letter forms so that they note the fine differences that distinguish one letter from another; they do not need to be overly drilled on the letter names.

Listening for Beginning Sounds

Most kindergarten teachers, whether with or without a commercial program, work with children on beginning sounds. As discussed previously, youngsters who speak English already *hear* sounds, so we do not have to teach that. But we do have to teach them what we mean by the "beginning" of a spoken word, and that is a difficult understanding for young children. However, the teaching job is always easier if we understand what it is we have to teach. Be certain your teachers understand that, with the exception of any child they have identified from a different language background, their children already hear sounds, discriminate sounds, and reproduce sounds in the English language.

Many teachers provide enjoyable experiences for young children in the process of clarifying "beginning sound" and providing practice in sorting spoken words according to beginning sound. The activities may involve making "sound pages," where pictures are collected whose names begin with the same sound. Often, teachers will have treasure hunts, where children collect small objects whose names begin with the same sound.

An important point in this teaching is the language a teacher uses. Do your teachers say what they mean? For example, does the teacher ask children if *fish* and *fan* "sound the same" when that teacher really means "Do they *begin* with the same sound?" Furthermore, if teachers are going to clarify what is meant by the beginning of a spoken word, it is best to avoid also having children identify rhyming words.

Associating Consonant Letters and Sounds

Phonics is a term that refers to any kind of instruction that leads to sound associations for printed letters, regardless of the method used. That method might be through experience with word patterns, as in "linguistic" reading instruction; it might be through learning to verbalize rules, as in some synthetic phonics instruction; it might be through analyzing known words, as in some meaning emphasis programs; and it might be through a stimulus-response technique.

While some basal reading programs would begin this kind of instruction with vowel generalizations, discussion of these will be presented in the next chapter. Most programs begin with letter-sound associations for consonants. One question you and your teachers ought to investigate is "What is the best way to develop these associations?" Methods vary from the use of color, special diacritical marks over letters, associated pictures with each letter (a tire with a nail in it going *ssss* for *s*), a collection of words children have learned at "sight" that have the same element (*man, mop, me* for *m*), or key pictures (a picture of sun with *s* superimposed on the picture).

We must begin by recognizing there is no logic or means whereby we can explain to anyone *why* the letter *s* represents the sound that it does. Hence, if we want to teach this association, we are left with either the repetition of stimulus-response training or the use of some makeshift clue.

Most effective, in my experience and research, is the key picture technique as used around the world by Frank Laubach in his world literacy campaign. There does not seem to be any particular picture that is "magic" for a given letter, so long as the picture follows the configuration of the letter reasonably well. The effectiveness of key pictures was demonstrated by McKee (1966) with a phony alphabet. For example, if you were trying to learn the following three "letters" and the sounds they represented, you might need quite a bit of practice before you mastered the sound associations:

These letters are called "en," "em," and "double you" and they stand for the sounds you hear at the beginning of "night/no," "moon/might," and "water/wind." Since the shapes are really the same symbol, you might even get them confused, just as children at the beginning stage of reading tend to confuse *b* and *d*.

These same letter-sound associations can be learned easily if you see the letters with a key picture:

(note)   (man)   (wagon)

Incidentally, because you can spell, you might also be able to remember the name of the letter, along with "note." If you were a kindergartener or first grader who could not spell, you probably would not remember the name of the letter, but you could remember that the letter stood for the sound you hear at the beginning of "note." In your reading, then, if you came to a word that began with that symbol, you could remember the beginning sound even if you could not remember the name. And it is the sound association that is important for reading.

Using Oral Context and Consonants to Read Words

If teachers are going to develop all of the letter forms, beginning sounds, and letter-sound associations before children use them, it will be a long time before application. Hence, it is a good idea to include some application as reading instruction moves along. For example, after a few letter-sound associations have been developed, the teacher can print a word beginning with the letter-sound association taught, can give oral context, and the children can read the printed word.

You didn't have any practice, but you saw the key picture for this letter: ──○ . Hence, if you could not read a thing but were given the following context orally, you should be able to read the last word:

"I'd like a cold drink of _____."

Furthermore, given the same context, you should not confuse that word with:

Teachers do need to be careful in providing this initial practice: The context they use should be such that no two words beginning with the same letter would make sense. For example, if a word beginning with *b* is used in the sentence "The boys went for a ride on a b___," the word could be *bus* or *bicycle*.

Sometimes early application of learned skills can be provided if teachers will take a story they plan to read to children and put a page or two on a transparency. Then, if children understand that the teacher will stop at times and let them read a word, they can get some realistic practice. Teachers do need to plan ahead and stop only when the word children are to read begins with a letter already taught and it is shown in context strong enough that no other word beginning with that letter would make sense. Incidentally, this technique of using a transparency on the overhead projector also begins to develop another basic skill—the habit of moving from left to right when faced with print.

Recognizing High-Frequency Words

Regardless of philosophy, from extreme phonic to extreme meaning emphasis programs, everyone acknowledges that the beginning reader must recognize some words instantaneously. Phonic programs may call these "irregular" words, while other programs may just call them "sight" words, but all realize they must be developed.

For example, we might be at the very extreme in the view that learning to read is not a matter of learning words, that it is a matter of learning the skill of using context and consonant letter-sound associations. Even so, we must recognize that a child may master that dual skill perfectly and still not be able to read a single page because that child would have no printed context to use—every word would be strange. Hence, early in the process we need to develop a recognition or "sight" vocabulary that will serve as printed context to use in identifying other strange words.

It is precisely at this point that we must help teachers walk a fine line between teaching skills and teaching words. There are only a few words so important that they are worth teaching for their own sake. For example, three words—*I, and, the*—account for 10 percent of all words in print. Just ten words account for 25 percent of all words in print. On the other hand, we rapidly reach a point of diminishing returns in teaching words: The one-hundredth word in frequency of use—still assumed to be relatively important—is used only 4 percent as often as the most frequently used word.

Research evidence suggests strongly that the best way to develop a recognition vocabulary is for the individual to meet that word repeatedly in a variety of meaningful contexts. Hence, you might talk with your teachers about introducing a few of the very important words and then immediately having children use them to read rebus sentences. For example, with just three words and a variety of picture cards, children can enjoy reading a great number of rebus sentences.

The teacher might introduce the three words: *the (The), is,* and *in.* With these words and a collection of pictures, the teacher and children can make and read sentences such as "The (picture of a dog) is in the (picture of a house)." Gradually, your teachers might substitute a few other high-frequency words, one at a time, such as *a (A)* for *the (The), was* for *is,* or *on* for *in.*

The six words just presented—*the, a, is, was, in, on*—account for over 12 percent of all words in print. This represents an excellent return for the investment of time and effort. On the other hand, if teachers are preparing youngsters for a specific preprimer, they may want to look at its first few words, especially the structure words such as above, and include them in the rebus sentence experience as well, so youngsters will be successful in their first attempt at reading.

In contrast to such words, the words that teachers too often try to teach first are nouns. They usually teach these nouns through labels, for example: *door, window, desk.* Yet, the concrete words are the easy ones for children to learn. If your teachers are going to do such labeling—and it might help to relate print to the referents and oral language it represents—at least have them include the structure words. Instead of *door,* they ought to put on the door the words *This is a door.* It takes innumerable exposures before some children will recognize *the,* but those same children will recognize *tyrannosaurus* after seeing it only once. Are your teachers giving the practice where it is most needed?

SUMMARY

This chapter has dealt with what readiness and beginning reading are all about. In terms of grade or age level, we have presented the kind of program appropriate for typical youngsters from nursery school or kindergarten through early first grade.

Readiness and beginning reading have been presented as a continuum, beginning with the oral English development and moving through the basic beginning reading skills where pupils learn to use context and consonant letter sound associations.

It was suggested that the readiness portion begin with diagnosis of the needs of entering children rather than with prediction or sorting of those children. A number of traditional "readiness" concerns that are merely predictive ought to be discarded to make time for those that are important. In their place, the following kinds of diagnostic information should be determined for each child and then followed up with indicated instruction: auditory discrimination, ability to understand instructional language, ability to follow oral directions, listening comprehension, ability to identify sequence, expressive language development, vocabulary, ability to categorize, ability to use oral context, and ability to discriminate letter forms.

The concern for *time* was evident also in the discussion of delayed entrance into kindergarten, where too often the child who needs help most gets it later than others. Related administrative concerns included questions about the possibility of extended-day or full-day kindergartens and the need for continuity from kindergarten into first grade and beyond. If progress is continuous, the time when children "begin reading" will vary with the child: some will begin in kindergarten and some in first grade.

Exploration of the question "What is reading?" led to some suggestions that indicated it was probably a compromise between extremes of phonics and learning words. Most important, this is a question that each staff must resolve for itself if teachers are to implement a reading program soundly and consistently.

A brief discussion of the strengths and dangers of a language experience approach led to presentation of some of the skills most often developed in beginning reading. These included: using oral context, discriminating letter forms, listening for beginning sounds, associating letters and sounds, using letter-sound associations to read printed words, recognizing high-frequency words, and ultimately, reading book material.

The major point of this chapter has been to encourage staffs to focus on the major skills that are important for success and to eliminate those activities that are irrelevant. While some basic skills can and should be taught, let's remember that time and interest are essential factors for success; children will learn to read if given enjoyable opportunities to do so.

Suggestions for Action

Following are some factors you may want to examine in your school and discuss with *all* staff members concerned with children in their first few years of school. You may even want to establish a task force of parents and teachers to investigate one of the broader topics such as "What should readiness consist of?" "What approach should we take to kindergarten diagnosis/screening?" "What is reading?" "What are the important beginning reading skills?"

You may want to read through the beginning levels of your adopted reading program. What "readiness" and "beginning reading skills" are included? Visit kindergarten and first-grade classes to see if these skills are actually taught. Meet with the teachers to evaluate the effectiveness of these skills. What changes are needed?

Bring your kindergarten and first-grade teachers together. How well do these two levels mesh in terms of curriculum? Is there an arbitrary division between "readiness" and "reading" in your school? Is there a smooth continuum of experiences from that first day of the first year through later years? How can you improve the articulation?

With members of the primary staff, you may want to discuss some of the following areas, establish priorities, and begin evaluating procedures:

1. What are some of the factors traditionally considered important for "readiness" that ought to be removed from our thinking and our kindergarten program? What are the factors that are important for a successful "readiness" program? Do we provide these effectively? When? How?

2. What information do we get on entering kindergarteners? Which items of information *don't* we need or use? What information do we need that we don't get? What is our purpose in collecting the information: to sort and classify? to diagnose and teach? How do we communicate and use the information?

3. Is there value in diagnosing at the kindergarten registration, where we might share the results and ideas with parents?

4. To what extent can we or should we use parent volunteers, senior citizens, and older students in helping to individualize the kindergarten program?

5. What is or should be our policy on both delayed and early admission to kindergarten? How do we justify that policy?

6. What might be the advantages and disadvantages of full-day kindergarten? of extended-day for children who need more help?

7. What is our philosophy of "reading"? Are we *practicing* this philosophy in terms of what and how we teach?

8. What do we include as the specific beginning reading skills beyond oral language development? Are these skills, as well as "readiness," taught in kindergarten? Which of our kindergarteners enter with deficits in oral language development? What are we doing for them? Which enter with excellent language skills? What do we provide for them?

9. If reading skills are taught in kindergarten, does the kindergarten teacher have commercial or locally prepared materials to assure consistency and continuity? How effective are these in the view of the kindergarten and first-grade teachers? What changes are needed?

10. Visit some classes to see if kindergarten and first-grade children are getting an *enjoyable* start in reading, regardless of their entering level of development. What improvements can you and the teachers plan?

References

Carpenter, Ethelouise. "Readiness is Being." *Childhood Education* 38 (1961): 114–116. A brief discussion of general readiness, including the definition quoted in this chapter.

Durkin, Dolores, *Teaching Them to Read.* Boston: Allyn and Bacon, Inc., 1978. A professional text on the teaching of reading.

Hammill, Donald; Goodman, Libby; and Wiederholt, J. Lee. "Visual-Motor Processes: Can We Train Them?" *The Reading Teacher* 27 (1974): 469–478. A summary of research studies indicating that current programs in visual-motor skills do not even develop those skills.

Hillerich, Robert L. *Reading Fundamentals for Preschool and Primary Children.* Columbus, Ohio: Charles Merrill, 1977. Chapters 2–4 present a detailed summary of research and direction for teaching the readiness and beginning reading skills.

Hillerich, Robert L. "A Diagnostic Approach to Early Identification of Language Skills." *The Reading Teacher* 31 (January 1978): 357–364. Summarizes the skills and results of research on a diagnostic approach used with entering kindergarten children.

Hillerich, Robert L. *Ready Steps.* Boston: Houghton Mifflin, 1981. A diagnostic test and instructional kit for identifying needs and teaching language skills to entering kindergarten children.

Humphrey, Jack W. *A Study of the Effectiveness of Full-Day Kindergarten.* Evansville, Ind.: Evansville-Vanderburgh School Corporation, 1980. Reports results of research showing the effectiveness of a full-day kindergarten program.

Jansky, Jeannette, and deHirsch, Katrina. *Preventing Reading Failure.* New York: Harper and Row, 1972. Reports predictive results of a study of thirty-seven different tests used with beginning kindergarten children.

Lapp, Dianne, and Flood, James. *Teaching Reading to Every Child.* New York: Macmillan, 1978. A professional text on the teaching of reading, used for the definition of readiness.

McKee, Paul. *Reading: A Program of Instruction for the Elementary School.* Boston: Houghton Mifflin, 1966. A professional text on the teaching of reading. Chapter 1 presents a clarification of what reading is all about.

Tinker, Miles A., and McCullough, Constance M. *Teaching Elementary Reading.* Englewood Cliffs, N.J.: Prentice-Hall, 1975. A professional text on the teaching of reading, used for the definition of readiness.

CHAPTER 5

What Are Your Priorities: Phonics and Structural Analysis

The beginning reading skills of using oral context and consonant letter-sound associations in initial position and the beginnings of a recognition vocabulary were discussed in the previous chapter. Once pupils have mastered these basic skills, they are ready to move to the next step, which will include reading in book material.

Among all the possibilities we need to be concerned with in order to continue to move pupils along toward success in reading, two stand out clearly as the most important. First, we need to be certain that each youngster moves to higher-level reading material only as he or she is capable of handling it; that is, youngsters must always be placed in the appropriate level of reading material. That placement will be discussed in Chapter 9. Second, a related concern is to see that youngsters get a great deal of experience in reading. It should come as no surprise that children also learn to read if they are given the opportunity to read.

This present chapter will discuss the additional elements, whether they are seen as "teaching" or merely as "providing experience," that will help move pupils along toward maturity in reading. Instructional efforts will include developing a larger recognition vocabulary, developing ability to use consonant letter-sound associations in positions other than the initial position, and providing some experience with the sound representations of vowel letters and with structural analysis. The latter includes experiences with the parts of words larger than letters or sounds; that is, with syllables and with prefixes and suffixes.

Of course, continuing with all of this experience will be the constant development of the reading comprehension skills that were introduced at the listening level in "readiness," which will be discussed in greater detail in Chapter 7.

CONTINUING PHONICS INSTRUCTION

You may recall from the brief discussion of the role of phonics presented in Chapter 3, that phonics is useful only when the word to be identified is already in the reader's listening/speaking vocabulary. No amount of phonics will help anyone get the pronunciation, much less the meaning, of a word like *ciscisbeo* if that word was never heard or understood before. Hence, phonics instruction may be considered appropriate for any individual at the early stages of reading; additional phonics instruction is of no value to anyone *reading* above about a third-grade level because such individuals face the problem of words that are not familiar even in their spoken form. With such words, the reader can only use context and the dictionary.

So that the preceding statement is not misunderstood, I would like to clarify this point. Additional phonics will not help anyone *reading* above about third-grade level, but additional phonics will undoubtedly help that individual *placed* in sixth or eighth grade (or the adult) who is *reading at* a first- or second-grade level.

Even at early grade levels, your teachers should not let themselves fall into the trap of looking upon skill in phonics as a *goal*. Skill in phonics is a *means*, and only one of the means toward the ultimate goal of skill in reading. There are some disabled readers in clinics who are better in phonics than you or I, but they cannot read.

The preceding statement should be obvious and unnecessary, but sometimes we may be so close to the reading skills that the obvious eludes us. For example, in one school the staff did an excellent job of individually diagnosing and properly placing each child in a newly adopted reading program. A third-grade girl moved into the school and naturally was given all of the diagnostic tests. The teacher found that the third grader was reading at a fifth-grade level, but she was assigned to remedial reading because she could not pass the phonics test!

Whatever phonics we teach has its limitations. Its purpose is to enable immature readers to "get close to" or to approximate the pronunciation of a word they would know if it were spoken to them. For example, a young reader might fail to recognize the printed word *target*. When applying the "rules," whether using /j/ or /g/ for g and whether accenting like *forGET* or *MARket*, the child might get close enough to recognize *target*, so long as that word is part of his or her speaking vocabulary.

On the other hand, if the youngster had been taught to use context efficiently, all of the phonic analysis might be completely unnecessary. Perhaps the story is about Sue, who received a bow and arrows for her birthday. "Sue got some paint to make a *target* on the back fence." In such context, the first letter should be adequate to trigger the word, if a child is reading for meaning.

Recognizing that phonics is a tool toward success in reading, let's examine some of the additional experiences your teachers should be providing children and some of the ways those experiences should be handled.

Consonant Generalizations

One of the important, albeit not difficult, tasks is to provide children with experience in using their single consonant letter-sound associations in positions other than the initial position. They must learn to use those associations at the ends of words and in medial positions when necessary. For example, all we need is context and initial consonant to decide on the missing word here: "We decided to go for a swim in the w___." *Water* is the only word beginning with *w* that would make sense. However, if the word was p___, we'd have to look at the last letter as well to decide if the word is *pond* or *pool*.

Having youngsters apply their skill to various positions in a word is not difficult. Usually this is accomplished primarily through experience in reading, with some teacher direction and questioning.

Consonant Digraphs

Digraphs are combinations of two letters that represent a single sound. The major ones of concern are *sh (ship)*, *ch (chair)*, and *th (thumb* and *this)*. Many programs also frustrate young children with the *wh (wheel)* representing /hw/. Since even most adults pronounce *wheel* and *which* as if they began with a *w* rather than an *h*, why not let children use the sound they know *w* stands for to identify such words? Considering all of the important things the beginning reader has to learn, the /hw/ might be dismissed as an insignificant "purist" item.

Consonant Clusters

Unlike digraphs, which represent a sound different from the sound usually represented by the letters that make up the digraph, clusters retain the sounds of the individual letters. Clusters are combinations of letters such as *bl (black)*, *st (stop)*, and *str (string)*. There are over twenty-five such consonant clusters, and at one time they were each taught as individual new elements for children to learn.

Most teachers and reading programs today recognize that these clusters are made up of consonants for which children already have established the sound associations. If a child knows the sounds *s*, *t*, and *r* stand for, that child also knows the sounds *str* stands for. Here again, the primary job of teachers is to provide experience, perhaps also calling additional attention to what the child already knows.

There are some children, however, who seem to have particular difficulty with clusters, even though they know the sounds the individual letters stand for. Depending on your philosophy of reading, you may go in one of two directions.

If children are in an intensive phonics program, they will be told to "sound it out," meaning to make a sound for each of the letters, and then to "blend" those sounds together by saying the sounds faster. This approach is not too satisfactory with a word like *string*, where isolated sounding might initially produce something like "suh," "tuh," "ruh" (or "er"), and so on.

In a meaning emphasis program, children may still have difficulty with the clusters. However, that difficulty is not compounded with the problem of "blending" the sounds back together. One technique teachers might use is to work backwards from a word youngsters know in order to acquaint them with clusters. The procedure is similar to a familiar activity most teachers use for practice with initial consonants called "consonant substitution." In that procedure, the teacher may put a familiar word on the board, such as *ran*, and have youngsters pronounce the word. Then the teacher will erase the *r* and substitute *p*, asking what the word is now.

In this same pattern, the teacher may put a known word, such as *ring*, on the board and have pupils pronounce it. The teacher may then add *b*, reminding pupils that they know the sound that letter stands for, and have them pronounce the word *bring*. The same procedure can be followed with *rain*, adding *t* for *train* and *s* for *strain*.

Important follow-up activities include having youngsters find other words with clusters, preferably in context, and giving lots of experience in reading.

Vowel Generalizations

Nowhere in the reading program do we have more time squandered and more children frustrated than when we deal with the vowel sounds. While there has been some easing up of the rules about vowels since the middle 1970s, most reading programs still devote a large portion of the time at primary levels to instruction about vowel generalizations. Here is an area where you and your teachers should be acquainted with some of the research evidence, since the practice in reading programs is often contrary to that evidence.

Most of the credit for unearthing the problem should go to Clymer (1963), who examined four major basal reading series at the primary level. From the teacher guides of those series, he listed only those generalizations or rules that were agreed upon in all four series. With such agreement, we might assume the rules certainly would be important. The list consisted of forty-five rules, dealing with consonants, vowels, and syllables. Of the forty-five rules, twenty-four (over half, to give you some idea of the emphasis on instruction about vowels) dealt with the vowels.

Clymer then applied the rules to the words used in the pupil books to discover how frequently each rule was true. He established 75 percent as his criterion, saying that a rule ought to be true at least 75 percent of the time if we are going to bother teaching it to youngsters. Of the twenty-four rules dealing with vowels, only six were true as often as 75 percent of the time in the very books used to teach those rules.

One of the most common rules, still often taught by teachers, is the rule that when two vowel letters are together in a word the first "has its long sound and the second is silent" as in *boat.* That rule was usually interpreted to children as "When two vowels go walking, the first does the talking." Do your teachers teach that rule? It is true only 45 percent of the time! The child who learns and faithfully applies that rule will be wrong more often than right.

Following are the six rules that the four programs agreed upon, and that Clymer found to be true more than 75 percent of the time:

1. The *r* gives the preceding vowel a sound that is neither long nor short (Example: *horn*):   78 percent
2. Words having double *e* usually have the long *e* sound (Example: *seem*):   98 percent
3. In *ay,* the *y* is silent and gives *a* its long sound (Example: *play*): 78 percent
4. When *y* is the final letter in a word, it usually has a vowel sound (Example: *dry*):   84 percent
5. When *a* is followed by *r* and the final *e,* we expect to hear the sound heard in *care* (Example: *dare*):   90 percent
6. When there is one *e* in a word that ends in a consonant, the *e* usually has a short sound (Example: *leg*):   76 percent

Notice that the first, third, and sixth rules barely made the 75-percent criterion. Besides that, the first rule is of little help, since it only tells us what the sound is *not.* Likewise, the fourth rule only tells us that *y* has a vowel sound. There are fifteen vowel sounds in English, so which sound does *y* represent in an unknown word?

Many other researchers have gone on from Clymer's study to do their own analyses of different collections of words. (See Hillerich, 1977, Chapter 6.) Essentially, they have verified Clymer's findings, regardless of the vocabulary used for analysis.

The largest study ever done of the relationship between sounds and letters in English was that done by Hanna and others (1966). This group examined 17,000 words to determine if there were rules that could be taught. They programmed a computer for over 300 rules, including rules about the position of the sound in the word. Further, they even built in the 8 most frequent spellings of the schwa sound (as at the end of *banana*). Despite all this help, the computer was able to spell only 49 percent of the words correctly! Its big problem came with the vowel spellings, and there is at least one vowel sound in each English word.

If you have difficulty in convincing your teachers about the fallibility of the vowel rules, you might refer them to Table 5–1. It presents the data related to vowel sounds and spellings direct from the Hanna study. This chart may be used to verify rules about vowels from either a reading or a spelling viewpoint. Across the top are the fifteen vowel sounds we identify in English. Down the left column, alphabetically, are the spellings of those vowel sounds. The figures on the chart represent the number of words where a given vowel sound was spelled in a given way.

To use the chart from a reading viewpoint, start with the letter or letters for which you want to find the sound. For example, if you see the letters *au-e* (the dash represents any consonant), you might want to know what sound those letters usually represent. To discover this, find *au-e* in the left-hand column, then go across, and you will see that there were nine words where those letters represented the vowel sound in *saw*. Continuing on, you find there was also one word where they represented the vowel sound in *ape* and two words where they represented the vowel sound in *boat*.

To use Table 5–1 to check on a spelling generalization, work in the opposite manner. In spelling, we begin with a sound in mind and have to decide on the letter or letters to represent that sound. Hence, if you want to find out how /ō/ *(boat)* is spelled, find /ō/ at the top of the page and go down that column. You'll find that there were three words where that sound was spelled *au*, two words where it was spelled *au-e*, and so on. Examination of Table 5–1 should be a fairly convincing argument about the fallibility of most of the vowel rules we teach. Those rules usually fall into one of two categories: (1) rules that apply to many words but are not true very often, or (2) rules that are true most of the time but do not apply to enough words to be worth teaching. We certainly ought to question the teaching of either of these kinds of rules.

Often, teachers are not easily swayed by research. You might want to give them a little demonstration about the vowels. On the chalkboard or an overhead projector, present the following list of vowel spellings: *ey, ay, i-e, ea, e, e-e, oe, ae, y, eo, i, ei, ie, ee*. Have teachers, preferably as a group, call out the sound each of these elements represents as you point to each one. You will hear many different sounds, and you will probably become aware that, where there are two letters together, they are using that misleading rule about "When two vowels go walking." After the entire list has been read, you might want to

Table 5–1   Sound-Spelling Correspondence for Vowels

Key Word Sound / Spelling	pin /i/	elf /e/	bat /a/	top /ä/	saw /ô/	foot /ù/	cup /ə/	ape /ā/	eel /ē/	kite /ī/	boat /ō/	oil /òi/	owl /aù/	moon /ü/	few /yü/
a	4	158	4192	80	683		1606	1002							
a-e	187	51	147		34		3	790							
ae		1							5						
ah					4										
ai	15	50	1				9	208							
ai-e		3						18		1					
aigh								4							
ao					2										
au					150		1				3				
au-e					9			1			2				
augh					12										
aw					75										
aw-e					2										
ay	1	1						131		3					
ay-e								1							
e	69	3320			5		2742	16	1765						
e-e	28	113					143	6	62						

Reprinted by permission from Hillerich, Spelling: An Element in Written Expression, Charles E. Merrill Publishing Co., 1981.

Table 5–1   (continued)

Key Word	pin	elf	bat	top	saw	foot	cup	ape	eel	kite	boat	oil	owl	moon	few
Sound	/i/	/e/	/a/	/ä/	/ô/	/ů/	/ə/	/ā/	/ē/	/ī/	/ō/	/ôi/	/aů/	/ü/	/yü/
Spelling															
ea	50	152			18		32	14	245						
ea-e	1	1					2		30						
eau											6				5
ee	42								249						
ee-e									9						
ei	13	6					2	14	16	6					
ei-e								2	6						
eigh								18		3					
eo		3					10		2						
et								9							
eu						1	6							4	28
eu-e															1
ew											3			22	38
ew-e															1
ey	40	1						14	6	1					
ey-e										7					
eou							8								

Key Word	pin	elf	bat	top	saw	foot	cup	ape	eel	kite	boat	oil	owl	moon	few
Sound	/i/	/e/	/a/	/ä/	/ȯ/	/u̇/	/ə/	/ā/	/ē/	/ī/	/ō/	/ȯi/	/au̇/	/ü/	/yü/
Spelling															
i	5349						1459		38	554					
i-e	339						7		44	555					
ia							2								
ia-e	3	4													
ie	43						22		33	26					
ie-e	4						4		23						
ieu															4
iew															6
igh										88					
o	1			1558	435	17	2044				1876			37	
o-e				20	21		48				370			12	
oa					9						127				
oa-e											3				
oe									5		13			4	
oh											4				
oi												92			
oi-e							2					8			

Table 5–1 (continued)

Key Word Sound Spelling	pin /ĭ/	elf /ĕ/	bat /ă/	top /ŏ/	saw /ô/	foot /ŏŏ/	cup /ə/	ape /ā/	eel /ē/	kite /ī/	boat /ō/	oil /oi/	owl /ou/	moon /ōō/	few /yōō/
oo						114	7				9			173	
oo-e														12	
ou						25	388				29		227	29	
ou-e							1				10		54	3	
ough					15						8		4		
ow				4							124		119		
ow-e											1		2		
oy										1		48			
oy-e												1			
u	3	2				200	1743							93	814
u-e	3					11	60							34	256
ue														16	27
uo														2	
ui	16													6	8
ui-e														4	
uy										3					
y	1801						29			211					
y-e	1									23					

show them that every one of these elements represents /ē/, as in *key, quay* (pronounced "key"), *gasoline, each, be, complete, amoeba, Caesar, any, people, ski, conceit, grief, tree.* Does anyone want to suggest a rule that can be used here?

Can We Teach About Vowels?

From the foregoing evidence, you might get one of two reactions. Some might say, "Forget about the vowels." Others, especially teachers, might say, "Forget about the college professors who sit in their easy chairs and analyze language. I teach children and they read better after I've taught them about the vowels."

Despite the latter reaction, research results with children from four different studies suggest that it is better to ignore the vowel rules than it is to teach those rules. However, there is one procedure even better than ignoring the vowels, and that is to have children explore the "possible" representations of vowel letters and sounds.

From second grade on, teachers and children can have a much more enjoyable and beneficial time with reading if they use this "exploration method." First, the teacher helps youngsters identify a given vowel sound that they will work with, such as /ē/, as in *he* and *eel.* Once pupils have identified the sound, they might reread a page from their basal reader and list all of the words they can find that have the /ē/ sound. The teacher may ask for the words and list them on the board. Then, with the class, that teacher will sort those words according to the different representations (spellings) of that sound. The chart may look something like this:

e	*ee*	*ea*	*y*
even	feet	eat	any
he	keep	dream	lady
she	sleep	east	daddy
	see		

After pupils get a little experience with this procedure, they may be encouraged to use library books or any printed material to add to the chart. The above chart may be expanded very early with *e-e (these), i (ski, radio), eo (people), ie (chief),* and so on. Certainly the discussion will lead to no rule or generalization other than the fact that the /ē/ can be represented in many different ways.

If teachers use this approach, they do not have to violate their reading program. Whenever the guide calls for the teaching of a rule, instead of "spoonfeeding" the rule to children, the teacher may introduce it and then have children collect appropriate words to see how often the rule is true and how often it is not. If it is a good rule, children will remember it better by having had this experience; if it is not a good rule, teachers should not want them to use it anyhow.

Another positive feature of this exploration is the fact that teachers are hard pressed to do all of the individualizing they would like. Here is an activity with its own built-in individualization. When children are set free to find other words with a given vowel sound, they will return with different collections. The bright child may bring in fifty words and fifteen different spellings, while the poorer reader may have only fifteen words and five different spellings, which is good for that particular child. In the ensuing discussion, all benefit.

If you are interested in initiating this kind of approach with your teachers, you might liven up a staff meeting. Give teachers a piece of printed material of several paragraphs. Have them read it and list all of the words they can find that have given a vowel sound, for example /ē/ or /ā/, as in *eel* or *ape*. Then make a chart similar to the one just shown. Your teachers may be surprised at the variety of spellings they find.

You might want to talk with your upper-grade teachers about this exploration of possible spellings as well. It serves another purpose at that level and should be continued. This experience is absolutely essential if students are going to learn to use a dictionary for spelling. This is a skill not often taught, and it involves "educated guessing." This exploration of possible spellings provides the education necessary so that students know the different possibilities when they attempt to find a word they do not know how to spell. Specifics for teaching this skill are discussed in Chapter 8.

Finally, this discussion about substituting exploration for rules is consistent with a theme that goes throughout this book. The true value of this exploration probably lies in the involvement of pupils as active participants in language. Anything we do that removes the dull drill and gets children actively and enjoyably involved with their language is going to contribute to their skill in that language.

As you and your staff look at the reading program, do you teach a lot of these rules that help no one? If you are using a management system with your reading program, this is a good place to begin doing a little housecleaning. As suggested in Chapter 3, management systems all have a lot of padding and a lot of "skills" that help no one. With the staff, you might go through the items included about vowels and make some decisions about which are important and which are not. A practice exercise that contributes to skill is worth doing, but one that merely practices a useless generalization should be removed to make more time for children to *use* reading.

Getting Application of Skills

One valid criticism of reading instruction, whether in a classroom or a clinic, is that too often youngsters are taught and given practice in a skill, but they never see what that skill has to do with real reading. In other words, it does no good to teach and give additional practice in a skill—no matter how important that skill is—if it is not then carried over to application in actual reading.

We cannot rely on "transfer" to get this application for us. The notion of "transfer" is a myth when it comes to pupils in school. We must not only teach and give practice, we must then take children by the hand and show them how that skill applies in the book they are holding.

One of the most important activities teachers can perform has to do with their behavior just before youngsters begin to read a selection in their basal reader or whatever other material they use. This has to do with *how* the teachers introduce new words to the group, or—if they do not introduce new words—how they alert pupils to ways of identifying new words.

If you use a synthetic phonics program, your teachers will usually not introduce new words. Nevertheless, the teachers should remind pupils what they are to do when they come to a word they do not know. In this case, the direction that the teachers should give and be able to get from pupils is to "sound it out."

If you use a meaning emphasis approach, the method of introduction of new words will vary, both in terms of primary or intermediate grades, and in terms of what each teacher instructs pupils to do.

In some meaning emphasis programs, at both primary and intermediate grades, the purpose for introducing new words is to teach those words. Under such circumstances, a teacher will put the new word before the class, usually in context, and ask if anyone knows the word. For example, the new word might be *chickens* in the sentence "We got lots of eggs from the *chickens* at the farm." In this circumstance, usually some child will then call out the word.

Then the teacher begins a discussion about the word, attempting to build all kinds of meaning and associations for the word and constantly calling attention back to that word. He or she will ask about chickens, who raises them, what they look like, what they eat, and so on, while repeatedly asking pupils to look at and say the word. All this is to be certain they will remember that word when they come to it in their reading.

If your teachers introduce new words in this manner, you might want to initiate a discussion with them about what they are doing. They are merely *teaching words*. This means that they are giving their pupils no independence in identifying a strange word. They are making their pupils dependent upon them as teachers to be givers of words. Under such circumstances, you would expect any child who comes to a strange word to have *one* word attack skill: that child will raise a hand and ask the teacher!

There is another way of introducing new words that can be helpful to youngsters. It will differ at primary and at intermediate grades. At the primary level, the teacher will still introduce the new word in context, as mentioned, but her or his purpose will be quite different and, as a result, the methods will be different.

That teacher may put the new word in context for the class. For example, the new word is *chickens* in the sentence "We got lots of eggs from the *chickens* at the farm." The teacher will point out the new word in the sentence and ask pupils how they can figure out what it is. They should be able to say (or the teacher will remind them) that they can use the sense of the other words and the sound they know *ch* stands for. Then the teacher may ask who has figured out the word. There need be no follow-up discussion of that word, nor any building of meaning so children will remember it. The teacher's point here is not to teach that word; it is to review with youngsters what they are to do when they come to a strange word.

At intermediate grades, the purpose should be the same, but the technique will be different in that older students will be meeting words outside their listening/speaking vocabularies. Hence, the technique they will use, and should be reminded to use, will be context (the sense of the other words) and the dictionary.

The point of this entire discussion is to suggest that teachers need to let youngsters know what they are to do when they come to a strange word in the material they are about to read. Often, basal reader guides fail to clarify or encourage this practice. If teachers do not direct them, children may learn the basic skills but never see how these skills apply to the material they are trying to read.

WORD RECOGNITION

So far in this chapter we have been discussing "word identification," the skills individuals can use to figure out a word they do not immediately know. Now we will examine "word recognition," the automatic reaction to a word that is known immediately when it is seen. Such words are said to be part of the pupil's "recognition (or sight) vocabulary."

While I do see reading as involving the use of skills, as opposed to remembering words, I must admit that anyone with *no* recognition vocabulary will have no context to use as part of the skill for identifying other words. Therefore, as discussed briefly in Chapter 4, at a very early stage we need to begin developing and expanding this recognition vocabulary.

What Words Are Important?

Interest in the counting of words goes back to the ancient Greeks. In the present century, there have been well over one hundred word counts reported in English research literature. Less than a dozen of these are large-scale tabulations; most deal with the limited number of words most frequently used and therefore deemed to be the most important for success in reading.

Teachers of reading are most familiar with the Dolch Basic Sight Vocabulary of 220 words (Dolch, 1939). However, since data for that list were collected primarily from basal readers of the 1930s, some educators today question that word list as being outdated. Probably the more accurate criticism is that the Dolch list, as well as most others, was made from basal reader vocabularies that were made from such word lists, and so on, ad infinitum. Do any of them represent the real world of language in which children should be reading?

In an effort to answer this question, Hillerich (1974) compared four major lists that were compiled from uncontrolled vocabulary; that is, from written or published material over which there was no effort to limit or control the vocabulary used. The four studies included a school vocabulary (Carroll, Davies, and Richman, 1971), an adult print vocabulary (Kucera and Francis, 1967), and two studies of children's writing vocabulary (Rinsland, 1945; Hillerich, 1978). For your information, in case you or your staff want original sources, detail on these studies is provided in the references at the end of this chapter. Except for the Rinsland study, which is older, they are the only recent, large-scale reports that have been done of uncontrolled English vocabulary.

Comparison of the 500 most frequently used words from each of these lists helped to explain why word lists are different. They do not seem to differ so much by date as they do by source. For example, on a composite list of the 500 most frequently used words from each of the four studies, there were 113 words on the Kucera and Francis list, within the first 500, that were not on any of the other lists. These unique words appeared to be a businessperson's glossary: *board, business, community, economic, federal,* and so on. Likewise, 48 words unique to the Carroll study included *check, circle, correct, list, slowly, quickly,* and *carefully.* Can you recognize where these came from?

To put this another way, word lists seem to differ by their source rather than by their date. This difference is important if teachers are to work with the appropriate words, whether they are concerned with reading or with spelling. It means that they must have a list that has been compiled from a variety of sources rather than from just one. If we go to a variety of uncontrolled vocabulary studies, such as the four listed, and find the words they all agree upon, then we must have a list of words that are important no matter what, when, or where we read.

Such a list is presented in Table 5–2 in case you and your teachers would like to use it. This list originated from the comparison just described. A check against each of the studies indicated that these 190 words represent about 70 percent of all words used by children in their writing and over half of the words used in adult printed material. This is a good return on the investment of time and effort to learn 190 words, and it represents 2 percent more word coverage than the 220 words on the Dolch list.

The words in Table 5–2 are arranged in order of frequency of use, so teachers can begin with the most frequently used words and gradually add on. In order for teachers to have some idea of what the "typical" child can do,

Table 5–2.   The 190 Starred Starter Words

Midyear norms based on individual testing in eight school districts:
+ = Grade 1 (N = 344)—118 words were known by 50 percent or more of pupils.
    Grade 2 (N = 329)—all words were known by 75 percent, except the 9 words marked "(2)."
    Grade 3 (N = 357)—all words were known by 90 percent, except the 12 words marked "(3)."

+ the	+ had	+ from	+ me	+ down
+ and	+ we	+ up	+ your	+ back
+ a	+ be	+ will	+ an	+ just
+ to	+ one	+ do	+ day	+ year
+ of	+ but	+ said	their	+ little
+ in	+ at	+ then	other	+ make
+ it	+ when	what	+ very	+ who
+ is	+ all	+ like	could (2, 3)	after
+ was	+ this	her (3)	+ has	people
+ I	+ she	+ go	+ look	+ come
+ he	+ there	+ them	+ get	+ no
+ you	+ not	+ time	+ now	because
+ that	+ his	+ if	+ see	first
+ for	+ as	+ some	our (3)	+ more
+ on	were (2, 3)	about	+ two	many
+ they	would	+ by	+ into	know (3)
+ with	+ so	+ him	+ did	made
+ have	+ my	+ or	+ over	thing
+ are	+ out	+ can	+ how	+ went
+ man	only	right	last	told
want	much	+ ask	+ away	why
+ way	+ us	most	each	small
+ work	+ take	should	never	children
which	+ name	don't	while (2, 3)	still
+ good	+ here	than	+ took	head
well	+ say	three	+ men	left
came	+ got	found	+ next	white
new	around	these (2)	+ may	+ let
+ school	any	saw	+ Mr.	world (2)
+ too	use (3)	find	+ give	under
been (3)	place	+ tell	+ show	same
think	+ put	+ help	once	kind (3)
+ home	+ boy	every (3)	+ something	+ keep
+ house	water	again	+ room	+ am
+ play	also (2)	another (2)	must	best
+ old	before	+ big	didn't	better
long	+ off	night	always	+ soon
+ where	through (2, 3)	thought (2, 3)	+ car	+ four

modest norms are indicated at the top of the list. You might remind your teachers that these "norms," just like test norms, indicate what the *average* child could do—half the children could not do this.

Since the Starter Words were compiled from both printed material and children's writing, this list may be used for both a reading and a spelling vocabulary. However, teachers should recognize that we expect words to enter the reading vocabulary half a year or more before we expect them to be added to the spelling vocabulary.

All that has been said about words for the recognition vocabulary up to this point has been based on a particular philosophy of reading. It is based on the assumption that pupils are going to be reading in a variety of materials, and that the goal is not merely to have them reading in the basal reader.

If, however, you and your staff feel that children should stay in a basal reader, your selection of words will then be quite different. You still cannot go to word lists compiled from basal readers because each basal series seems to have somewhat its own vocabulary. In comparisons of basal reader vocabularies at the primary level, different researchers have found that they do not agree on more than about one hundred words. Hence, it would seem that if concern is with the words in the basal, you had better just take your own basal and teach those words.

This lack of agreement among basal readers has another implication. Many times teachers want a supplementary reader to use with their pupils, and they believe another basal is the answer. With this lack of agreement about vocabulary, there is as much difference between any two basal reading programs at the *primer* level as there is between any one of these and a "beginning-to-read" library book. Why not use the library book?

How Many Words?

We have already suggested that we quickly reach a point of diminishing returns in teaching words. For example, in the Carroll study, the first one hundred words represent 50 percent of all words in print. By adding another one hundred words, we increase that coverage by only 9 percent. Adding a third group of one hundred words adds only another 5 percent.

We might say that the Dolch 220 words are more than we need, and that the 190 words are about the right number. Based on an expanded study of the 190 words, using over 40 additional word counts, I could add that the 190 words may be *more* than enough. Actually the last 20 words may not be worth undue concern. It appears that the 170 words can be clearly justified from any standpoint, but the last 20 are in that gray area to be questioned.

Fortunately, the 190 words are listed in order of frequency of use. This has important implications for that teacher who has a child who can learn only 10 words this year. Those words ought to be the most frequently used ones, so that child at least has automatic recognition of one-fourth of all the words in print.

Expanding the Recognition Vocabulary

Once the words are decided upon, the next concern is how to teach them. I have already suggested the use of rebus sentences in the kindergarten and early first grade in order to give practice with the very high frequency words in meaningful context.

Researchers who have studied what makes words easy or difficult to learn usually consider factors such as word length, familiarity in spoken language, concreteness, configuration, and frequency of use. Of these factors, we can rule out configuration (the shape of the word) because it has nothing to do with learning that word. Word length and concreteness often conflict with each other, so research is unclear on the importance of word length. In terms of concreteness, we have few high-frequency words that are picturable, so that factor is academic. If the high-frequency words are not already in the child's oral language, that child should be working at the oral language, not the reading, level. Thus, we are really left with frequency of use as the most important consideration in the development of this recognition vocabulary.

This importance of frequency of use is certainly borne out in practice. In connection with the norms on the list of Starter Words in Table 5–2, we have indicated with a plus (+) those words recognized by the average first grader in mid-year. If you will look at that list again, you will notice that most words in the first column, the column of most frequently used words, have a plus beside them. The next column has fewer pluses, and so on. In other words, children tended to recognize the more frequently used words—the ones they saw more often—and tended not to recognize less frequently used ones.

Other research verifies the importance of exposure to words in a variety of meaningful contexts. Do your teachers assure this opportunity by providing time for children to actually read?

To put it bluntly, research is not completely clear on this question of how best to develop vocabulary. There is evidence that pictures will detract from such learning. The compromise, to avoid this danger, is to be certain that teachers also call attention to some elements in the word itself. If children look only at the picture to decide what the word is, they have no clues about the word itself that they can use when the picture is no longer there.

Other than this caution, we can safely say that teachers should be most concerned about developing into the recognition vocabulary those words that are used most frequently in natural or uncontrolled language. This is most sensible for two reasons: (1) these are the words that will be met most often in print, so they are the ones that provide most of the context to be used in identifying other strange words; and (2) these words are the most difficult to learn because they are most often the structure words, those that are least concrete and carry the least amount of imagery.

In terms of the techniques for teaching, it is also clear that learners need to be active participants rather than passive recipients. Hence, do your teachers provide for meaningful participation with words in context rather than for isolated drill with flash cards? Again, however, the experience in context will be further facilitated if the learners have their attention called to some graphic features of the word—those letters that help to distinguish that word from others.

Is it any surprise that research has demonstrated that children tend to use techniques they have been taught? If they have been taught only a drill kind of "look-and-say" with flash cards, their only strategy when they come to an unfamiliar word is to "try to remember" or to ask someone. If they have been taught some phonics and the use of context, their strategy is to use that knowledge in order to decide, from several options, what the word might be.

A final comment: Have your teachers recognized the importance of writing experience as another way to reinforce that recognition vocabulary? While there is little support for "preferred modalities," we do know that the more senses brought to bear in a learning situation, the more likely learning is to take place. As soon as children have control of the mechanics of forming the letters, they should be involved in writing sentences or even simple stories. In the process, they will be using these same structure words that are so difficult to recognize and that must become a part of their automatic recognition vocabularies.

STRUCTURAL ANALYSIS

Thus far, our attention has been primarily on letters and sounds (phonics)—the smallest parts that make up the language. Now we turn to larger chunks as we discuss structural elements. These will include compound words, contractions, syllables, and affixes—the prefixes and suffixes that are used in English. Most of these elements are taught to some extent beginning in first grade and continuing through the later grades.

Compounds and Contractions

Experience with compound words can be helpful to the young reader. The only generalizable skill involved is an awareness that some long words are made up of two shorter words that are known, and usually the meaning of the longer word is related to the meanings of the two short words. A word of caution is in order here. Teachers should never have pupils look for "little words in big words." To do so is to mislead them more often than to help them. In other words, youngsters should be taught to look for *two* known words that make up the larger word, or else they will have to handle that word in another way.

As with any other language skill, do your teachers turn this into an enjoyable exploration or a dull drill? Often, children enjoy hunting for compounds and illustrating literal interpretations, such as *rain* and *bow* for *rainbow*.

In teaching about contractions, teachers should remember that these contractions are *natural words* in the child's language. The teacher is not teaching a foreign language and should not be teaching children to translate. Why have youngsters translate *we'll* into *we will* when they consistently use *we'll*? Instead, the meaning, as contrasted with *we won't*, ought to be the focus. By the same token, *isn't* should be discussed as the opposite of *is*, rather than broken down into *is not*.

Even in writing, the translation is not the most important point. Here, youngsters may need some experience with translation in order to be guided on where to put the apostrophe. Often in writing, practice sheets provide a reverse kind of experience. Even for writing, the experience ought to be going from *is not* to deciding how to write (spell) the contraction rather than the practice of going from *isn't* to decide what two words make up the contraction. Is this something that needs to be discussed with your staff?

Syllable Rules

Not satisfied with the amount of time already wasted in teaching children about vowels, most basal reading programs continue on in a worse manner. They provide for the teaching of a group of useless rules about syllable division. Fortunately, most teachers are about ready to rebel on this point, and they need only a little encouragement from their principal.

Let's begin with the first rule that is usually taught. It is *relatively* the best. That rule indicates, "When there are two consonants between two vowels, we divide between the two consonants unless they are a digraph or a cluster," in which case we must go to the next rule. This rule is sometimes further complicated by being broken into two identical rules, one for "like consonants" and one for "unlike consonants." The rule is usually abbreviated as the VCCV rule, where the division is shown as VC/CV.

As an example, according to the rule, the word *yellow* would be divided as *yel-low*. If you would like to check a dictionary, you will find this is the way the entry word is divided, showing us how to divide the word if we run out of space at the end of a line. It is a *writing* convention, and an arbitrary one at that. A part of *reading* is the act of converting, mentally or actually, from print to speech. Hence, to pronounce the word we should use the pronunciation syllabication: /yel'-ō/. You will note there is no /l/ in the last syllable, so how can there be the letter *l*?

To be practical, however, where do you break that word when you say "yellow"? Do you say /ye'-lō/, /yel'-lō/, or /yel'-ō/? From my own pronunciation, I'll tell you frankly that I *don't know* where I break it. In fact, I will go a step further and admit that I *don't care!* And why should anyone care? The important point is that youngsters should realize that longer words can be pronounced in chunks—"syllables" if you will. The precise point of that division is certainly immaterial.

Linguists have trained ears and are more adept than most of us at interpreting fine distinctions in speech, including the pauses we make within words. One linguist was asked where the word "water" is divided when the speaker says it. The linguist replied, "About in the middle of the *t*." Other linguists have pointed out that there is no "truth value" in syllabication; it is an arbitrary convention and even dictionaries differ on where they divide the same word.

However, not satisfied with the VCCV rule, most reading programs go on to teach the VCV rule: "When there is a single consonant between two vowels, try dividing before the first consonant following the first vowel, and try the long sound of the vowel; if that doesn't sound like a word you know, try dividing after the first consonant following the first vowel and try the short sound of the vowel." (The rule doesn't say what to do if it *still* doesn't "sound like a word you know.")

First of all, do you understand the rule and have you learned it? Second graders are supposed to. To put it simply, the options are V/CV as in *ba-by* or VC/V as in *cab-in*. However, how could anyone pay attention to the meaning of what is being read with rules like that swimming around in his or her head?

If your teachers believe this kind of instruction is worthwhile, give them a little test. First, to be fair, you might want to review the rule with them, since some might not remember it. Then ask them where they would divide the word *notum*. Most often they will appear puzzled and will be afraid to admit that they do not know what the word is. If it is pronounced /nō-tum/ you divide it as *no/tum*; if it is pronounced /not-um/ you divide it as *not/um*. Since this is not a real word, you can contradict their syllabication with the opposite pronunciation. The whole point is: In order to use the rule, we must know the word. And if we know the word already, why would we *want* to use the rule?

Not only does common sense militate against teaching the syllabication rules, research does too. Consistently, studies of the effectiveness of teaching these rules to children indicate that such instruction contributes nothing to their reading achievement.

By third grade, many reading programs spend so much time on this that some "end of level tests" in those programs are devoted almost exclusively to syllable division. Teachers and children become frustrated, and for no good purpose. Here is a point where you and your staff can easily do some housecleaning.

All this is not to suggest that we ignore the fact that words have parts. However, it is to suggest that the exact point of division is not important to reading success. Even at mature levels, where the point of division may be important in some formal writing, the wise writer—if this end-of-line exactness is that essential—will use a dictionary to check on the syllabication of most words.

Prefixes, Suffixes, and Common Syllables

Unlike the comments about syllabication rules, we can say that there are some important instructional goals related to prefixes, suffixes, and common syllables.

To begin with, we should clarify the obvious: A syllable is a speech unit or print unit that may be smaller than a word but that is pronounceable without distortion. The latter point distinguishes "syllable" from consonant "sound." For example, *apt* is a word of one syllable, and it is a syllable in *aptness*. (Interestingly, it is not a syllable in *aptitude* because of the strange way we divide words.) A syllable may or may not have meaning by itself.

Common Syllables

Some syllables are used so frequently in English words that it is beneficial if their recognition (for pronunciation) is automatic. For example, *com* is a syllable that has lost its meaning in most English words, but it is among the most frequently used syllables. Anyone who recognizes it immediately has a quick pronounceable chunk of any word beginning with *com*.

Another important syllable is the "consonant-*l-e*" (C*le*) ending of so many English words, such as *table, candle, turtle,* and so on. Often pupils are taught that they divide the word before the C*le*. Once more, that point of division is not important, but the quick pronounceable unit is. After children meet several words ending in C*le*, the teacher might have them collect additional words with that ending. Then, in pronouncing the list, pupils will discover that they all end with that consonant sound plus schwa plus /l/: /bəl/, /dəl/, and /təl/ in the case of *table, candle,* and *turtle*.

Suffixes

There are two kinds of suffixes in English. There are derivational suffixes, such as *-able, -less, -ful,* which change the meaning of a base or root word, and there are inflectional suffixes, such as *-ing, -tion,* which do not change the meaning of a base but usually change the part of speech. Before youngsters can deal effectively with suffixes or prefixes, they must also look at affixed words to determine if there is a base they recognize. Otherwise, they could be in the same trap as when taught to look for "little words in big words." Having been taught the adjective-forming suffix *-ive*, which changes *act* to *active*, they may think they see the same suffix in *live*.

In terms of the derivational suffixes—those that change meaning—modern basal readers are fairly sensible in limiting the number. There are not too many of these suffixes that are worth teaching for meaning, if you accept as your criteria that you will teach only those that (1) are frequently used, and (2) are consistent in meaning. On the latter point, why teach students the six or seven meanings of a suffix? How will they know which meaning it has in a strange word?

Most important of the derivational suffixes, in terms of frequency and consistency, are *-ful*, *-less*, and *-able*. These can be developed for meaning in both reading and writing.

Many basal programs have apparently gone out of their way to create problems for young children when it comes to the most common suffixes in English: the plural marker *(-s)* and the past marker *(-ed)*. At first grade level, in many of these programs, children are taught to identify the three sounds for each of these suffixes. Most educated adults who speak English are not aware that *-s* and *-ed* both have three different sounds!

This is a point you ought to check with your first- and second-grade teachers. Are they teaching children about *-s* by having them identify if it is pronounced /z/ *(toys)*, /əz/ *(bushes)*, or /s/ *(hats)*? Are they teaching children to identify whether *-ed* is pronounced /əd/ *(hunted)*, /d/ *(played)*, or /t/ *(stopped)*?

If those first and second graders speak English, they will automatically pronounce the endings of such words correctly when they know that ending signifies a plural or a past event. (And, if they do not speak English, they should not be attempting to read that material anyhow!) All that children need to be taught about these suffixes is that they indicate plural or past. A speaker of English is hard pressed to use the /z/ pronunciation of *-s* in the plural of *hats*, or to switch any of the pronunciations of either the plural or the past marker.

While first- and second-grade teachers have no business teaching these different pronunciations for the past and plural markers, this is not to say that there is anything wrong if an upper-grade teacher gets students involved in this kind of exploration in order to further understand the nature of the English language. That, however, is quite different from thinking that this knowledge will improve beginning reading.

Prefixes

In terms of the total to be taught, prefixes also are usually well handled in basal reading programs. There are only a few that fit the criteria for teaching. Those prefixes to be taught for meaning usually include *un-*, *dis-*, *mis-*, *re-*, *pre-*, and *in-*.

The latter presents a problem because it assimilates: It is spelled *in-* in *incorrect*, *im-* in *immeasureable*, *ir-* in *irreversible*, *il-* in *illegible*. However, because it is so frequently used and because it usually means "in" or "the reverse of," most educators believe it is worth instruction.

Finally, there is one word of caution about the teaching of prefixes. Teachers should be careful in teaching children to note first if there is also a base word along with the supposed prefix. An analysis of 2,650 basic words indicated that there were ten times as many instances where a word began with the spelling of a prefix (that was not a prefix) as there were instances of the true prefix. Supposing pupils have been drilled on the idea that *pre-* is a prefix meaning "before"? What happens when they come to a strange word like *preach*? Does that mean an "ache" that comes "before"? Hence, awareness of the existence of a base word is essential before the reader jumps to any conclusion about a prefix.

This limited number of prefixes and suffixes is not the total story about such items for instruction in the elementary school. As students get into upper grades, with a heavier emphasis on the content areas, they will have need for additional items, including some of the Greek and Latin combining forms used so often in technical terms. Those will be discussed later, in connection with examination of the content areas, in Chapter 8.

SUMMARY

This chapter has presented some of the highlights dealing with additional instruction in phonics, word recognition, and structural analysis.

Phonic skill was suggested as a means toward success in reading rather than as an end in itself. Additional instruction is needed to extend pupils' use of consonant sound associations to positions other than initial position in words. Vowel generalizations were questioned. While pupils can benefit from exploring the nature of the symbol-sound relationships for vowels, the teaching of fallible rules can be worthless if not misleading.

The importance of application of skills was discussed. Regardless of the approach taken in reading instruction, pupils need to be directly reminded of what they are to do when they come to a word they do not know. Without such reminding, they may learn skills but never understand how those skills relate to the printed material before them. A specific technique for introducing new words is one way to guide pupils to application.

The development and expansion of a recognition vocabulary is an essential element if individuals are to move toward maturity in reading. No one can read successfully if that person has to analyze every word in a sentence. Less than 200 words make up 50 to 70 percent of the words anyone meets in reading or will need in writing. Such words will become part of the automatic recognition vocabulary through repeated exposure in a variety of meaningful contexts.

Structural analysis relates to the parts of words larger than single letters or sounds. Here we discussed the importance of providing experience with compound words and with contractions. Certain common syllables, prefixes, and suffixes need to be taught, but those taught should be only those frequently used and, in the case of prefixes and suffixes, consistent in meaning.

The usual teaching about syllable division was discouraged. No one needs to know the precise point of syllable division in order to be more successful in reading. Furthermore, evidence from studies with children indicates that knowledge of the syllable rules does not contribute to improved reading ability.

In conclusion, suggestions have been made that you and your staff examine the reading program and possibly do a little housecleaning on the vowel and syllable rules. Doing so will free time so that pupils can get more use of reading and thereby increase their recognition vocabularies as well. Yes, children do also learn to read by reading.

Suggestions for Action

The following are some items you may want to consider for possible examination in your program and for possible discussion with your staff. You may want to do some preliminary planning with a local or area reading specialist in terms of some of the specific items. While any of the suggestions will require observation on your part, some of the follow-up may be on a one-to-one with individual teachers, while other items may be handled best in a total staff meeting.

1. How do your teachers view the role of phonics in the school? Is phonics instruction seen as one of the means toward success in reading, or has it become an end in itself? How is this view demonstrated in the classrooms?

2. What rules are being taught about vowel sounds? Are they helpful in reading? Talk with some of your teachers about trying the "exploration" approach in dealing with vowels, or go into a class and try it yourself.

3. To what extent do upper-grade teachers provide for exploration of both vowel and consonant spellings as necessary background for success in using a dictionary for spelling?

4. How concerned are your teachers about a recognition vocabulary? How do they go about developing it: through flash cards and drill, or through

lots of experience in reading and talking about words? What source do they use for the word list?

5. What provision is made for application or carry over of skills? Visit some classes to see if teachers are introducing new words. If they are, how and why are they doing it? If they do not, what, if anything, are youngsters told to do when they come to a strange word?

6. What prefixes and suffixes are taught in primary grades? What criteria are used for their selection? Which ones should be deleted and which added to the program?

7. What syllable rules are being taught? What are teachers' reactions to inclusion of these rules?

8. Ultimately, are there some areas of the "skill" program or management system where you and the staff should clean house so that children also have more time to truly read?

References

Carroll, John; Davies, Peter; and Richman, Barry. *The American Heritage Word Frequency Book*. Boston: Houghton Mifflin, 1971. A word frequency count based on tabulation of 5,088,721 words from 1,045 texts in grades 3–9. Reports 86,741 different words by rank and frequency of occurrence.

Clymer, Theodore. "The Utility of Phonic Generalizations in Primary Grades." *The Reading Teacher* 16 (1963): 252–258. Reports the utility of forty-five generalizations agreed upon in four basal reading series at the primary level.

Dolch, Edward W. *A Manual for Remedial Reading*. Champaign, Ill.: Garrard Publishing Co., 1939. Contains the Dolch Basic Sight Vocabulary of 220 words.

Hanna, Paul R.; Hanna, Jean S.; Hodges, Richard E.; and Rudorf, Edwin H., Jr. *Phoneme-Grapheme Correspondence as Cues to Spelling Improvement*. Washington, D.C.: U. S. Office of Health, Education and Welfare, 1966. Reports results of a computerized study of 17,000 words to determine sound-symbol correspondences.

Hillerich, Robert L. "Word Lists—Getting It All Together." *The Reading Teacher* 27 (1974): 353–360. Provides details and the original study to develop the 190 Starred Starter Words.

Hillerich, Robert L. *Reading Fundamentals for Preschool and Primary Children*. Columbus: Charles Merrill, 1977. Chapter 6 contains a detailed analysis of research about the value and teaching of vowel rules.

Hillerich, Robert L. *A Writing Vocabulary of Elementary Children*. Springfield, Ill.: Charles C. Thomas, 1978. A word frequency count based on tabulation of 380,342 words used in creative writing by elementary children, grades 1–6. Provides an alphabetical list of 8,925 different words, with frequency of use at each grade.

Kucera, Henry, and Francis, W. Nelson. *Computational Analysis of Present-Day American English*. Providence: Brown University, 1967. A word frequency count based on tabulation of 1,014,232 words from 500 samples of adult printed material. Reports 50,406 different words by rank and frequency of use.

Rinsland, Henry. *A Basic Vocabulary of Elementary School Children.* New York: Macmillan, 1945. A word frequency count based on tabulation of 6,012,359 words used by children in writing, grades 1–8. Provides an alphabetical list of 25,632 different words, with frequency of use at each grade level.

CHAPTER 6

What Are Your Priorities: The Role of Independent Reading

Throughout this book you have found, and will continue to find, a recurring theme: Children also learn to read by reading. Yes, there are some important skills to be taught, but experience in reading is also an essential factor in learning to read at more mature levels. Even your best teachers of reading are wasting their time teaching children *how to read* if, in the process, they are not helping them *want to read* and actually getting them *to read*.

Certainly your teachers recognize the importance of teaching reading, but do they recognize the equal importance of *using* reading? The *teaching* is assisted through use of a basal reading series, but that is only half of the total program. The *using* is accomplished through library books, by whatever name that portion of the program is called: trade books, independent reading, or library reading.

Most parents and many teachers seem to think the total reading program is in the basal reading series. This is certainly not true. The basal is adopted for the convenience of teachers, to serve as a vehicle for the consistent and sequential development of basic reading skills. The workbooks accompany the basal for additional reinforcement—isolated practice—of the skills taught. Then the enjoyable application and additional practice needs to be provided in the independent reading program.

Even teachers, who themselves recognize the importance of the inde-

99

pendent reading program, will often hesitate to practice what they believe. A frequent comment from such teachers is: "What will my principal think if all we are doing is sitting there reading library books and talking about them? The principal will think I'm not doing my job."

It seems that the first step for the principal is to let teachers know that they are "not doing the job" if they are not making use of independent reading. Nor is it wishful thinking that the independent reading should be half of the total program in reading instruction. That position is clearly substantiated by the evidence from Individualized Reading.

INDIVIDUALIZED READING

One of the approaches to reading instruction that has not been discussed up to this point is that of Individualized Reading. This is not to be confused with the "individualization" of reading of the 1970s, with its diagnostic/prescriptive teaching and management systems. In fact, the philosophy of Individualized Reading is just about the opposite.

This approach arose as a concerted movement in the 1960s out of the concern of a number of educators about the "lockstep" of basal readers. Since all children do not like the same stories, why should they all read the same ones in a basal? Since children move at different rates, why are they all kept together in a basal? Such thinking led to the self-selection of books, self-pacing through books, and the use of library books instead of a basal reader for reading instruction.

The basic plan in Individualized Reading is to have children select their own library books. Then the teacher moves about the class, having individual conferences with youngsters. In those conferences, teacher and pupil discuss the book being read, and the teacher identifies and teaches needed skills. Throughout the program, youngsters also share and discuss their books with the rest of the class.

Like the Language Experience Approach, the philosophy was beautiful, but there were often some pitfalls in application. Often, with a class of twenty-five or more, the conferences became superficial. Children were reading and usually enjoying it, but there was a minimum of skill instruction. Despite neglect of the skill instruction, any summary of research comparing Individualized Reading with basal reading programs will usually have to conclude that there was no significant difference in reading achievement.

Such a finding makes us wonder! How much better would children in Individualized Reading have achieved if some organized skill instruction had been included along with the enjoyment and practice of reading? Conversely, how much better would children in basal reading programs have achieved if some of the enjoyable application of reading had been included along with the skill instruction? Let's see to it that children have the best of both worlds!

We have already suggested some of the "skills" in a basal reading program that might be removed, or at least minimized, in order to make more time for using reading. You, as principal or supervisor, must also let teachers know that such use of reading is not a frill but a necessary component of a good reading program.

Even among some teachers who do use library reading in class, the handling of that reading often implies that it is a frill. Too often a teacher will tell students, "You can read your library books when you are finished with your work." Who gets to read the library books? It is only those youngsters who already read well and who enjoy reading anyhow. Meanwhile, the poor readers will often be "rewarded" with an extra worksheet on syllabication or vowels because they didn't do well on the previous one.

THE NEED FOR AVAILABILITY OF BOOKS

Even if teachers and pupils do want to use library books, it is difficult for them to do so if the books are not available. Books need to be at hand *within the classroom* if youngsters are going to make the most use of them. This, and other arguments to be presented later, can make a strong case for a classroom library as opposed to a central library in the elementary school. On the other hand, most elementary schools already have central libraries, and it is pointless to suggest that they be eliminated. Besides, here again we can have the best of both worlds: We can have the advantages of a classroom library along with the advantages of a central library. The need is for the principal to step in and provide some leadership.

The Classroom Library

One of the advantages of the classroom library is the availability of books. Several research studies have pointed out that two to three times as many books are checked out if they are in the classroom rather than in the central library.

Second, if books are kept in the classroom, they provide a common background of knowledge. As a result, pupils are able to talk with each other, to have discussions about characters and authors, and in many ways to share and enjoy this common background.

Probably most important, if books are in the classroom it is clear that the teacher is responsible. They are as much a part of the reading program as that basal reader. Such a situation also makes the teacher better acquainted with those books and, therefore, more able to stimulate and guide the reading.

Not one of these advantages needs to be lost, and several additional ones can be gained, with the central library. Most often, however, the gains are not automatic. The principal must see to it that the library and librarian function as an extension of the reading program and that teachers are directly involved.

The Central Library

There are all degrees of "central library," ranging from an unattended room where books are kept, to a library manned by volunteers, to a library with a full-time, qualified librarian.

To begin with, if your "library" is in one of the former categories, you might begin with an assessment of the entire concept. Should most of the books be turned back to classroom libraries, with only the major reference works remaining in the "library"? A central file of the library cards can be kept in the office or reference room, each checked with the name of the teacher who has custody of the books. In this way, anyone looking for a specific title or author can find where that book is. If you go in this direction, several other considerations are important:

1. Books should be divided so that there is a range of reading levels in each classroom. Not all third graders can read at the third-grade level, and not all are interested in those titles.
2. Teachers should plan to exchange collections, at least at grade level, once or twice a year so that the collection in the room is varied.
3. The card catalog can still be maintained so that upper-grade teachers, usually sixth grade, can continue to teach use of the card catalog.

Of course, if you have aides or volunteers who do a satisfactory job of keeping books available and moving in the library, you may want to continue in the same manner as if you had a qualified librarian. That gets us to some points about the "proper" operation of a good elementary school library.

Does your librarian, whether qualified in library science or not, understand the role of an elementary school librarian? The job is not merely to keep books neatly shelved, cataloged, and dusted, and it is certainly not to keep dirty little hands off the books! The best librarian is the one who gets the books out so much that they become worn out from use. In other words, the good librarian goes around to classes, if not storytelling, at least "selling" the books.

Related to this, how many hurdles are set up in your library to keep youngsters from checking out books? Do you have an "open" library, or do you only schedule classes to the library? Why should a child go to the library only at 9:30 on Wednesday morning? Perhaps that pupil was ready to go back at

10:00 last Wednesday because he or she did not like the book that was checked out, or perhaps that child has not finished with the book yet on this Wednesday at 9:30. Children should be allowed to go to the library at any time they and their teacher decide it would be a good idea. There is nothing wrong with scheduling entire classes to the library as well, in order to assure a weekly visit, but individuals should not be limited to that schedule.

In defense of librarians and children, perhaps a word is in order about that "class visit" to the library, too. That is not the time for the classroom teacher to drop off her or his class in the library and go for a cup of coffee. Who knows those youngsters and their interests better than the teacher? That is the time for the teacher to be mingling with the group, making suggestions and giving reactions.

Does the librarian understand, too, what a visit to the library should be like? We have all seen those signs in libraries requesting "Quiet Please." In one school, at least, the librarian understood the function of the elementary library. Just above the "Quiet Please" sign, she had hung another sign: "NO." The library is not a place to slip into, silently select a book, and quietly sit down to read. If the library is to serve its true function, it must be a place for the class to go where there will be a great deal of chatter as youngsters and teacher exchange comments about the different books they know or think someone else should know. The quiet reading of those books can take place in the hallway, the classroom, or even outdoors if the weather is appropriate. Just sitting in the library quietly reading as a group is a waste of that space.

The checking in and out of books should be as simplified as possible in order to remove that hurdle from children. Does your library charge a "fine" for overdue books? Some libraries have an "amnesty week" when borrowers can bring back overdue books without paying the fine. I have known individuals who kept an overdue book for months in order to return it during amnesty week! Think how much sooner that book would have been back if every week had been "amnesty week."

In one school, the staff completely eliminated the entire checking procedure. If you wanted a book from the library, you went in and took it. When you were finished, you put it back. In comparing inventories before and after a year of this experiment, the staff found they ended the year with more books than when they started. While you might not want to go this far, at least you can see to it that procedures are kept as simple as possible, so that more books get into the hands of children.

Picking up on the advantages of a classroom library, the good school librarian will also encourage teachers to take out a collection of twenty or thirty books and keep them in the classroom until pupils tire of that collection. Then it can be exchanged for another. In most communities, the public library also encourages this procedure by allowing teachers to check out a collection of books for class use and return it when a new collection is desired. Do your teachers take advantage of these means of making library books available at all times to children?

THE SELECTION OF BOOKS

Who selects the library books in your school? Is this very serious responsibility left to the librarian? If so, your teachers are neglecting an important opportunity to become more knowledgeable about those books and to assert some direction in their selection.

Without a librarian and with the books in the classroom, the teacher is the only one who knows about the books and selects new ones. This advantage of the "classroom library" need not be lost. With your direction, classroom teachers, in cooperation with the librarian, can and should become active in the selection of books.

As we all know, publishers' catalogs cannot be used in this selection process. Has there ever been a publisher who admitted to publishing a book that was not "the best"? Relying on a publisher's catalog for the selection of books is a good way to make poor choices, if not to get into serious trouble.

In this half of the century, we are most fortunate to be literally swamped with children's books. Our problem is not to search out a book for children; it is to find the best or the most appropriate from the thousands that are recommended by reliable authorities each year. To do this, your teachers need to have available and to become acquainted with the tools used by the children's librarian. These tools are not the private domain of the school librarian. In fact, if you have a school librarian, that person would already have some of these tools and would undoubtedly welcome an opportunity to share them and to explain them to teachers. With or without a librarian or central library, every elementary school needs a *Children's Catalog* and at least one monthly publication about children's books. Following is a brief description of some of these publications:

Children's Catalog, H. W. Wilson Company, 950 University Avenue, Bronx, NY 10452. (Latest revision.) This is the standard reference for children's books. It is the most comprehensive and includes listing by classification, subject, author, and title, as well as indications of outstanding quality. A listing here is, in itself, a recommendation. Revisions are made every five years, with annual supplements between those revisions.

School Library Journal, R. R. Bowker, 1180 Avenue of the Americas, New York, NY 10452. (Nine issues per year.) Contains many reviews of children's books in each issue, as well as articles about authors, illustrators, and awards.

The Horn Book Magazine, 585 Boylston Street, Boston, MA 02116. (Six issues per year.) Contains detailed reviews, as well as some illustrations and articles, related to children's books. More literary than *School Library Journal*, but with fewer reviews per issue.

The Booklist, American Library Association, 50 East Huron Street, Chicago, IL 60611. (Issued twice a month.) A recognized authority, this

journal includes reviews of nonprint media, reference works, and so on.
Wilson Library Bulletin, H. W. Wilson Company, 950 University Avenue, Bronx, NY 10452. (Ten issues per year.) Includes reviews of adult, as well as children's, books. Also includes reference works and news about literary awards.
The Calendar, Children's Book Council, 67 Irving Place, New York NY 10003. (Semi-annual.) For a one-time cost of about $5.00, your school can be put on the mailing list for this publication. It includes notes about book awards, dates related to children's books, and some lists of free or inexpensive materials such as book marks, dust jackets, and so on.

A good spot for these resources might be in the teachers' room, so they can be examined when teachers have some free time. You may want to spend some time in staff meetings on the subject of children's books and their selection. With the availability of these publications, teachers can assume their responsibility as partners in selection, and they can gain additional knowledge about children's books.

There are other ways to gain this knowledge. Teachers may share about books at a staff meeting, so that all can capitalize on each other's knowledge. Most teachers have had a course in Children's Literature, but have they kept up?

One "painless" method of getting better acquainted with children's books was demonstrated to me by a beginning sixth-grade teacher who, within a period of three years, became one of the most knowledgeable people on the staff about children's books. When asked how she did it, she replied, "Oh, I just started taking a few books home each Friday and read them over the weekend." With a little encouragement and opportunity for sharing, your teachers can get "hooked" on children's books, too. After all, most chidren's books are more interesting than many adult books.

Once you have your teachers aware of the importance of this aspect of the total reading program, the real enjoyment begins. We cannot really *force* children to read, but we can coax, nudge, persuade, inveigle, tease, and otherwise edge them into it. Important first steps are taken if the books are available and if teachers realize how important this part of the reading program is. Now, however, we also need to incorporate ideas on how to *use* the library reading that we are trying to encourage.

This "using" of library reading is another important step and one that can also be an enjoyable opportunity for your teachers to share with each other. All of us, adults as well as children, can enjoy reading a book or story, but our enjoyment is increased if we have an opportunity to share that reading with another interested party. This is one of the points that came out of Individualized Reading. The conference with an interested teacher, no matter how superficial, was an important motivator in the continued reading done by that youngster.

While it is not our point here to inundate you with the many specific ideas that can be used in motivating and sharing about books, a few examples seem pertinent to stimulate your thinking. With just these sample items, you might conduct a sharing session among your staff about their ideas. Every teacher has some excellent devices that he or she has used with students. Get them out so everyone can benefit, either by copying or by adapting them.

IDEAS FOR USING LIBRARY READING[1]

While the availability or accessibility of books is a necessary prerequisite, this is not enough. The opportunity or time to read books is an essential part of the independent reading program, but there is much more. In addition to reading books, youngsters must do something with that reading—they must "use" reading.

We can organize this "using" of reading into several categories, all of them serving a secondary function as further motivation to do more reading. They include activities aimed at: developing awareness of books, providing a sense of accomplishment, and sharing. The latter may be through talking, writing, and/or creative activities. Of these sharing activities, the talking and writing are the most important since they involve further language development.

Developing Awareness of Books

With all of the other demands for children's attention, we must make a concerted effort to insure that they know about books and how enjoyable they can be. Of course, one way to do this is to read to them. Some reading to children ought to take place every day in every classroom. Does it in your school?

Besides reading to youngsters, there are many activities teachers can provide that will help to develop this awareness of books and thereby motivate the reading of them. Following are just a few examples:

1. "Sell" the books to youngsters. Each time the teacher brings a new collection of books into the room, that teacher might hold each book up, make a comment about it, and hand it to anyone who would like to examine it. Or the teacher may just pass each book around the room after a comment about it.
2. Have a book fair at school. These are book exhibits, where books may be purchased by parents and children.
3. Book contests may be held in classrooms, or school-wide, where pu-

---

[1]For many additional ideas, see Hillerich (n.d. and 1977) and Huck (1976, Chapters 11 and 12).

pils try to convince others that theirs is the best book for anyone to read.

4. "Commercials" on the school public address system can provide motivation. With your morning announcements, let youngsters take turns presenting a commercial about a book or books that ought to be read. (No book recommendation is more forceful than that of a peer.)

5. Quizzes may be held. At primary levels, these may simply be envelopes with questions on cards: "I'm an elephant who's faithful 100 percent. Who am I?" Of course, that would be Horton, from *Horton Hatches the Egg*. Upper levels may have such questions in a grab bag or on the bulletin board: "I won fifty dollars for eating worms. Who am I?" Any fourth grader ought to know that is Billy, from *How to Eat Fried Worms*.

6. A book Laugh-In provides a favorable atmosphere for quizzes. The teacher may set up a "wall" with window-like doors similar to the old "Laugh-In" television show. Different students may pop out with a quiz question or an original riddle about a book, author, or character. The rest of the class must guess the answer.

7. Filmstrips, movies, and television shows about books are good motivators. Keep teachers informed about any book that will be televised, either on commercial or educational TV. Excellent filmstrips are available from Weston Woods (Weston, CT 06880) for Caldecott and Newbery Award books.

8. Some primary teachers may like to start a grab bag. This is a collection of odd trinkets that can be associated with different books in the class, for example, a fire hat, truck, puppet, and so on. A pupil reaches into the bag, or may request an item, and the teacher reads that book to the class.

9. Older students who are poor readers may read easy books without stigma if they are to review those books for primary classes. Any older students might even enjoy reading these books and making a book "bingo" game for primary pupils. Bingo cards are set up with either the names of familiar characters or titles of popular books. Small cards—to replace the "caller's beans"—are then made with the opposite, the titles or characters. To play the game, the "caller" pulls and calls a card while players cover the matching item on their bingo cards.

Providing a Sense of Accomplishment

"Progress" in reading is a very intangible thing. Youngsters need to feel success, a sense that they are getting somewhere. Any kind of record is acceptable, except the kind where each pupil is competing against all of the others. In a class competition, the good reader moves ahead, but the poor reader quits because he or she has no chance of winning. If individuals are to compete, they must be competing only against equals. Under all other circumstances, the record keeping ought to be private or on a group basis. Here are some suggestions: suggestions:

1. Footprints provide a class record. Each time someone reads a book, the title of that book is put on a construction-paper "footprint" and fastened to the wall or ceiling. Sometimes classes have attempted to get their footprints out of the class, down the hall, and to the library before the end of the school year.

2. Individual "bingo" cards may be kept. These cards, laid out like bingo, contain a topic or category in each square: horses, mystery, adventure, biography, and so on. Whenever the pupil reads a book on a particular topic, that square gets colored in. This device encourages some variety in reading, but it does not present the pressure that some, such as "My Reading Design," can create. The top priority in elementary school is to get youngsters to read, whether or not there is variety in their reading.

3. Logs, graphs, or other kinds of personal charts may be kept by individual students and discussed periodically with their teachers. The teacher conference is important.

4. Title I, remedial reading, and learning disability teachers who work on a one-to-one or a small-group basis have an easier time of keeping open but noncompetitive records. Here, each student should have a chart, a poster, or some kind of record of progress. It is usually best if the youngster makes or helps to make the decision on the format for this record. You might want to check the rooms of your special teachers to see if they are showing youngsters records of progress or success.

Sharing through Creative Activities

Certainly any kinds of activities that involve use of language, either in talking or writing, are the most important. However, there is also a place for some of the construction and art kinds of sharing.

1. A travel poster may be made, advertising the setting of one of the books read.

2. Shadow boxes, dioramas, mobiles, and murals may be constructed by individuals or small groups who have read the same book.

3. Factual books may lead to construction or demonstration. A cookbook may be used at home to bring the class a sample serving. Craft, con-

struction, or hobby books may result in sharing the end product, whether the student brings to school a birdhouse or a collection of rocks, stamps, cans, or what have you.

4. Book jackets, posters, or bookmarks may be made, relating to the book read.
5. The teacher may like to section off the bulletin board for "favorite animals," "favorite characters," "favorite real people," and so on.

Obviously, the activities previously mentioned and those to come do not fit neatly into only one category. These "sharing" activities are also motivational and present some sense of accomplishment. The important goal of this whole presentation is to keep pupils actively involved in the world of books.

Sharing through Talking

Talking and writing are the most important of the kinds of activities engaged in. Just as youngsters learn to read by reading, they also learn to use language by using it. Furthermore, these activities not only benefit the presenter, they are motivational to the listener or reader as well.

1. Individual conferences need to be held with the teacher. During the class time that pupils are reading, the teacher may be moving about, talking with them about the books they are reading, how they compare with books previously read, and so on. However, this should not occupy all of the teacher's time, since that teacher should also be reading some of the time. In fact, one of the best ways to get a youngster interested in a book is if the teacher has been reading and enjoying that book. Most teachers who read children's books have had the experience of putting that book down on their desk only to find several children rushing up to ask for it.
2. Reading to kindergarten or first grade is an excellent way for older students who are poor readers to have an excuse to read easy books and to get more experience in reading.
3. Students may interview a person who has read a book. The interviewer can make a list of questions about the book in advance. That interview may even be "broadcast" on the school public address system.
4. Especially in upper grades, various kinds of comparisons can be made. Students may read several versions of a biography or historical event. Then they might discuss the similarities and differences as a panel in front of the class. Or individuals might like to compare illustrations in two books, or a movie or TV version of a book with the book itself.

5. Panels of "experts" may ask questions in order to discover what a "guest" has just read or what character that guest has in mind.
6. Each day someone might present to the class the most unusual, most exciting, or funniest part of a book.
7. Puppet shows may be used to dramatize a book. The overhead projector is helpful here. Pupils can draw the characters and scenes on transparencies. The characters can even be cut out and taped on cotton swab sticks so they might be moved about. The story can then be presented, complete with action, on the screen.
8. Two youngsters might play the parts of author and character. In a conversation between the two, what would the character have to say to the author, or vice versa?

Sharing through Writing

The more students can use writing, the more they will gain in their language skill. This, however, does not mean writing *book reports*. If your teachers require traditional book reports, the elimination of that requirement will be the greatest contribution you can make to increased interest in reading in your school.

You may have some students similar to two boys I knew as a principal. These two were inseparable from kindergarten on, and both of them always had a library book under their arm—until third grade. One day I stopped them in the hall to ask if they didn't like to read anymore. They responded, "Sure!" Follow-up questions got vague answers, including the fact that they always got their books from the public library rather than from their classroom. Finally it came out: If they took a book from the class collection, they had to write a book report on it!

If you have teachers that insist everyone must have the experience of writing a book report (and some seem to think this is necessary for survival!), at least convince them that one is enough. That unique task can be salvaged. Each pupil can write a book report about his or her favorite book—in whatever format the teacher desires. The finished product can be placed in a class book for all to use. Any student can go to that reference in order to get some ideas about a book that might be worth reading. Further, establish a rule that no one can have more than one report in that class book. If anyone reads a better book than the one reported on and *wants* to put it in the class book, the original report must come out.

A better alternative, *if the class likes the idea*, is to keep a card-file on books read. Each card should contain author and title, plus a brief statement about why the book is or is not a good one to read. With this reference, the entire class can get ideas about which books are good.

There seem to be an unlimited number of activities involving writing that can replace the traditional book report. Here are just a few examples:

1. Students can do original writing of the type read. A book of poetry may lead to the writing of poems; a riddle book, to riddles or jokes. These kinds of materials may also lead to scrapbooks in which favorites are collected from a variety of sources and shared with others.
2. Pupils may be "on-the-spot reporters," writing a news article about a book they have read as if what happened in the book occurred here and now in their hometown. Complete with headlines, this provides for some interesting creative writing and also serves to motivate others to read. In fact, some class newspapers have consisted entirely of such accounts.
3. Headlines themselves can provide for writing and can also be used as riddles for others to guess the book referred to. For example, "Ben Franklin Declared a Fraud" is a possible headline from Robert Lawson's *Ben and Me*. This use of headlines can also be a way to give poor readers at upper levels an excuse to read easy materials. In fact, they might even go back to nursery rhymes. Give each small group a nursery rhyme and have them make a headline of it. From "Mary Had a Little Lamb," one group—obviously not poor readers—came up with the headline: "Schoolboard Says Baaa to Ewe!"
4. Students might enjoy compiling dictionaries of the unusual words they meet in their reading.
5. In a language log (notebook), youngsters may copy down unusual or interesting descriptive paragraphs. For example, descriptions of characters may be recorded and shared with the class for comparison. This activity can be followed by creative writing, where ideas from the literary models might be used to write descriptions of characters or of people in the class.
6. Letters may be written to publishers, or to authors through the publisher, of books read. (If this is done, they should also be mailed, and your students will most likely receive a reply.) Letters may also be written, for fun, to characters to criticize, compliment, or question something in the book. Perhaps others in the class will take the part of the recipient and answer the letters. Letters may also be sent to the school or public librarian, recommending a certain book.
7. Students might make a crossword puzzle using ideas from a book. Then someone who has read the book can attempt the puzzle.
8. Older students may rewrite books they have read as picture books for younger ones to read. They may even rewrite them as easy-to-read books, using the 190 Starter Words as a guide.
9. The class may compile a *Who's Who* of favorite characters, with brief biographical sketches about each. Booklets might also be compiled of favorite types, such as "Great Girls," "Great Guys," or "Mighty Mice."
10. Students may enjoy writing parodies of poems or fairy tales: "Coal Black and the Seven Giants."

FOCUS ON READING

In addition to finding creative ways to motivate and use library reading, teachers can do a great deal through physical arrangements. There is no law that says children must sit, with both feet on the floor, while they read a book. Few do at home. Do the physical settings in your school encourage independent reading?

At the primary level, many teachers have found that everything from old bath tubs to packing crates can serve as "hideaways" for reading. Anything a youngster can crawl or climb into may be more inviting to reading than a chair or desk.

At any level, children will enjoy using a small rug, cushions, or throw pillows. Reading seems to be more enjoyable to many children in a horizontal position than it is in the vertical.

Sustained Silent Reading (SSR)

The use of SSR is one way to give practice in reading and to provide a model for reading. SSR may be practiced within a class or within the entire school. It is a set time when everyone reads silently: teacher and pupils in the class, or everyone in the school, including principal, clerk, custodian, cooks, and so on. Furthermore, it is an activity that can be practiced from first grade through high school, if not college.

Initially, SSR may extend only for a five-minute period, but everyone must have a book and must continue reading during that period. Gradually, the time may be extended to ten, fifteen, or twenty minutes, but it is always uninterrupted silent reading. The value of this approach is enhanced if the teacher, at times, reads some of the same books youngsters are reading. Not only does the teacher get better acquainted with the books, but pupils discover that even adults can enjoy the books they are reading.

SSR is a part of independent reading, but it does not replace the need for students to do something with that reading. In other words, the ideas for motivating and sharing are still important parts of the independent reading portion of the total program.

Dealing with Poor Readers

The "poor reader" is the one who does not read as well as the typical child; that is, the one who is reading below grade level. The mere definition of "grade level" and the structure of our reading achievement tests dictate that there are youngsters in each classroom who are "poor readers."

Unfortunately, library books tend to be written at about the reading level of their interest appeal. For example, the library books of particular interest to a fifth grader are usually written at about that reading level. Nevertheless, there are ways that poor readers can enjoy library books written at their reading level. The only hurdle to be removed is the stigma that such youngsters often feel they are reading "baby" books.

On this point, is your library arranged so that it reinforces this stigma? Do you have sections for primary pupils and other sections for middle graders? Sometimes this kind of arrangement is carried to such an extreme that middle grade students are not even allowed in the section with the "baby" books, and conversely, primary pupils are not allowed to take an upper-grade book, no matter what their interest or reading level may be. If you have such an arrangement, you might ask the person in charge if he or she has never read a book that was easier to read than it needed to be. There are many ways to organize books without implying that everyone must read at a certain level. Even if the books are so arranged, the children need not be.

One way to get older students into easy books is to ask them if they would like to take a look at first- and second-grade library books to see what they look like to them now "that they're grown up." In one sixth-grade class, this approach was taken with the low reading group. The ensuing discussion became so exciting and enjoyable that the teacher had to let the entire class in on the project.

This same approach was taken with a low group of junior high readers. They were asked if they had time to examine some primary books to help determine if they were good enough to put into classrooms. These junior high students, who did not like to read, did not read, or did not read well, became so involved in the primary books that—entirely on their own—they made notes on cards about the books. In a discussion about two weeks later, they spent an entire period giving reactions to the books and insisted that these books remain so they could finish their "reviews." Needless to say, when the books were finally picked up, another box of primary books had to be delivered.

This kind of reaction should not be too surprising. Even adults can enjoy primary books. In fact, some are more interesting than the adult fare we often get. Furthermore, youngsters will discover that these "baby" books are not too babyish, especially in terms of vocabulary. That sixth-grade group got into quite a discussion of some of the words used in picture books. For example, in Marcia Brown's *Once a Mouse*, the expression "ungrateful beast" is not exactly a beginning-to-read expression.

Another technique that has worked very well is to have a grade level, or several if you prefer, responsible for reviewing outstanding books for the school. If you have book fairs, for example, you might make your fourth graders the reviewers. Perhaps they will decide to review for the school the Newbery and Caldecott award winners and/or runners up.

Since the Newbery Award is given to the outstanding book in terms of literary quality, those books tend to be written at about a middle-school level. The better readers in fourth grade can be responsible for the review of these books to upper-grade classes.

The Caldecott Award is given for the outstanding book each year in terms of artistic quality. As a result, these books tend to be primary or picture books. The poorer readers in fourth grade can be responsible for the review of these books with lower-grade classes. Not only is this a method for getting poor readers into library books that they can read, it is a way of promoting the books throughout the school.

Reluctant Readers

Unlike "poor" readers, "reluctant" readers are those who can read but do not. Of course, many poor readers are also reluctant readers.

If we recognize the importance of practice in reading, then the first priority is to get such youngsters to read, no matter what. In my view, even comic books would be acceptable. The difficulty with comic books is that youngsters usually only "read the pictures." We might question the value of this kind of "reading."

Often, reluctant readers can be started with books that do not have to be read in their entirety, such as books of riddles, jokes, or poems. Again, we might remind you, such reading is more highly motivated if there is continued opportunity for sharing the results with others. Time must be provided to tell the joke or riddle to the class.

Nonsense poetry seems particularly motivating, especially if the teacher reads a poem or two to the group to get the book started. Among the most popular of the nonsense poetry books are John Ciardi's *I Met a Man*, and the particularly delightful (for any age!) *Where the Sidewalk Ends* by Shel Silverstein. You would be surprised at how many more you can turn up if you raise this question at a staff meeting. Every teacher has discovered some little book that is a prize to that teacher and class. Let your staff share their prizes.

Related to this kind of book are the primary ones that use idioms, figurative language, homophones, or just plain puns. The "Amelia Bedelia" books by Peggy Parish can be used at any level to acquaint students with idioms. *The King Who Rained* or *A Chocolate Moose for Dinner* are other examples of fun with language in easy books. Such fun, incidentally, may be a jumping off point for more creative writing in the same vein.

Some teachers are concerned about developing good "taste" in books too early. The first priority is to get youngsters reading. Besides, if a child has never experienced some of the poor quality, there is no basis for comparison in order to recognize good writing. Specifically, that boy or girl who happens to be hooked on the Hardy Boys or Nancy Drew can still get practice in reading. After a few of these books, the teacher might suggest taking "a look at this book before you read the next Nancy Drew." A kind of alternating along this line will help. Even if your suggestion does not work, that youngster is still getting practice in reading—and there are only fifty or sixty Nancy Drew books available anyhow!

A Young Authors' Conference

We have been touching on the importance of writing as it relates to reading. Some schools have had great success in carrying this even further by having a "Young Authors' Conference." Such a conference can be as simple or as elaborate as you and your staff desire.

Short of this kind of conference, older students may merely write books for younger ones to read. Such a practice helps both ages. The older students get their writing "published," and the younger ones enjoy reading a book written by "Timmy's older brother." The older authors of such books ought to be guided by their teachers, at least to the extent that they are aware of the need to keep vocabulary simple and to appeal to their readers. Their books may be bound and placed in the library just like any other book. You may even have a "kick off," where the books are reviewed in advance of cataloging them.

A "Young Authors' Conference" goes further. It may be school-wide, district-wide, area-wide (and eventually state-wide). Under such programs, guidelines are distributed and evaluation committees formed. Everything from poems and short pieces to books written, illustrated, and bound by students are submitted. On a set day, participants and other interested parties gather for a read-in of the materials, and the winners are announced. Often, the decision to pick a few "winners" is eliminated, and all participants receive a certificate of participation in the conference. Usually the wind-up activity for such a conference includes a presentation by a children's author or illustrator.

A Word about Censorship

The school is supported by public money. Educators have a responsibility to be prudent custodians and allocators of those monies. At the lowest extreme, this means that tax money should not be used to purchase poor quality materials. In terms of library books, should tax money be used for Nancy Drew, Hardy Boys, or similar materials that youngsters can, and probably will, find anyhow? This is a beginning point that might be discussed with your staff if there is any question about it.

In these days, questions go much further. Social, religious, ethnic, and political groups of all kinds find the school an easy target. Sometimes a single—and to most people, "innocent"—book can set off a great upheaval in the school community. One memorable parent attacked a beginning-to-read book as "communist propaganda" because, in that book, community members co-operated to build a snow hill for youngsters to slide down. The "final proof" was the fact that the family lived in a *white house* and there was a *red bird* in the yard.

Unfortunately, too many attacks are not by a single individual; neither are they quite so easily discouraged. Are you, as well as your teachers, super-intendent, and board of education, aware of positions and procedures should something like this come up in your school? For example, among other positions in the American Library Association's "Library Bill of Rights" are the following positive and helpful statements:

> The American Library Association affirms that all libraries are forums for information and ideas, and that the following basic policies should guide their services.
> 1. Books and other library resources should be provided for the interest, information, and enlightenment of all people of the community the library serves. Materials should not be excluded because of the origin, background, or views of those contributing to their creation.
> 2. Libraries should provide materials and information presenting all points of view on current and historical issues. Materials should not be proscribed or removed because of partisan or doctrinal disapproval.
> 3. Libraries should challenge censorship in the fulfillment of their responsibility to provide information and enlightenment.
> 4. Libraries should cooperate with all persons and groups concerned with resisting abridgment of free expression and free access to ideas.[2]

As you see, the first two points indicate the library's positive responsibilities in furthering our cultural heritage in a pluralistic society. Such positions recognize the rights of all, but they may create conflict in the case of individuals or groups who seek only their rights to the exclusion of the rights of others. Hence, the next two points encourage a steadfast position.

Your school district must go a step further. You need to have a written statement, approved by the board of education, establishing procedures that will be followed when anyone objects to or attempts to censor books or materials in the school. Such a procedure is imperative. In most cases, it will avoid much unpleasantness that could arise when individuals become personally involved in a disagreement. That procedure ought to state the objectives for selection, who is responsible for the selection (ultimately this is the board of education), criteria and procedures to be used in the selection of materials, and, finally, the course of action to be followed by anyone challenging or objecting to any materials selected.

---

[2]Reprinted by permission of the American Library Association from the Library Bill of Rights, adopted June 18, 1948; amended February 2, 1961, June 27, 1967, and January 23, 1980, by the ALA Council.

Because this is such an important area, the procedures for objections to material should be spelled out in detail and distributed to all staff. Following is a brief outline of some of the kinds of things you should clarify in your directions for handling challenged materials.

Initial Complaint

Teachers should be given some important pointers about handling objections. While your ideas may vary somewhat, you will probably want to include the following suggestions:

1. Teachers should be courteous and demonstrate their shared interest in the welfare of the child.
2. Teachers should not immediately defend the book. Inform parents that it was carefully selected and that it will be reexamined.
3. Teachers should notify the principal.
4. Teachers should set a date, or have the principal set a date, for a conference with the parent.

Follow-up

The principal and teacher will reread the material and get information from professional reviews or designated individuals. At the parent conference, they will hear the specific complaints of the parent again and will present the justification for keeping the book. If that parent is still not satisfied, he or she will be invited to submit a formal request for reconsideration of the material. The procedures for the formal complaint will be initiated.

Formal Complaint

Here, additional steps must be spelled out, such as:

1. The parent will be given a copy of the form for written complaints (see Figure 6–1) and invited to return it to school when it has been completed.
2. The superintendent will be informed.
3. The material objected to will be temporarily withdrawn, pending a decision of the Materials Evaluation Committee.
4. The Materials Evaluation Committee will conduct a thorough investigation of the book, its merits, possible faults, other reviews, and so

on. That committee will make a written report of its findings and recommendation to the superintendent.

5. The complainant will be notified of the decision.

In your district, ultimate responsibility for a decision may be retained by
the board of education, or it may be delegated by them to the committee.
This, too, should be clearly defined, including the fact that authority ultimately rests with the legally elected members of the board of education.

Figure 6–1 is a sample of a formal request for reconsideration of material. It is an adaptation of forms recommended by the American Library Association and the National Council of Teachers of English (National Council
of Teachers of English, 1978). As you see from the foregoing, this procedure
is not designed to hinder any legitimate complaint. It is, however, a protection
against the whims of an individual or group who would attack material used
within the school. If you establish a clear procedure, including a required writ-

Author: _____ Book: _____ Periodical: _____ Other: _____
Title: _____ Publisher: _____
Request initiated by: _____
Address: _____
City: _____ State: _____ Zip: _____ Telephone: _____
Do you represent yourself: _____ An organization/group (name): _____
1. What do you object to in the work? (Please be specific. Cite pages.) _____

2. What do you feel might be the result of exposure to this work? _____

3. Is there anything good about the work? _____
4. For what age group would you recommend it? _____
5. What do you think is the theme of this work? _____

6. Did you read (view or hear) the entire work? _____ What parts? _____

7. Are you aware of judgments of this work by literary or other critics?
(Specify): _____
8. What would you like the school to do about this work?
_____ Do not assign/lend it to my child.
_____ Return it to the Selection Committee for reevaluation.
_____ Other. Explain: _____
9. In its place, what work of equal literary quality and subject treatment would
you recommend? _____
Signature of complainant: _____ Date: _____

Figure 6–1   *Sample: Citizens Request for Reconsideration of Material*

ten statement on the specifics of the complaint, you will find little difficulty with the self-appointed censors.

Work with Parents

The teaching of reading is a primary function of the school; however, good readers are not made by the school alone. Parents also play an important part. For example, research indicates that children who are read to at home will be better readers than those who are not. If parents did nothing more than read to their children, their children would be better readers; but you can be more specific in your suggestions to parents.

Most educators agree that parents should not become involved in teaching reading skills. The emotional relationship between child and parent usually makes such teaching difficult, if not impossible. However, parents play a significant role in the development of good readers through the part they play in modeling reading, showing an interest in reading, reading to children, and discussing books with their children.

You and your staff can help and encourage parents in this role. Do you ever use a meeting of your parent organization to talk about children's books and the uses of this kind of reading? For one thing, in a total group of parents it is amazing how knowledgeable some are about children's books, but it is also sad how little others know about them.

A major area for such a discussion can be the role of attitudes in reading and how parents can help in their proper development. Youngsters need to find out from parents that *reading is important*. Are there newspapers in the home? Are there books and magazines? If the parent does some reading, the child learns that it must be an important activity.

Do parents let children know that *reading is fun?* Do they ever talk about and chuckle over something they have read? Do they share some of their reading with children? With each other?

Parents can also let youngsters know that *reading is informative.* Do they ever say, "I'll have to look it up"? Do they use other reference materials, including a dictionary? Do they refer to sources of information, such as the newspaper or encyclopedia? If they do, their child will learn that reading can provide information.

Probably most important of all is the attitude that *I can do it.* Do parents realize the value of justified praise? Instead of a critical remark, can they find something positive to say each day? Each bit of praise is a taste of success, and success leads to more success, just as certainly as failure and criticism lead to the "I can't" syndrome.

Do parents of your younger students realize all of the basic readiness skills they are developing merely through reading to the child and discussing the story with that youngster? They are developing everything from basic sound discrimination, through acquaintance with the patterns of printed English, to the basic comprehension skills. You could spend an entire meeting merely tying in the act of reading and discussing wtih the "reading readiness" skills presented in Chapter 4.

You and your teachers could even "sell" books to parents. Have a good collection of the books available, just as the teacher would with a class. Then make a few comments on the books, maybe even read a bit of some, and pass them out to the group. If the parents are very knowledgeable about these books, they, too, may want to get into the act and tell about some favorites they have discovered and used.

Nowhere is this kind of experience more important than when you and/ or your teachers meet with the Title I parents. Some of these parents do not have books in the home, and they might not be aware of the different ones that are available. Here, you usually have a small group and can have a good time talking about and distributing the books for examination.

It is with these parents, too, that you should share some of the ideas about the relationship of reading-to-children to "readiness" and how books can and should be discussed with their youngsters. You may also want to make a point about oral reading. Some well-intentioned parents think they have to "listen to" the child read. While they might invite oral reading of a part the child wants to share, they should also encourage some silent reading with a follow-up discussion.

Finally, they should understand that a follow-up discussion is most helpful, but that it should be a *discussion* and not a quiz. If they will talk about the book *for fun*, the purpose will be accomplished, and the comprehension skills will begin to take care of themselves.

CREATIVE READING

This important element in the total reading program could be discussed in the next chapter in connection with the comprehension skills, but it seems more appropriate here. It is different from the specific skills we usually talk about under "comprehension," but it does involve basic understanding of what is read.

In "creative reading," readers go beyond the ideas in print to generate, expand, or elaborate their own thoughts. Print becomes the jumping-off point for novel ideas, those that represent divergent or productive thinking.

One of the important values in developing creative reading is the encouragement of youngsters to become involved personally in the material they have read. Most often this kind of reading is practiced through the questions teachers ask. Youngsters also should be encouraged to ask these kinds of questions themselves.

An obvious first question that might be asked about any piece of material read is "Did you like that story? Why? (or Why not?)" Personal involvement of creative reading questions can go on: "Have you ever been in a situation like that?" "What would you have done if this happened to you?" "If you wrote that story, how would you have made it end?" "What are some of the other ways that character could have gotten out of trouble?" "What other story have you read that this reminds you of?"

Do your teachers get youngsters involved personally in the material they read? Do they provide opportunity for pupils to generate new ideas out of what they read? While not developing specific comprehension skills, this kind of involvement is basic to any of those skills and to interest in reading itself.

SUMMARY

This chapter has been devoted to the independent—or library—portion of the reading program. It included ways of using that reading to share and to motivate additional reading. This element of the reading program was justified with evidence from Individualized Reading, where pupils who read library books and discussed their reading, often with a minimum of skills instruction, achieved as well as those who were in basal reading programs. These two portions of the total program—basal and library book—ought to receive *equal* time and attention.

If library books are going to be read, they must be available to pupils. Classroom libraries are one assurance of the availability of books. Central libraries need not keep children from books if those libraries are open to youngsters at all times and if procedures are simplified. The school librarian can be one of the promoters of library reading in the school, but teachers also must assume their part of this responsibility. The teacher's role in library book selection, in knowledge of the books, and in their use is as important as his or her role in the selection and use of the basal reading program.

To help in the selection of books, some of the tools of the school librarian were suggested. These should be available and used by teachers. *Children's Catalog* and one of the periodicals about children's books ought to be a minimum in each school.

So that youngsters also have an opportunity to use the reading they do, a number of ideas were suggested as examples of the kinds of activities teachers might promote. These included ideas designed to (1) develop an awareness of the world of books, (2) provide a sense of accomplishment, and (3) provide for sharing through talking, writing, and creative activities. Sustained silent reading (SSR) was also suggested as one procedure that might be used to enhance the reading program.

Since poor readers often are neglected in the library program, ideas were presented that would encourage them to read easy books by removing the stigma often associated with "baby" books. Reluctant readers need to be teased into reading, often through the kind of sampling they can do in books of jokes or riddles.

The importance of writing was again brought out. A "Young Author's Conference" can be a helpful stimulus to the language arts, as well as a means of providing easy material for younger readers and motivation for older ones.

Objections to materials or attempts at censorship, as might be made by individuals or a small group in the community, are a concern to all. Every school should have an established policy, so incidents are not dealt with in an inconsistent or personal manner. An example form for a written complaint, along with an outline of procedures to consider, were presented.

Parents need to be made more aware of children's books, of the importance of these books, and of their own role in this aspect of the reading program. Suggestions were presented for parent meetings. While not instructors in skills, parents serve essential roles as models of reading behavior, developers of attitudes about reading, and builders of language as it relates to print.

Creative reading is equally important with the comprehension skills. Through involvement with and elaboration from ideas presented in print, youngsters will find reading a more meaningful activity.

Suggestions for Action

The body of this chapter contained a number of ideas you might want to implement with your staff or parent group. In addition, the following questions represent some thoughts for you to consider and possibly discuss with your staff.

1. What proportion of your total reading program is balanced by independent reading as opposed to skill instruction? Observe some classes to determine if this is an important topic for discussion with your staff.

2. Check on the number of library books available in classrooms. How often do teachers take collections into the rooms?

3. Are you and your staff satisfied with the operation of the library? How does it complement rather than hinder the reading program? What procedures promote rather than interfere with the circulation of books? To what extent does the librarian work with teachers in the selection of books? Can the physical layout of the library be improved to encourage browsing and talking about books?

4. Do you have the necessary "tools," such as *Children's Catalog* and at least one periodical about children's books? Check to see if your teachers know how to use, and do use, *Children's Catalog*.

5. Perhaps your teachers could use more ideas about ways of "using" li-

CHAPTER 7

What Are Your Priorities: Comprehension Skills

Comprehension is the heart of all reading. It has to do with approximating and reacting to the ideas an author has represented in print. In other words, it has to do with understanding.

OVERVIEW

As indicated in Chapter 3, most reading professionals list three categories of reading comprehension: literal, inferential, and critical. Literal comprehension has to do with understanding or with answering questions about what an author said. Inferential comprehension refers to understanding what an author meant by what was said. Critical reading has to do with evaluating or making judgments about what an author said and meant. Edgar Dale (1965) put it well when he referred to these three categories as "reading the lines . . . reading between the lines . . . and reading beyond the lines." These three categories are too often misunderstood as "levels" of difficulty. They are too often considered as follows:

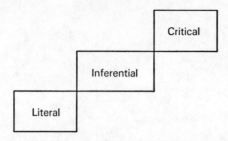

Most educators, including myself until recently, refer to these as "levels." My terminology was changed abruptly when, in reference to the "levels," a teacher commented that this was convenient: her low group worked at the literal level, the average group at the inferential, and the top group with critical reading! Certainly no one intended "level" to refer to difficulty! We might ask easy or difficult questions about any of these three categories. For example, suppose a student is asked to read the following:

> Dogs are friends, always loyal and playful. Cats are sneaky creatures that scratch and bite.

In terms of difficulty in responding, it is easier for a child to understand the inclination of this author in terms of a preference for dogs or cats than it is to be able to give a specific literal definition of *loyal*.

To be more exact about the three categories, let's examine some questions that might be asked about the two sentences just presented. In the literal category, we might ask: "What did the author say about dogs?" "What did the author say about cats?"

Inferential questions might be: "Which kind of animal do you think the author likes better?" "Which do you think the author believes would make better pets?" In the case of both questions, we would follow with: "What made you think that?" or "How do you know?"

Critical reading questions might include: "What is there in the author's background that might have led to these attitudes?" "Is what the author says about dogs and cats true of *all* dogs and cats?" We might also ask about the word choice: "What words did the author choose that are emotionally loaded to encourage us to agree with that author's position?" Incidentally, you will notice that the first two critical reading questions require information or knowledge beyond the selection actually read. This is typical of critical reading.

The only relationship these categories have to "levels" is the fact that literal understanding is a prerequisite for the other two. In fact, a more appropriate illustration of these three categories is as follows:

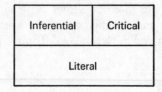

This diagram is supported by research, which indicates that one can understand literally while not necessarily being able to infer or to react critically. On the other hand, if the reader can make inferences or react critically, that individual has obviously understood the literal facts; that is, what the author said. (Lauer, 1977; Lowerre and Scandura, 1973–1974).

Obviously, if the reader did not understand the words the author used, there would be no way to answer the inferential or critical questions. Conversely, the reader might understand literally what the author said, yet that reader might not be able to draw conclusions about the statements nor evaluate the remarks the author made. Furthermore, research indicates that inferential and critical reading are somewhat independent of each other: Instruction in inferential skills may lead to increased comprehension scores without improving critical reading; instruction in critical reading skills may increase critical reading ability without affecting general comprehension.

Origins in Experience

Thus far, you may have the impression that the ability to comprehend presupposes skill in word recognition/identification, use of context, and, at times, use of the dictionary. In recent years, interest and research in schema theory (the theory about knowledge) suggest that, in addition to these skills, an "encyclopedia" is even more important. In other words, the knowledge of the world that a reader brings to the printed page provides the substance or enables the inferences that lead to the underlying information; the print serves only as clues or guidelines to "meaning."

This line of thinking suggests that, in order for a reader to comprehend print, the reader must find a reasonable match or fit between that print and schemata or stored experiences. If there is no fit, meaning is not achieved, despite the fact that the writer did represent certain ideas in the print and some other reader, with the appropriate background, would be able to comprehend that writer's meaning. For example, consider the following excerpt:

> The two men tied the youth, spreadeagled, securely to stakes driven into the hard earth. Without a word, each withdrew a sharp knife from its sheath and began slowly to carve deep gashes into the boy's forearms and chest, apparently oblivious to his quiet whimpers of pain.

Did you comprehend this selection? Was this an example of some sadistic torture? Were the two men cruelly punishing the boy for some misbehavior? Such questions, with affirmative answers, would fit quite naturally into your schemata. However, if you were a member of this primitive tribe, your schemata would be entirely different, and you would recognize this as a perfectly natural and praiseworthy case of ritualistic tattooing.

Evidence from schema theory indicates that the reader must "bring meaning to print" in order to get any meaning from that print. Practical implications are that teachers must be aware of this need. Youngsters cannot be expected to comprehend material, no matter how many "skills" they are taught, if they have no experience to match against the ideas represented in a particular passage. While we will be talking about various comprehension skills, teachers must also check on the background their pupils have for understanding whatever selections they are about to read.

Origins in Oral Language

Comprehension skills do not begin with the beginning of reading instruction. Actually, they begin long before this, in the preschool years, as thinking skills. These thinking skills developed in the preschool years include inferential and critical skills, as well as literal skills. For example, imagine the four-year-old who comes into the house with mud on his shoes and tracks it across the clean floor. He gets what his mother thinks he deserves. The next time that child comes into the house with mud on his shoes, he draws a conclusion. Specifically, he predicts an outcome: "This is what will happen if I track mud on the floor again." This is an inferential thinking skill.

An important part of the kindergarten program is the further development and extension of these so-called "reading comprehension skills" at the listening/thinking level. Hence, as you continue with this chapter, think of these as skills not only to be taught as part of reading instruction, but also to be developed orally in the kindergarten. When the kindergarten teacher reads a story to the group, does that teacher then ask questions that require operating within these three categories? Equally important, does that teacher actually *teach* these skills, as well as provide opportunity to practice them? This latter point is the subject of the next section for teachers at all levels.

Questioning Techniques

Teachers provide most of the practice in the area of reading comprehension through asking questions about material read or, in the case of kindergarten, listened to. The questioning provides *practice;* however, practice presumes that some teaching is taking place. If teachers use only questions for practice, they are leaving children to their own devices to figure out how to learn the skill. Unfortunately, evidence from observing teachers (Durkin, 1978–1979) and from analyzing basal reading series (Durkin, 1981) suggests that little, if any, *teaching* takes place.

Most teaching, except as will be discussed with critical reading skills, is accomplished through demonstration—by giving examples—by taking children back to the text and asking "How did you know?" To illustrate, suppose children read the following paragraph:

The boy ambled down the street. He gazed in a store window. Tarrying by store after store, he shuffled home.[1]

After children read this paragraph, the teacher may want to give practice in the inferential skill of drawing general conclusions. A very easy conclusion can be drawn by asking: "Was the boy in a hurry?" If the teacher settles for the response "No, he wasn't," that teacher has not gone far enough. Or perhaps the children cannot answer—an unlikely possibility in this paragraph. In either event, the teacher should go back to the paragraph and ask "How do you know?" or "How can we find out?" Then children (or, if necessary, the teacher) should point out the clues, such as *ambled, gazed, tarrying,* and *shuffled.* Other examples of teaching will be mentioned in connection with each of the skills later in this chapter.

Even our questioning techniques, which often represent the sum total of the "teaching" of comprehension skills in too many schools, leave much to be desired. Evidence from a variety of studies indicates that 75 to 95 percent of questions teachers ask are literal questions. This is true, whether those observed are primary or secondary teachers.

Analyses of basal reading programs suggest that they are little better, since about 50 percent of the questions in those programs are literal. Yet, why should this be? Why should teachers be so confined and limited to the literal if, as we know, anyone who can answer inferential or critical questions has already mastered the literal understanding? Hence, questioning ought to begin, and ought to primarily remain, in the inferential and critical categories; it might drop back to the literal when there is a disagreement that seems to be based on some misunderstanding of the literal facts.

Another major problem with our questioning techniques is the rapidity with which teachers ask questions. Lucking (1975) reported that adults require an average of 14 seconds to begin responding to a question. Teachers allowed children an average of 5.6 seconds. This same study also reported that teachers asked an average of 5.17 questions per minute—almost machinegun fire!

In another study, the researcher reported that teachers waited three times as long for a bright child to respond to a question as they did for a slow child. Does this suggest that the teacher wants to give Johnny "a turn," but will then go to Suzie to get the answer?

Thus far in this chapter, we have presented some basic concerns that are certainly important enough for you, as principal or supervisor, to check on. Are your teachers operating primarily with literal comprehension? Are they merely giving practice, with no instruction or explanation on the comprehension skills? Are they allowing *time* for children to respond to the questions asked? After all, there is something about silence that invites response.

---

[1] Reprinted by permission from Robert L. Hillerich, *Reading Fundamentals for Preschool and Primary Children* (Columbus, Ohio: Charles E. Merrill Publishing Co., 1977).

LITERAL COMPREHENSION SKILLS

The foregoing discussion is in no way meant to imply that we should never be teaching the literal comprehension skills. It is just to call attention to our over-emphasis on them in the past, to the almost complete exclusion of the other two categories. There is a place for the teaching of each of these skills.

Naturally, even literal comprehension presumes use of the basic decoding skills discussed in previous chapters. Specifically, it requires use of context, phonics, and, depending on reading level or difficulty, structural analysis, dictionary, and necessary typographical aids such as punctuation or special type. It also presumes experience, so the reader has the necessary schemata to make a mental fit with the text.

Even in the literal category, teachers must be careful not to settle for mere repetition of word patterns. They must translate or ask for translations, or they will not know if the child truly comprehended. For example, pupils may read: "The boy saw a dog." If the discussion follows the usual pattern, you will hear something like:

"Who saw a dog?" . . . . "The boy."
"What did the boy see?" . . . . "A dog."

Such an exchange proves nothing about comprehension, except that the respondents understand the structure of English sentences. They could answer with similar ease to those kinds of questions about this sentence: "The stripling beheld a canine" or even "The yap yipped a yop."

In other words, even when working with literal comprehension, teachers must ask for translation rather than for regurgitation of the same words. With such a basic sentence, this is difficult, but we could at least ask, "Who saw the animal?" or "What kind of animal?"

Beyond this, the literal comprehension skills are outlined here. They are the common skills that are included, if not taught, in most reading programs. Following the outline, each skill is discussed specifically in terms of how teachers might develop that skill:

1. Identifying referents for pronouns and adverbs
2. Recognizing and recalling detail
3. Recognizing and recalling main idea
4. Recognizing and recalling sequence
5. Recognizing and recalling comparisons
6. Recognizing and recalling cause/effect relationships
7. Interpreting similes

Identifying Referents for Pronouns and Adverbs

Use of this skill requires that the reader identify the words represented by pronouns or adverbs, such as *she*, *it*, and *there* in the following sentences:

May found her book on the table. She wondered who put it there.

At the oral level, four-year-olds easily demonstrate the ability to understand such words; yet, in reading, even third graders have problems with them. Although without definite research evidence, I suspect the problem children have lies with the mechanics of typical workbook pages.

Usually such pages consist of a selection to be read. Within the selection, pronouns and/or adverbs are numbered. At the bottom of the page is a numbered list of these words, beside which the child is to write the referent. In contrast, if children are given a list of pronouns and a selection with blanks into which they are to write the appropriate pronoun, they seem to have little difficulty. Of course, this is an expressive rather than a receptive act, such as reading. However, taking a clue from that, I have told children to ignore the lower part of the page and merely to write in the referent for each word at the point where that noun substitute appears. They seem to find this task much easier. Yet, if they can do this, they certainly must understand what are the referents for those words. You might check this out with your teachers.

Recognizing and Recalling Detail

First of all, if the teacher wants children to practice this skill, that teacher should establish this *purpose for reading* before children do the reading. Second, the teacher should provide the practice with material in which detail is a significant part of the selection. In other words, children should not be asked to read for detail that is insignificant to the selection.

For example, perhaps students are going to read an article about stamp collecting. It might be a good reason to read for detail to recall what materials are necessary in order to begin a stamp collection. Conversely, if students are reading a story in which a character just incidentally happened to be wearing a raincoat, there is certainly no reason to ask pupils what color the raincoat was—unless, of course, the color of the coat was significant to some event in the story.

In the case of this and the remainder of the literal skills, pupils are given practice in both *recognizing* and *recalling*. To "recognize," pupils will have the material before them and will need merely to locate the answer to a question. To "recall," pupils will not have the material before them; they must remember from the previous reading in order to reply to a question. Some believe the latter is a memory and not a reading skill. However, both behaviors are essential to good readers and ought to be practiced in reading classes.

Recognizing and Recalling Main Idea

There are some who would say this is an inferential skill only. However, if a main idea is stated in so many words, then its recognition is a literal skill.

In the early stages of reading, children are asked to identify the main idea of a one-paragraph story. Later, they deal with longer selections. In both instances, there seem to be two basic methods of giving practice: (1) the teacher may ask children what title (or name) they would give this story, or (2) the teacher may mechanically ask, "What is the first sentence about?" "What is the next sentence about?" and so on, until finally, "What are all the sentences about?"

As an example, young children may read the following to decide what "name" they would give this story:

Fire engines are usually red. They carry hoses and ladders. They also carry fire fighters. We need them to put out fires.

The teacher may ask "What name would you give this story?" and expect the literal response "Fire Engines." Once more, however, the reinforcement—or teaching, if children cannot respond—should include "Why did you decide that?" with the expectation that the children will point out that all of the sentences tell about fire engines.

Recognizing and Recalling Sequence

Work on this skill begins with sequence of events. At higher levels, it may also include recognizing or recalling a sequence of character development or of the development of an argument.

This is another skill for which workbook pages cause children problems as a result of unrealistic practice. When adults use this skill, they usually recall three or four significant events which then serve as an outline—as hooks on which to hang the details of a story they want to tell to someone. In contrast, workbooks often list a dozen to fifteen insignificant details, arranged in jumbled order, for pupils to sort out. Some would be a challenge to any college graduate. Is it any wonder young readers get lost in the details and have difficulty with this kind of assignment?

Check with your teachers on this skill. If they are giving their pupils such unrealistic practice activities, have them go through, with the class, to strike out all choices except for four or five of the most significant. Then let pupils determine the sequence in which those four or five occurred. Such practice is realistic.

Recognizing and Recalling Comparisons

This is an easy skill to develop in the literal category because the comparisons are stated in so many words: "Sue can run faster than Jerry." Here again, it is wise for the teacher to ask, "Who is slower?"

Recognizing and Recalling Cause/Effect Relationships

This skill is relatively much easier in the literal category than in the inferential because, in this former instance, the reader is given answers in so many words. Teachers can help youngsters become even more adept at identifying cause/effect relationships if they will alert them to the clue words that can be so helpful. After providing several examples in sentences, teachers should have pupils look for and list the clue words, such as *because, as a result, since,* and so on, that signal a cause/effect relationship. Be sure pupils are finding the words; it does not help them much if a teacher just hands them a list to memorize.

Interpreting Similes

Children usually have little difficulty with similes because they explain their meaning in so many words: "It was as scarce as a snowflake in July." Similes ought to be dealt with more from the standpoint of appreciation and effect rather than out of concern for interpretation of meaning.

INFERENTIAL COMPREHENSION

Inferential comprehension goes beyond what an author said, to get at what that author meant or implied by what was said. It requires selecting facts that were stated and putting them together in order to arrive at a conclusion or inference that was not stated in the selection.

In this sense, drawing conclusions is much like working a math problem: We are told that Fred has two marbles and Mary has three; how many marbles do they have together? We take the given facts, *two* and *three*, to arrive at a fact not given—*five*.

While their practice is usually to the contrary, teachers should devote most of their comprehension instruction to this and to critical reading. There are several reasons for this statement. First of all, we can presume understanding of the literal if children can answer questions in the inferential and critical categories. Second, inferential comprehension requires thinking beyond mere recall. Finally, inferential questions lead to more sophisticated language usage, as well as to more thought (Smith, 1978). This can be demonstrated very easily with a simple sentence that children might read, such as, "Dottie wore a yellow raincoat." If a teacher asks the literal question "What color was the raincoat?" children will likely respond with one word: "Yellow." However, if the teacher asks the inferential question, "Why do you think she wore the yellow one?" those children will respond with much more than one word—probably with a complex sentence beginning with "Because. . . . "

Actually, all inferential comprehension is a matter of drawing conclusions; however, we usually break this category down into a number of subskills because there are different kinds of conclusions that can be drawn. These different kinds of conclusions make up the inferential comprehension skills as follows:

1. Drawing general conclusions
2. Inferring main idea
3. Inferring sequence
4. Inferring comparisons
5. Inferring cause/effect relationships
6. Making judgments
7. Identifying character traits and motives
8. Predicting outcomes
9. Interpreting figures of speech: metaphors, personification, idioms

Part of the reason teachers spend so little time on inferential skills seems to be the fact that they do not know how to ask inferential questions. There is no rule of thumb to suggest that if we drop *who, what, when,* and *where* as question markers we will get away from literal questions. Some inferential questions may begin with these markers, and some literal questions may begin with *why.* For example, suppose children have just read: "The girls remained in the house because it was raining." A literal cause/effect relationship question may be "*Why* did the girls stay in the house?"

The closest we can come to a rule of thumb to guide teachers in identifying inferential questions is to suggest that if their natural inclination is to follow a question with "Why?" or "How did you know?" the initial question was probably inferential. For example, suppose pupils read "Dottie wore a yellow raincoat." If the teacher asked the color of the coat (literal) and received the response "Yellow," that teacher is unlikely to ask "How did you know?" since the child would most likely say "It says so right there!"

On the other hand, if the teacher asked "Why did she wear a yellow raincoat?" (inferential) and the child responds, a natural inclination would be to follow up with "Why did you think that?" or "How did you know?"—asking for clues from other parts of the selection to justify the initial response.

Children often learn more than we intend to teach. Since they are accustomed to being asked literal questions, children tend to read literally. Hence, if a teacher is going to do a better job by asking inferential questions, that teacher had better be sure to inform pupils in advance of their purpose for reading a selection. Otherwise, they may read literally and then be surprised when the teacher asks questions that require making inferences.

Drawing General Conclusions

To draw a conclusion, the reader must take literal facts that are given in the story, put them together, and arrive at a decision (conclusion) that was not stated in the selection. At a very basic level, this skill may be developed through riddle-type experiences. Perhaps young children will read something like this:

> Terry walked into the store. All she saw was tools, paint, nails, and screws. "I must have made a mistake," she thought. "I'll never find the milk and bread in here."

To get a general conclusion from the clues, the teacher might ask "What kind of store was Terry looking for?" "What made you think that?" Of course, the teacher might also ask "what kind of store did Terry go into?" However, if the above paragraph represents the entire selection read, the latter question might be classified as asking for the main idea of that paragraph (a hardware store). While this is also an inferential skill, let's get teachers to sharpen their focus on what they are asking of children and on the skill they want practiced.

In order to clarify the individual skills, in addition to an explanation of each one, I will use a common story to serve as a basis for example questions. With each following skill, the example questions relate to "Goldilocks and the Three Bears," since that is a story everyone is familiar with. As principal, you might like to use the same technique with your staff, having them make up a question about the story for each of the inferential skills.

In the story of Goldilocks, a question seeking a general conclusion might be "Why do you think Goldilocks went into the house when no one was home?" Depending on the version of the story, possible answers might be that she was tired, hungry, lost, and so on. All pupil responses should be followed with "Why do you think that?" "How do you know?" or some similar question. If not, children may just be making wild guesses. Such guesses may help to develop some creativity of response, but they do nothing for developing the skill of drawing conclusions. Furthermore, *teaching* will include pointing out, or having pupils point out, the clues they used to decide on the response they gave.

Inferring Main Idea

Most often, getting at the main idea of a paragraph or a selection is an inferential skill. However, questions asked are the same kind that can be asked when the skill is applied literally, either by asking for a title for the story or by examining specifically what each sentence or paragraph is about.

A more creative approach to inferred main idea might be to have children pretend they are newspaper reporters and that the story they just read occurred here and now in their town. When they write up the news story, what headline would they give it? For example, with the story of Goldilocks, they might suggest a headline such as "Break-in at Bear House."

If you work with teachers to practice developing questions, always ask them what answer they anticipated from their question. In this way, you can be more certain that the question has been thought through and that it is on target. I was using the Goldilocks example with graduate students when one student suggested the novel approach of asking pupils for the moral of the story. This is another worthwhile method for many stories, but never having considered Goldilocks as having a moral, I asked the student what answer she expected. Her reply was: "Little girls shouldn't go around sleeping in strange beds."

Inferring Sequence

Basal reading programs usually neglect this skill. While its omission may not be overly serious, it is an inferential skill that can be taught and practiced. It involves determining what must have happened between two events when the author does not say. For example, pupils may have read a story that included the following end and beginning of two paragraphs:

> . . . The wind increased and the sky darkened, so the boys decided to quit the ball game and go into the house.
>   After the rain stopped, the boys took their equipment and returned to the field.

A very simple question requiring pupils to infer sequence would be to ask "What must have happened in the time between those two paragraphs?" The obvious answer is that it must have rained.

With Goldilocks, assuming the author has not stated it literally, teachers might ask what Goldilocks must have done between the time she finished the porridge and the time she sat in the first chair. The inferred sequence might be that she moved from the kitchen to the parlor where the chairs were.

Inferring Comparisons

While questions for this skill are the same as those used in the literal category for recognizing or recalling comparisons, the answer to the question is not stated in the selection. Again, the reader must use the information given in order to get at an implied similarity or difference. For example, as a literal comparison, the author might have stated that John was taller than Mary, and we could ask the literal question "Who was taller?" As an inferential comparison, we might only have read that the two went to explore a cave. At the entrance John had to bend over to get in, but Mary could stand straight up. Now when we ask "Who was taller?" it is an inferential question.

With Goldilocks, teachers might ask which bear was most like Goldilocks, expecting comparisons with the porridge, chairs, and beds. The teacher might also push this further by asking if Goldilocks was larger or smaller than Baby Bear, expecting the inference that she might have been a little larger since she broke Baby Bear's chair.

Inferring Cause/Effect Relationships

In working with inferential skills, children are not given the helpful clue words that they have when they identify literal cause/effect relationships. They are not told "because" or "as a result." Nevertheless, the kinds of questions asked are the same, whether the answer is literal or inferred. In the literal category, pupils might read "Because it was raining, the game was called off." In the inferential, they might also be asked why the game was called off, but the text might only have stated "It was raining. The game was called off."

With Goldilocks, teachers might ask questions such as "Why did Goldilocks run when she saw the bears?" or "Why do you think Baby Bear's chair broke when Goldilocks sat in it?" In any case, teachers should always follow the inferential questions with "Why?" or "How do you know?"

Making Judgments

When anyone makes a judgment, that person must bring his or her own values to bear on a situation to evaluate it. No one is born with a set of values. Each individual goes through a growth process, beginning without an awareness of choice, moving to a recognition that there is a choice, developing a preference,

138 Chapter 7

and ultimately having a very strong preference, or "valuing" one choice over others.

Teachers can play an important role in helping pupils develop values. Questions to develop this skill may begin "Why do you think . . . ?" "Should . . . ?" or "Would you have . . . ?"

Relating to the story of Goldilocks, teachers might ask "Do you think Goldilocks should have gone into the house when no one was home?" "Why?" (or "Why not?") Similarly, they could ask "Would you have gone into the house when no one was home?" "Why?" (or "Why not?")

Identifying Character Traits and Motives

There are a number of ways teachers can develop this skill. Always, however, they should take pupils back to the selection to justify their responses. One technique is to have pupils list all of the characteristics they can think of for people they have met. Then, from the list, they will associate pertinent ones with a character or characters they have read about. For many stories, pupils may create a chart with each character serving as a heading for a column in which the characteristics of that individual will be listed.

Another method is merely to recall actions of a character and then associate the traits one can infer from those actions. Goldilocks might be considered nosy, unthinking, selfish (in eating another's food), and so on. In terms of questions to be asked, if that is the preference, teachers can use questions such as "What kind of person was Goldilocks?" or even "Would you like Goldilocks as a friend?" "Why?" (or "Why not?")

Predicting Outcomes

Too often, teachers and basal reading guides provide practice in this skill by interrupting a story to ask students what they think will happen next or how they think the story will end. This kind of practice leads to a convergent kind of thinking, as if there were only one "right" answer—the answer the author concludes with. Admittedly, there is no research to tell us for certain, but it seems more appropriate to allow students to finish a story. Then we can provide practice in predicting outcomes by changing an event and asking "What do you think would have happened if . . . ?"

Following this procedure, a whole world of possibilities is opened, and no single answer is required as the "right" one. With the story of Goldilocks, an obvious question might be "What do you think would have happened if the bears had been home when Goldilocks first got there?"

It is important that teachers also remember to hold students to the nature of the characters, the situation, and so on. Encouraging wild guesses as responses will not provide practice in this skill. For example, even a kindergartener should not respond to the above question by saying "The bears would have eaten her." In reply to such an inappropriate response, the teacher should ask "Is that the kind of bear who lived in the house?"

Interpreting Figures of Speech: Metaphors, Personification, Idioms

Metaphors are difficult for elementary children to interpret because they tend to read material literally. While they can understand a simile such as "Dad was as grouchy as a bear this morning," they have difficulty with the metaphor "Dad was a bear this morning."

A typical approach to metaphors is to have children analyze in three steps: (1) What two things are being compared? (2) In what ways could they be alike? (3) From the rest of the context, how did the author intend for us to compare them?

I prefer more language involvement and writing. By third grade, children can collect examples of similes. Then the teacher may demonstrate how the similes can be converted to metaphors. After some practice in converting, pupils can make up new metaphors. Finally, they can search out and interpret metaphors in their reading.

Personification, attributing human qualities to nonhuman elements, is not a difficult figure of speech for pupils to interpret. When they read "The trees reached out their arms," pupils know that trees do not have arms and that the author is referring to the branches.

Idioms are so much a part of our language that we do not even realize how prevalent they are. For example, do you really "put out" the lights when you leave a room? Native speakers are familiar with most common idioms, but children from another language background have unique problems with them. Also, children today are not familiar with some of the more antiquated idioms such as "whip up dinner" or localized idioms such as "pick up the floor."

All children can get good experience with idioms by having teachers use the Amelia Bedelia books by Peggy Parish. Amelia is a household maid who follows all directions literally. She "dresses" the chicken for dinner, "puts out" the lights, "draws" the drapes, and so on. Although the books are directed to third or fourth grade, they can provide an enjoyable jumping-off point even in high school.

CRITICAL READING SKILLS

While we have indicated that inferential comprehension skills are neglected, we can say that the teaching of critical reading is practically nonexistent. Yet, if we do not develop skill beyond the literal, we are merely doing as Bartolome

(1969) suggested: developing "higher level illiterates." These higher level illiterates might present a more serious problem than those who cannot read at all. Perhaps it is worse in a democratic society to have enough skill to be able to read literally and to believe that everything in print is true than it is not to be misled at all.

Critical reading is essentially the same kind of process as critical thinking, except that the former is applied to print. Most authorities who talk about critical reading see it as involving evaluation or judgment. Unfortunately, some reading authorities also get critical reading confused with creative reading. While also important, this latter is a nonskill process that was discussed in Chapter 6.

Critical reading may be defined as a thought process applied to printed material that results in justified action or conclusions on the part of the reader. It involves determination of an author's stated or implied conclusions, based on objective evaluation of that author's supporting statements, as well as on analysis of the means—the language and the logic—used to arrive at those conclusions.

There are a number of problems to overcome if we are to teach critical reading. Teachers have not been prepared to do this kind of teaching, and professional books on the teaching of reading usually offer only brief comments about it. Basal reading programs do very little in this area, and other materials are only now becoming available.

A second major problem lies again in the misunderstanding about comprehension *level*. Some people have believed that raising general comprehension in reading will result in more critical reading skill. This is just not so. Research evidence is clear that general comprehension can be raised without affecting critical reading skill, or vice versa.

Related to this last point, too many teachers seem to think that critical reading skills are so sophisticated that they cannot be taught until high school. Wolf, Huck, and King (1967) demonstrated that a number of critical reading skills can be taught as low as first grade, and that children so taught will read more critically than those not taught the skills.

Fourth, while we have already discussed the problem with teacher questioning, critical reading skills usually require *more* than mere questioning. Their development most often requires that the teacher do some specific, and often isolated, teaching and practice. Then the class will return to textual material and apply that skill.

Fifth, since critical reading is an evaluative act, children must use other sources of information in order to have a basis for comparison. Being locked into a single text in social studies or science does not facilitate this kind of alternative information, and the teacher must not be afraid to "rock the boat" a little by discussing controversial issues.

Finally, critical reading skills are normally used when reading informative or persuasive material. In contrast, most teaching of reading is done with basal readers, consisting primarily of fiction. Who reads "Goldilocks and the Three Bears" critically?

Rather than merely list the critical reading skills as I listed the other two categories, I have presented them in a chart form that follows the definition of critical reading, grouping the skills according to their relationships. Specifically, Figure 7–1 indicates that the critical reader must evaluate in four major areas: central issues, support for those issues or conclusions, language style, and logic used to arrive at the conclusions. As shown in this figure, the reader obviously must begin with a selection to be read and must use the basic decoding and comprehension skills. Also, after using appropriate critical reading skills, the reader should adjust thinking or action accordingly.

Beyond these points, there is no intent to imply a sequence for use of the skills. The critical reader may begin reading an article and be struck by the emotionally-loaded words. Then the first critical reading skill used would be the recognition of slant and bias. From that recognition, the skilled reader might decide to investigate the author's background in order to understand the bias. In other words, the sequence on the chart is merely an effort to provide a logical organization from which to discuss each of the skills.

Not all of the critical reading skills listed on the chart will be discussed here. Specifically, "levels of abstraction" and the elements of "logic" are omitted. Principals interested in these are referred to Hayakawa (1949) for the former; Wolf (1965) and Lowerre and Scandura (1973–1974) provide some ideas for the latter. To deal with these here would go beyond the limits of this book and would give the lie to the promise that you, as principal, do not need to be a reading specialist.

Furthermore, any teaching of critical reading will undoubtedly come as a result of the few skills included in the basal your teachers are using. Those are essentially the skills discussed here, with the addition of a few that are easily developed with the staff. If you do nothing more than help teachers become more aware of these skills and their importance, you will have made a great contribution to the improvement of critical reading instruction.

Central Issues

The reader must use inferential skill to determine the main ideas presented. An important skill for teachers to develop on this point is that of reserving judgment. A number of research studies have indicated that negative attitudes toward the content of material will handicap a reader's use of critical reading skills. Since this is true, we must look at what happens when we pick up a newspaper article. The first thing we see is the headline—and headlines tend to be very succinct and biased. Before we read further, we may already have developed some preconceived notion or bias from the headline. Thus, teachers should call attention to this need and give students practice in withholding judgment until they have the facts.

It seems to me that attention to currency of a book is often mistaught. On the one hand, if a reader is interested in space exploration, and notes that the book in hand was published in 1948, it would be wise to find another book

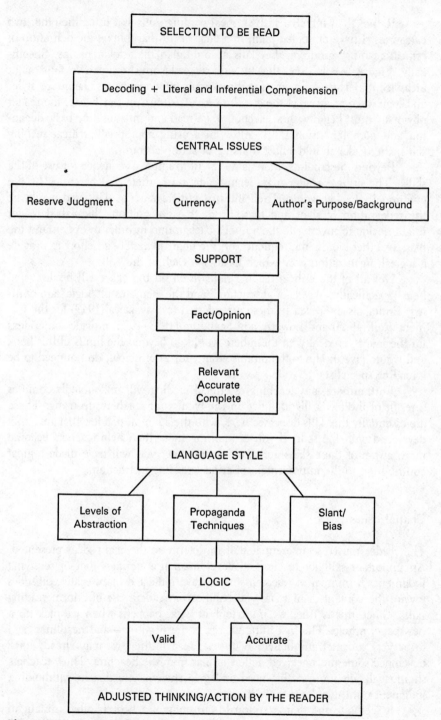

Figure 7–1   *The Critical Reading Skills*

on the subject. On the other hand, if a reader is interested in a biography of Robespierre, choice of a book should be based more on the competence of an author than on the copyright date. Teachers ought to relate their discussion of copyright date to the content of a book and the possibility of new findings about that content.

Determination of an author's purpose and background are important to critical reading. Comparisons of the background of two authors can be made at the kindergarten level, where children can be told about two authors who wrote on the same subject. For example, they may have listened to a story about the white-tailed deer. Then the teacher may tell them about two different authors of such books. One was a forest ranger who followed a herd of such deer for several years, taking pictures and keeping notes on their habits. The other author is a television announcer who lives in an apartment in New York City. Pupils can then discuss which would appear more qualified to write a story about the deer. The point of such discussion at any level ought to be that success in one field does not automatically qualify a person as an authority in another: A top movie actor ought to know about acting, but that does not qualify him or her as an authority on international relations.

We previously suggested that no one reads "Goldilocks and the Three Bears" critically. Even the statement might not always be true. In determining an author's purpose, students might look at "entertainment" articles to see if they have a subtle message. For example, many readers apparently enjoy the humor of columnist Art Buchwald. Recently, he quoted formal statements such as "Cars don't kill people; people kill people." Then he added his own humorous translations of the formal statements. Very funny, but why were two of his barbs aimed at the automobile industry?

Support

The next block of skills deals with the question of the kind of support an author offers for the conclusions arrived at. First of all, the reader needs to determine if the author is using facts or opinions as persuasive vehicles. Students should recognize that there is nothing wrong with opinion, but they should look for support, through fact, for the opinions expressed.

Distinguishing fact and opinion usually begins with practice in kindergarten and first grade in distinguishing fantasy and reality. Distinguishing fact and opinion is one of the few critical reading skills that may already be taught—or at least given practice—in your school. It is also a skill that is frequently *mistaught* by leading pupils to believe that anything that is not true is an opinion.

Children need to be taught how to distinguish the two. Only when they are given criteria are they being *taught* instead of merely being given *practice* in the skill. A factual statement is one that can be verified objectively. It is a statement to which we can answer "Yes, that's true" or "No, that's not true," and we can prove it. An opinion is a statement that cannot be verified objectively. We can respond to opinions only with "Yes, I agree' or "No, I disagree." Of course, an author can marshall facts to help persuade or to support the opinions.

Students have little difficulty identifying opinions or identifying statements of fact that are true. For example, given moderate instruction, children could identify the following easily:

> There are twenty-five people in this room.   (Fact—true by count)
> There are too many people in this room.   (Opinion)
> There are not enough people in this room.   (Opinion)

Where children have difficulty is when they are given a statement of fact that is false. For example, too often they would incorrectly identify the following statement about their classroom as opinion because they know it is not true:

> There are 250 people in this room.

This is a statement of fact (false, I hope!) because we can verify it objectively by counting. Youngsters need to be given isolated instruction on this skill, additional practice with it, and then they need to apply the skill by reading persuasive or informative articles to identify the kinds of statements—fact or opinion—that an author has used.

Determining relevance, accuracy, and completeness require experience or outside reading on a topic. Students must have other information against which to evaluate an author's statements in relation to these points. Here the teacher's role is one of assuring that other information is brought in for comparison.

Through discussion and examples, the teacher can show children the importance of relevance of an author's facts to that author's conclusions. How often does an author use what we might call the "Sales Syndrome," presenting a series of true but irrelevant facts merely to get the reader responding "Yes, yes, yes"? Then, when presented with the conclusions, the reader is still saying "Yes, yes, yes."

Teachers must also provide opportunity and practice for students to evaluate the accuracy and completeness of an author's supporting statements. Accuracy refers to the question "Are the supporting facts true?" The critical reader must also evaluate completeness to guard against getting only one side of the story. Use of both of these skills requires gathering information from a variety of sources and comparing. In cases of disagreement, it may also involve falling back to check on the authors' backgrounds.

Language Style

Choice of language style is one of the means an author uses to encourage us to agree with the conclusions presented. "Levels of abstraction" refer to the degrees of concreteness in word or sentence choice, which may vary significantly between the vague and the very specific. "Propaganda techniques" are devices used to persuade through psychological impact, while "slant and bias" refer to the use of emotionally-loaded words.

Many teachers seem to be familiar with the propaganda devices, so just a few words of clarification might be helpful here. First, teachers should not be overly concerned about the accuracy of applying a particular label or name to a piece of propaganda or advertising. Most examples overlap and can be classed under more than one label. For example, Wheaties uses sports figures for endorsements. This practice can be classed as an example of "testimonial," since the hero is testifying that he or she eats Wheaties. It can also be classed as an example of "transfer," since it implies that if you eat Wheaties you, too, will be athletic.

Second, the act of collecting and labeling items is a waste of time if students and teachers stop there. The teacher must have students apply their knowledge of propaganda techniques by examining a piece of writing to determine if that author is using any of the devices. The classic propaganda devices are as follows:

> Bandwagon—"Everybody's doing it, so you'd better too."
> Transfer—"You'll be like . . . if. . . . "
> Testimonial—relies on endorsements by famous people.
> Glittering Generalities—good-sounding statements that convey no information.
> Common Folk—"We're not fancy; we're just like you."
> Snob Appeal—"Expensive, but aren't you worth it?"
> Appeal to Research—"Our survey of doctors shows . . . "
> Veiled Threat—"This could happen to you."
> Card Stacking—giving only one side of a story.
> Name Calling or Ridiculing—making fun of the opposition.

Of all the critical reading skills, one most needed by readers is that of identifying slant and bias (Kimmel, 1973). The writer interested in convincing a reader seldom relies on lies or half-truths; more likely, that writer will use emotionally-loaded words to gently ease the reader over to the desired view. Readers must be alert to this kind of writing.

This is an example of a reading skill that may be developed initially through writing. As with a number of critical reading skills, pupils may more easily understand what an author is trying to do to them as readers if they, first of all, perform the same act themselves as writers.

Teachers may begin with words pupils are very familiar with, asking pupils for other words that mean about the same thing. For example, starting with the word *house*, the teacher may elicit *home, abode, hovel, shack, palace, mansion,* and so on. Then the teacher can have the class sort the words according to their positive ("good sounding") or negative ("bad sounding") connotations. While all of these words denote or mean about the same thing—a place where people live—their connotations or emotional impacts are different: Would you rather spend the weekend in a hovel or in a mansion?

After pupils have done this kind of sorting with a variety of words and have become aware of the connotations of words, the teacher may give them a story without adjectives and have them insert adjectives to slant the story negatively. Then they may take the same story and slant it positively. Aesop's fables also make good material for this kind of experience. For example, the fable of the Fox and the Stork may be slanted by half the class to make the Fox the "good guy" and the Stork the "bad guy." The other half of the class may do the reverse. Then the two versions should be compared.

A reminder once more: This kind of experience is worthless unless pupils ultimately examine a piece of writing to determine if the author has used emotionally-loaded words to persuade. Pupils may underline the particular words, delete them if they are adjectives, and see if they are still persuaded of the conclusion. They may even substitute words with reverse connotations to see the effect on the reader.

Incidentally, Kimmel (1973) also found that the most biased kind of writing in any part of a newspaper was on the sports page. Sports writers cannot seem to report a score objectively. Rather than write "The Bluebirds Beat the Redbirds 9 to 7," they seem to prefer, depending on their favorite team, "The Bluebirds Clobbered the Redbirds 9 to 7" or "The Bluebirds Squeaked By the Redbirds 9 to 7." In any event, teachers who work with older students will find the sports pages ideal beginning material for teaching those students to identify slant or bias.

SUMMARY

This chapter dealt with the three categories of comprehension skills: literal, inferential, and critical. They have been presented as thinking skills applied to reading. While literal comprehension is a prerequisite to the other two, none of the three is seen as differing in terms of difficulty.

Evidence suggests that too much time is spent on the literal skills, to the exclusion of the other two categories. Inferential skills are neglected partly because most teachers do not seem to know how to ask inferential questions. While they need to improve their questioning techniques, teachers also need to do more: They need to teach through demonstration and example. This latter point is especially true when dealing with critical reading.

Finally, each of the skills was spelled out, with examples of how they might be developed.

Suggestions for Action

1. How much time do your teachers allow for pupils to answer questions asked in a discussion? Present the evidence from this chapter and some suggestions at a staff meeting. Observe a few classes. You might also suggest that teachers evaluate themselves by tape recording a class discussion and listening to the tape to see how much time they allow for responding to questions.

2. You, or your individual teachers, might evaluate the degree of emphasis or amount of time devoted to (if not squandered on) work with literal questions.

3. Ask each of your teachers to examine some of the practice materials they use for *literal* comprehension. If the practice is to recognize or recall detail, how important is that detail to the selection? If for recalling sequence, how important is sequence to the selection and how many details are listed to be arranged in sequence?

4. Before pupils read, how many of your teachers establish purposes for the reading? Do they also remember to discuss the selection in terms of the purposes established?

5. To help teachers understand how to ask inferential questions, you might devote a staff meeting to this kind of practice. Use a short story—or even the Goldilocks examples used in the inferential section of this chapter. Have each teacher make up a question for each of the inferential skills. Then share and discuss the questions to evaluate if they are good inferential questions and if they assess the skill intended. This kind of bootstrap inservice will raise the level of teachers' questions. Incidentally, teachers may enjoy this more if you have them work in groups of two or three to develop the questions.

6. Observe a class discussion. Tally the total number of questions asked. Keep a separate column for the follow-up "Why?" or "How did you know?" questions that get children to identify the clues they used to answer the initial question. What percent of tallies are in this latter (inferential) column? Of course, you'll want to follow the visit with a conference.

7. You might also encourage your teachers to tape record their discussions with pupils and listen to them in privacy in order to evaluate the kinds of questions they ask.

8. With middle-grade students, teachers might discuss the specific skills and then ask students to make up and evaluate inferential questions that they can ask each other about a selection they have read.

9. What critical reading skills are provided for in your basal? Which ones are your teachers teaching? At a staff meeting, you might get teachers to discuss what critical reading skills they are teaching and how they are doing this. Be sure to help them distinguish between *instruction* and mere *practice*.

10. If critical reading skills are being taught, how do teachers provide for application of those skills in real reading?

References

Bartolome, Paz I. "Teachers' Objectives and Questions in Primary Reading." *The Reading Teacher* 23 (October 1969): 27–33. Suggests a wide gap between the objectives teachers have in mind for the comprehension skills and the kinds of questions they ask to attain those objectives.

Dale, Edgar. "The Critical Reader." *The Newsletter* (Ohio State University) 30 (1965): 1. A brief discussion of the categories of comprehension and of the importance of critical reading.

Durkin, Dolores. "What Classroom Observations Reveal About Reading Comprehension Instruction." *Reading Research Quarterly* 14 (1978–1979): 481–533. Based on observation of social studies and reading classes, the author reports that practically no comprehension instruction was seen; most time was spent on assessment and help with assignments.

Durkin, Dolores. "Reading Comprehension Instruction in Five Basal Reader Series." *Reading Research Quarterly* 16 (1981): 515–544. Like the preceding study of classrooms, reports most effort is in direction and practice with very little instruction on how to perform the skill.

Hayakawa, S. I. *Language in Thought and Action*. New York: Harcourt, Brace and World, 1949. An excellent presentation of ideas in the field of semantics, including levels of abstraction and connotations of words. This is a good one to read in its entirety.

Hillerich, Robert L. *Reading Fundamentals for Preschool and Primary Children*. Columbus, Ohio: Charles Merrill, 1977. Chapter 7 presents a more extensive discussion of the comprehension skills as they are taught in primary grades.

Kimmel, Thomas H. "What Critical Reading Skills are Important in Evaluating Informative and Persuasive Writing, as Represented by News, Opinion, and Advertisements in Print." Master's thesis, National College of Education, 1973. An analysis of twenty-two samples, seven newspapers, and nine styles of writing, indicating all skills are related. Major ones needed for critical reading were adequacy/completeness, fact/opinion, and slant/bias.

Lauer, Ruth C. "A Causal-Comparative Study of the Existence of a Hierarchy of Reading Comprehension Skills." Master's thesis, Bowling Green State University, 1977. A comprehension test, based on a selection read, indicated that students could answer literal questions without being able to answer inferential or critical. Conversely, those who could answer inferential or critical questions were able to correctly answer the literal.

Lowerre, George F., and Scandura, Joseph M. "Conceptually Based Development and Evaluation of Individualized Materials for Critical Reading Based on Logical Inference." *Reading Research Quarterly* 9 (1973–1974): 186–205. Developed some of the basic logic skills with pupils in grades 2–4. Results indicated pupils could learn the skills, and that there was a hierarchy of skills.

Lucking, Robert A. "Comprehension and a Model for Questioning." ED 110–988, April 1975. Reported on the rapidity with which teachers ask questions.

Smith, Charlotte T. "Evaluating Answers to Comprehension Questions." *The Reading Teacher* 31 (May 1978): 896–900. Found that inferential and critical questions— as opposed to literal—elicited more sophisticated language responses.

Wolf, Willavene. "The Logical Dimension of Critical Reading." In *Reading and Inquiry*, ed. J. Allan Figurel. Newark: International Reading Association, 1965, pp. 121–124. Discusses two elements of logic: validity and reliability.

Wolf, Willavene; Huck, Charlotte; and King, Martha. *Critical Reading Ability of Elementary School Children*. Final Report. U.S. Department of Health, Education, and Welfare, Office of Education, Bureau of Research. Columbus: Ohio State University Research Foundation, 1967. With 651 pupils, grades 1–6, reported significant differences in critical reading skill in favor of those taught the skills, regardless of IQ or sex.

CHAPTER 8

What Are Your Priorities: Dictionary and Study Skills

This chapter will review the basic dictionary and study skills usually developed in an elementary school program and continued to whatever levels are necessary. In the process, it will point out some of the areas often neglected in most reading programs. Although taught in "reading," the study skills will also be discussed in the context of the content areas, where they should be applied.

While the foundation for most dictionary and study skills may be laid as early as kindergarten, these skills are more formally taught beginning at about third-grade level and their development continues throughout the formal educational years.

THE DICTIONARY PROGRAM

Dictionary skills provide the bridge to maturity in reading. The beginning reader works at a level where the words read are within the listening-speaking vocabulary and where context and phonics and/or structural analysis enable that reader to arrive at meaning. At more mature levels, words are not within the listening-speaking vocabulary and only context and the dictionary will enable the reader to arrive at the meaning of a strange word.

The dictionary skills of concern include (1) readiness for dictionary use, including picture dictionaries; (2) locational skills, including knowledge of alphabetical order and use of guide words; (3) use of a dictionary for meaning; (4) use of a dictionary for pronunciation; and (5) use of a dictionary for spelling.

Selection of Dictionaries

Why is it, when a new text is going to be adopted in reading, math, or any other subject area, the school district forms a committee and proceeds with a careful examination and analysis of available materials? On the other hand, when dictionaries are needed, too often someone just "orders dictionaries." These dictionaries are not only "textbooks" to be used in teaching skills, they are also tools to be used in reading, writing, and in all subject areas.

Dictionaries are as different from one another as any textbooks, and just as much care should be taken in their selection. However, many adults, including some teachers, have the mistaken notion that dictionaries are all the same. This idea must be changed among teachers, and it must not be allowed to develop among students.

Where are the guide words in a dictionary? True, they are at the top of the page, but in some dictionaries they are on opposite sides of each page. In others, there is only one guide word on the outside edge of each facing page. In some dictionaries, the guide words are one above the other on the outside edge of facing pages. Dictionaries differ.

Where is the pronunciation key in a dictionary? In many traditional dictionaries it is across the bottom of facing pages. However, in another dictionary, it is in a box at the top right-hand corner of the right-hand page. In another, it is in a box in the lower middle of the left-hand page.

How are definitions organized in a dictionary? In one, they are organized historically, with the oldest definition first. In another, they are organized in groups according to the relationships of meaning. In still another, they are organized according to frequency of use.

Where is the accent mark placed in the pronunciation of a word? Even here, dictionaries differ. Traditionally, the accent mark followed the accented syllable. In Merriam-Webster dictionaries the accent mark precedes the accented syllable.

Still more obvious differences exist in terms of the diacritical markings used for pronunciation. Not only do the symbols differ, but the ways in which the same word is to be pronounced may differ. For example, in one dictionary, the word *course* would be pronounced giving the -*our*- a pronunciation as "are." In another dictionary, the -*our*- is pronounced as "oar." Naturally, more sophisticated dictionaries, such as *Webster's New Collegiate* or *Webster's Third New International Dictionary*, will give the variety of pronunciations found in different dialect regions of this country.

Furthermore, perhaps your teachers should realize that the name "Webster's" on a dictionary does not mean anything. That name is not copyrighted, and it can be used by anyone on any kind of dictionary. Only "Merriam-Webster" is copyrighted by the G. & C. Merriam Company in the lineage of Noah Webster.

After teachers understand the great differences among dictionaries, you may want to insure that students understand these differences by requiring different dictionaries at every grade level or so. Then you can be assured that students will learn how to use *dictionaries* rather than how to use *a* dictionary.

There are many different dictionaries published. Among those you should be certain to include in your examination are the following, organized approximately by grade level of application:

Grades K–2 (Picture Dictionaries)
> *My First Dictionary* (600+ words), Oftedal and Jacob. New York: Grosset and Dunlap, 1948.
> *Picturebook Dictionary* (1,000 words), Hillerich, English, Bodzewski, and Kamatos. Chicago: Rand McNally, 1971.

Grades 2–3
> *The Ginn Beginning Dictionary*, Morris. Lexington, Mass.: Ginn and Company, 1973.
> *My First Dictionary*. Boston: Houghton Mifflin, 1980.

Grades 3–4
> *Beginning Dictionary*. Boston: Houghton Mifflin, 1979.
> *Scott, Foresman Beginning Dictionary*, Thorndike and Barnhart. Glenview, Ill.: Scott, Foresman, 1979.
> *Webster's Beginning Dictionary* (Grades 3–6). Springfield, Mass.: G. & C. Merriam, 1980.

Grades 5+
> *The American Heritage School Dictionary* (Grades 3–9). Boston: Houghton Mifflin, 1972.
> *Scott, Foresman Intermediate Dictionary*, Thorndike and Barnhart (Grades 5–8). Glenview, Ill.: Scott, Foresman, 1979.
> *Webster's Intermediate Dictionary* (Grades 5–9). New York: American Book Company, 1972.

Advanced (Grades 6+)
> *Webster's Third New International Dictionary*. Springfield, Mass.: G. & C. Merriam, 1971.
> *Webster's New Collegiate Dictionary*. Springfield, Mass.: G. & C. Merriam, 1974.
> *The American Heritage Dictionary of the English Language*. Boston: Houghton Mifflin, 1969.

As with any new book, at each grade level teachers should familiarize their pupils with the dictionary. They should acquaint youngsters with what the dictionary is for, how it can be used generally, and what it contains. For example, many students do not realize that dictionaries not only contain pronunciations and meanings, they contain tables of measure, flags, prefixes, suffixes, idioms, and various other kinds of information.

At middle grades and beyond, teachers and pupils should make a thorough examination of the introduction in their dictionary. It is here that they find how *that* dictionary is organized and how it can be used most efficiently. In a good dictionary, such as *Webster's New Collegiate Dictionary*, your teachers will find that the introduction contains a tremendous wealth of information, not only about that dictionary, but about the nature of the English language as well.

Dictionary Readiness

Several copies of good picture dictionaries ought to be available in every kindergarten and first-grade classroom. Picture dictionaries you select should be simple, not overly cluttered, and attractive to youngsters. (Two good ones have already been listed.) Picture dictionaries provide readiness for more mature dictionaries. They should be in the format of true dictionaries, where words are arranged in alphabetical order, so youngsters begin to get the idea of how words in a dictionary are arranged.

These dictionaries are not used in the manner of more advanced dictionaries. Children do not look up meanings of words, since they do not know any words for which they do not have meanings (or pronunciations). The books are used as picture books, eventually as a means of becoming acquainted with some words in print, and they are sometimes used in first grade both to get ideas for writing and as a means of checking the spellings of words that pupils want to use in writing.

Locational Skills

The locational skills include knowledge of alphabetical order, handling of a dictionary, and the use of guide words. By and large, these skills are pretty well developed in most basal reading programs and in most classrooms.

Youngsters have no real need for knowledge of alphabetical order until about second grade. If the proper preliminaries take place beginning in kindergarten, very little teaching will need to be done regarding alphabetical order.

Do your teachers have picture dictionaries, beginning in kindergarten, so that youngsters can get the idea of what this thing is that we call "alphabetical order"? In first grade, teachers often have pupils make their own little "spelling dictionaries," where they have one page or section for each letter—arranged alphabetically—and where they record their own words used frequently in their writing.

First-grade teachers also often have pupils use the alphabet at the front of the room along with phonograms, such as *-an*, *-ick*, *-ing*, and so on, to explore the language. Pupils go through the alphabet, letter by letter, to see what letters can be added to a given phonogram to make a word.

If all of these kinds of experiences are taking place in kindergarten and first grade, by the time youngsters get to second grade they will be fairly familiar with alphabetical order. In providing whatever additional practice is needed, you and your teachers need only watch for two major problems that exist in some practice materials.

First, children should *not*, at any level, learn alphabetical order through the alphabet song or any other system that merely provides practice in running through the entire alphabet beginning with *a*. They should be given chunks of the alphabet and asked to decide what letter would come "before," what would come "after," or what would come "between." Otherwise, the only way a child can decide what comes after *y* is to begin reciting the alphabet with *a*.

Second, some workbook pages and practice sheets contain exercises where pupils are to arrange words in alphabetical order. When they use such exercises, teachers should be certain that the sets of words to be alphabetized do not exceed five or six words in a set. Otherwise, youngsters get lost in the mechanics of having too many words to decide upon. They can still get the needed practice with sets of five or six words without the confusion of a dozen to fifteen words to arrange.

There is some evidence that initial practice in alphabetizing should be with nonsense words. Alphabetizing is a mechanical process that requires no concern for meaning. Use of nonsense words can demonstrate to pupils that they need not read the words, and it will also keep them from becoming distracted with the meanings of the words to be alphabetized.

Pupils need considerable practice in using guide words. This is usually provided through exercises where they must decide what word from a given list would appear between two guide words in alphabetical order. This skill of using guide words must begin with the knowledge of where the guide words are on a dictionary page and what the guide words represent. Most of the practice provided in workbook pages on this skill is realistic, and teachers should make use of such materials.

Where we often fall down in locational skills instruction is, once more, in application. After the isolated practice, do teachers then have youngsters take out a dictionary and do they have dictionary races—timed exercises to see how fast pupils can find a given word that the teacher presents to them orally?

Another way teachers can get application of locational skills is to pair youngsters, two to a dictionary. One child will hold the dictionary with its spine toward him or her and will announce a word. The "buddy" will then take a card and stick it into the dictionary pages at about the point where the dictionary should be opened to find that word. They check to see how close the guess was. Then they exchange dictionary and card and repeat the activity. Whoever comes closest to the page where the words are is the winner.

Using a Dictionary for Meaning

Children are usually taught how to use a dictionary for meaning before they are taught its use for pronunciation or spelling. This is true for at least two reasons. First, use of the dictionary for meaning is easier to learn than the other two uses. Second, the major concern of an individual is for the meaning of a word in reading, before worrying about its pronunciation and/or spelling.

This is also a skill that is usually fairly well developed in most basal programs and classrooms. Most often, such practice begins with a familiar word used with an infrequent meaning. For example, pupils know what a net is, but they may have difficulty with the meaning of *net* in the sentence: "The builder hoped to *net* a good deal of money." This meaning of *net* would undoubtedly be strange to a third grader.

This kind of practice is also important because it helps make youngsters aware that the dictionary will usually not help us decide on the meaning of a word unless we are also using context. Teachers should repeatedly remind students of this point. Of course, this has implications for the kind of practice teachers give children in using a dictionary for meaning. They should never give lists of words, or words in isolation, for children to find meanings. No one can use a dictionary effectively for meaning unless that individual knows the context in which the word is used. Otherwise, practice is meaningless.

Unfortunately, teachers do sometimes put lists of words on the board for youngsters to look up in the dictionary. Do your teachers do this? Worse, I've seen a commercial workbook page where students were directed to look up "meaning number 2" for a word. When have you ever looked up "meaning number 2"—or any other numbered meaning—for a word?

Using a Dictionary for Pronunciation

Teaching pupils to use a dictionary for pronunciation involves a number of understandings and subskills. Youngsters must understand (1) that the strange spelling following the entry word shows how to pronounce that word, (2) that the pronunciation key shows how to pronounce the strange symbols, (3) where the key is and how to use it, and finally, (4) how to use this information in order to pronounce a strange word, which means students must get practice in this skill, usually beginning in second grade. Most of the practice and teaching is effective up to the point of application. Then it falls down terribly. Neither teachers nor workbook exercises have managed to do a good job of teaching children the ultimate application of this skill.

It is easy enough for students to understand where they are shown a pronunciation for a word and where and what the key is. Nor is it difficult for youngsters to use the key to pronounce a given vowel sound. For example, if they are to find the pronunciation of /ā/, they can look in the key and find the word *bake* beside that symbol, indicating that the vowel sound is pronounced as in that word. They can even isolate that vowel sound without too much difficulty, saying "ā."

The difficulty arises when they attempt to carry that vowel sound back up to the strange word and say it in the context of the other sounds represented. Obviously, this is an oral-aural skill, and this is where classroom practice fails miserably. Most classroom practice relies on workbook pages, and this skill can not be learned through pencil and paper activity. Youngsters must repeatedly practice saying and hearing these sounds and words. If your teachers doubt the difficulty of this activity, give them, in print only, the pronunciation of a two- or three-syllable nonsense word. Have them use the dictionary key to decide on the pronunciation. You will notice that they are somewhat hesitant to say the word.

Some of the better workbook exercises try to come close to realistic practice by giving a pronunciation and then having the pupils identify, from among three or four other words, the word that has the same vowel sound. For example, with the word *feint*, pronounced /fānt/, pupils may be given the choices *paw*, *page*, *pan*, and *prance*. Such exercises are an attempt to get at realistic practice, but application of the skill will not be accomplished unless there is the oral kind of activity previously mentioned.

Of course, there are still some exercises that are an absolute failure and waste of time. For example, some workbooks provide lists of words pupils know, and the youngsters are to put the proper diacritical marks over the words. When have you ever had to put diacritical marks over a word you knew? Only the people who *write* the dictionaries have to be able to do that!

With appropriate oral practice, youngsters can learn to use a dictionary to pronounce a one-syllable word. Then teachers need to teach them how to use the accent mark. (And this is the only place where instruction in the use of accent is appropriate in reading.) Here again, the job will not be accomplished with pencil and paper activities. It is easy enough for pupils to understand what the accent mark signifies. Their problem comes in deliberately putting stress on the appropriate syllable. Up until this point, all words children used were picked up in their oral language development, and they learned the appropriate stress automatically along with the word. In fact, it is difficult to put stress on the wrong syllable of a word you know.

To give students conscious control of their ability to stress a particular syllable is a tough job. It might be made a little easier if the teacher begins with known words that shift stress, such as *pre'-sent* and *pre-sent'*, *rec'-ord* and *re-cord'*, and so on. Once pupils get some feeling for this control of stress, the teacher might go on to two-syllable nonsense words and finally to actual words in the dictionary. Here again, we might add the obvious: Practice in writing the accent marks over known words is a completely worthless activity.

Practice in using a dictionary for pronunciation, except in the case of words that shift accent, does not need to be in context. We can look up and find the pronunciation of a word without attention to its meaning or context.

Using a Dictionary for Spelling

While the previous two uses of the dictionary are generally taught relatively well, the use of a dictionary for spelling is usually not taught *at all*. What have you found in your school when you walk into a class—even at sixth grade— where a student asks the teacher for the spelling of a word? The teacher will usually say, "You know how to use a dictionary. Look it up." And the student's usual reply is, "How'm I gonna find it if I don't know how to spell it?"

What is the procedure for anyone who needs to use a dictionary to check on the spelling of a word? It is a matter of "educated guessing." This means that we must provide students with the "education," and then we must take them by the hand and show them how to apply it in their "guessing."

The beginnings of this skill should be found in late first grade or very early second, where the teacher turns the "reading phonics" around. Youngsters have learned in reading that *m* stands for the sound they hear at the beginning of "moon," "mice," and so on. Now the teacher can ask what letter they think would begin a word like *mischief*. Going a step further, when dictionaries are available, the teacher can ask what section of the dictionary pupils would check to find *mischief*, and they should be able to reply "in the *m* part."

The more difficult task has to do with the spellings of the vowel sounds. If your teachers are providing the kind of exploration of possible spellings of vowel sounds suggested in Chapter 5, pupils are getting the "education" necessary. Then youngsters can be "taken by the hand" in somewhat the following manner. The teacher may give the second graders a word like "mean" and ask how they think its spelling might begin. They should decide "with *m*." Then the teacher might ask how the vowel sound could be spelled, and youngsters may suggest *ee* from experience with *meet* or *feet*. When they check the dictionary for *meen*, they will not find it, so the teacher will ask for another "guess." Perhaps Pete is in the room, so they suggest *e-e*, as in his name. When they check for *mene*, they again will not find the word. Ultimately, they should suggest *mean* and find it in the dictionary.

With this kind of experience behind them, students in third or fourth grade can be given additional practice or "challenge" activities by trying to find the spellings of difficult words the teacher may put on the board in their pronunciation form. Youngsters will use the dictionary key to decide on the pronunciation and then will use their educated guessing to try to find the spellings of those words in the dictionary. For example, pronunciations such as /māl'-strəm/ *(maelstrom)* or /pen'-wär/ *(peignoir)* can be challenges for sixth graders.

If upper-grade teachers get students involved in some of the preceding activities as a special treat—for fun—those students may themselves try to find other words to stump their classmates. There is no better way to develop skills and to build vocabulary than to get youngsters interested in words for the fun of it.

Other Related Skills

In addition to the basic understandings and skills about dictionaries that need to be taught, upper grades can and should go further. At upper levels, teachers should acquaint students with use of a dictionary to discover word origins and etymologies. To do this, they must have access to more advanced dictionaries, such as the ones listed previously. Every sixth grade should have several copies of *Webster's New Collegiate Dictionary*, and they should have access to an unabridged dictionary such as *Webster's Third New International Dictionary*. The latter, or an equivalent, is that big, thick volume that usually collects dust in most school offices.

A related tool is the thesaurus. Use of a thesaurus is important if students are going to improve their word choice in writing. To begin with, they need to be taught what a thesaurus is and how to use it. This teaching can start by about third grade with some of the more simple versions. For lower levels, good beginning thesauruses are:

> *In Other Words: A Beginning Thesaurus* (Grades 3–4), Schiller and Jenkins. Glenview, Ill.: Scott, Foresman, 1977.
> *In Other Words: A Junior Thesaurus* (Grades 4–6), Schiller and Jenkins. Glenview, Ill.: Scott, Foresman, 1977.

These two books are an easy introduction to a thesaurus and will get pupils accustomed to discovering the fine nuances that distinguish "synonyms." They are the foundation for work with a real thesaurus.

By sixth grade, or even fifth, you teachers should acquaint students with *Roget's International Thesaurus* (New York: T. Y. Crowell). Every sixth grade should have at least one copy of this thesaurus and pupils should be taught how to use it. You may find that many of your teachers do not know how to use a thesaurus, so clarification with them is an essential first step.

THE STUDY SKILLS

In this section we will discuss the study skills, those skills required in order to read effectively in the content areas, such as the social studies and science. This kind of reading presumes some mastery of the skills previously discussed. No one can gain information from reading without using the basic decoding skills and the comprehension skills discussed in preceding chapters. Furthermore, the critical reading skills should be an integral part of reading in the content areas.

In addition, reading in the content areas presents some unique problems not found in other kinds of reading, and requires additional skills, such as the ability to locate information, to organize that information, and to read for different purposes. Under each of these headings, a number of specific skills to be developed will be discussed.

The teaching of the study skills has been neglected according to the evidence. Undoubtedly, one of the reasons we have not done a better job with these skills is the fact that the teaching of reading is usually done with basal readers, and they contain mostly literary materials. In contrast, the study skills need to be taught and applied in factual materials. Why would anyone want to outline or retain the specific content in a piece of fiction?

There are, however, additional problems that hinder the development of the study skills. Some are inherent in the nature of the material, but many are a result of our own lack of clarity in this area. Let's take a look at some of the concerns about the content areas in general before dealing with the skills.

Problems in the Content Areas

The "content areas," or subjects, are those that have a body of information to be taught. In the strict sense, probably only reading and written expression are not content areas but would be classed as skill subjects. Even math, which is usually considered a skill subject, is also a content area in terms of certain concepts that need to be developed. All of the content areas share in presenting common problems to the learner, but to keep within limits in this book, let's focus on the social studies and science as examples of the content areas and their problems.

Despite the handicap of having primarily literary materials in basal readers, the specific skills for the content areas are usually fairly well taught. The skills are not the *major* problem. Our biggest problems lie elsewhere, and until principal and teachers identify and resolve them, we will continue to do poorly in teaching reading in the content areas.

Recognition of these problems is a necessary first step toward their solutions. They include (1) lack of clarity of purpose, (2) heavy load of concepts without clarifying detail, (3) reading difficulty of materials used, and (4) unique content vocabulary.

Lack of Clarity of Purpose

A number of years ago, Harold Allen did a survey of secondary English teachers, asking them to state the objectives for teaching English. He collected over a thousand objectives and rightly concluded that any area with that many objectives has no objective! Have you and your staff clearly determined your objectives for teaching subjects such as the social studies or science in the elementary school? We should certainly hope that the declared purpose is not to "teach the facts." Yet, a glance at the kinds of tests most teachers develop in these areas would quickly destroy our hopes.

How will such teachers of facts keep up with the rapid accumulation of these facts: teach twice as fast each year? delete some of the "important" facts from last year to make room for the new? Do they realize that students will retain only about 5 percent of those facts by the next year?

Finally, what are facts anyhow? In the social studies they are most often collections of observations as reported by others; in science, they are too often merely substantiated theories. These "facts" change. Depending on your age, you may have learned facts that are now wrong. Did you learn that there were forty-eight states in the United States? How many elements were there in science when you went to school? And was the atom the smallest indestructible unit?

While teaching as if their goal is the facts, most teachers would *claim* their objective is to teach "concepts." These are supposed to be broad generalizations or understandings in the content areas. Even the specialists in various disciplines that make up the social studies have been unable to state clearly what are the most important concepts from their disciplines that should make up an elementary school social studies program. Perhaps we had better rethink that objective.

I would like to suggest that the primary goal for teaching the social studies and science in the elementary school is to use those subjects as the vehicles for developing the study skills. This is a worthy goal at the elementary level, the junior high, and probably even at the high school level. If we use these areas to teach youngsters *how* to locate, organize, evaluate, and retain information, they can apply these skills to learn whatever is necessary in the future. No one can guess the concepts, much less the facts, these elementary students are going to need in the year 2010, when they will be young adults. What they certainly will need are the skills—the tools—that will enable them to get their own information.

This is a "process" approach, and we saw it in the teaching of science, where pupils actually participated in science instead of merely reading about it. This "process" approach is just as valuable in the social studies.

If teachers accept this goal, the teaching that takes place may not appear too different on the surface. In U.S. history, for example, the class may still study "the causes of the Civil War." However, instead of studying this topic in order to learn and remember those "causes," they will be developing their study skills in order to learn how to sift out information and draw conclusions from it. Such experience is going to be more valuable than knowing the causes of the Civil War if these students are to be instrumental in avoiding a final world war.

Whatever goals or objectives you and your staff accept, it is important that you make them explicit. If teachers are going to be effective in any manner at all, they had better understand what their objectives are.

Heavy Load of Concepts

Another problem, especially in the social studies, has to do with the heavy load of concepts without illuminating detail. Have you looked at a middle-grade social studies text recently—from the eyes of a youngster? Usually these books present concept on top of concept, bare bones with no meat. For example, as you know, most sixth grades study old world backgrounds in the social studies. In one year they do a quick overview of European history, governments, economics, customs, and so on. Here is one sentence from a sixth-grade text, where five paragraphs were devoted to Hungary: "Hungary is less industrialized than East Germany, Czechoslovakia, and Poland but more so than the other Eastern European nations."

Imagine yourself a sixth grader asked to read "the next ten pages" of this kind of thing and then to answer the questions at the end. Of course, one of the questions will be "How industrialized is Hungary?" Do you know? Being able to do more than verbalize back the words from that sentence would require understanding how industrialized those stated nations are and how industrialized the "other Eastern European nations" are. Most sixth graders do not even know *what* the "other Eastern European nations" are, much less how industrialized they are.

In the same sentence is exemplified another problem that persists in social studies texts: the use of vague quantitative terms such as "less" and "more so." What does the author mean by "less"? Only 10 percent as industrialized? Only 50 percent as industrialized? Maybe 90 percent as industrialized?

In other words, if the teacher of that text is serious in wanting students to understand how industrialized Hungary is, the preceding sentence could represent weeks, if not months, of work. Those youngsters would have to investigate the kinds of industry found in Hungary, where it is located, the amount of employment in industry, and so on, and then they would have to relate that information to something they know, such as the industrialization in the city or state where they live—assuming that they know or have investigated that, too.

With your staff, it would pay to take a look at some of the social studies or science materials in your school—from the viewpoint of a naive pupil. Then, if a problem is identified, the next step is to determine how to solve it. The solution will depend on your objective in the subject. If the objective is merely to teach facts, then teachers can help youngsters to pull them out and memorize them. If the objective is to reach either concepts or skills, you will need to have children reading in a variety of other materials on the same subject. In other words, if your fifth grade is studying "the Westward Movement," they will need to get into a lot of different history books, as well as biographies, and even historical fiction of the period. Consistently, the evidence indicates that the best way to develop broad understandings is to read about the topic in a variety of sources. Furthermore, how can anyone use critical reading skills in an unfamiliar area without comparing information from a variety of sources? Such locating, organizing, and evaluating is basic to the study skills.

Reading Difficulty of Materials Used

Another major problem in teaching the content areas has to do with the reading level of the textbooks. In one study of twelve junior high school science books published between 1971–1974, only one had a readability level at grade level; over half were two or more years above grade level, and one was *five* years above grade level. In a more recent study of elementary social studies texts, most of them were written at grade level. However, you must realize what that means. If a fifth-grade text is at fifth-grade reading level, it means that in a typical school only half of the pupils in fifth grade can read it. Furthermore, the readability formula most often used—the Dale-Chall—is based on a comprehension accuracy of only 50 percent! Finally, shouldn't material used to gain information be written at an easier level than the maximum level at which a person can read?

On this point, you usually do not need to have your teachers go to the labor of doing readability formulas on texts. Publishers can supply that kind of information for you. They do not lie about it, but you do need to ask whether the reading level they give you includes the technical words. Some publishers claim that, since technical words are defined in the text, they should not be counted as difficult words. This exclusion results in a lower readability level for the book, which is misleading. Those technical words are still in that book, and the pupil must face them and handle them just as he or she would any other words.

Once you and your staff have reviewed this problem, you again need to arrive at a solution in terms of your objectives. If the objective is for pupils to get facts or concepts from the textbook, alternate means, other than reading, will have to be found for the ones who cannot read the text. Alternatives include reading that material to those pupils or having it tape recorded so they can listen to it. If the objective has to do with the study skills, then you need to have a variety of reading materials on the subject, including some at levels below the grade level, so all pupils can read on the subject and can exchange findings as they attempt to arrive at conclusions.

Perhaps one of the reasons teachers fail to do a better job in the content areas is the often-expressed concern with the pressure of so much material that is included in the curriculum by middle grades. This frequently is translated as a concern to "cover the book." Someone once said that the best way to "cover a book" is to sit on it! Better, as Edgar Dale once said, we ought to be less concerned with *covering* material and more concerned about *uncovering* it.

Do your teachers feel this kind of pressure? Again, clarification of purpose and use of appropriate materials instead of the single text will help to relieve it.

Unique Content Vocabulary

No one can hope to get meaning from reading unless that person can understand the meanings of the words used in print. Vocabulary in the content areas
presents problems from several points of view.

For one thing, there are often common words used in a special or technical sense. Young children are familiar with "fruit," but that word takes on a
new meaning in science. They know what a "body" is, but what about a "heav-
enly body"? Even the youngest knows what a "table" is, but a "table" in science is different from any that child has eaten off of. In math, one junior high
student seriously had a problem in accepting four as a factor of twelve. He had
been taught that the factor of a number was any number that divides evenly
into the original—and three is an "odd" number! Besides, are "odd" numbers
any more odd than "even" numbers?

Usually it is easier to learn a completely new word with its meaning than
it is to get an additional—and often, contrary—meaning for a known word. Do
your teachers just assume the new meaning is clear, or do they assure it?

A second problem with vocabulary has to do with the abstract terms so
often found in the social studies. What meaning does *freedom, peace,* or *de-
mocracy* have for a fourth grader? a sixth grader? Would you like to give a brief
definition for each? These are words whose meanings cannot just be discussed
once and assumed learned.

A third vocabulary problem relates to the technical words: *plateau, lati-
tude, orthoptera, hemiptera, hemisphere,* and so on. Here a twofold attack can
be made, as discussed in the next section.

Another vocabulary problem has to do with what we might call "loaded"
words. *Photosynthesis* is not just a word to be defined, it is a book—a whole
process. Yet, too often such new terms are merely defined parenthetically. For
example, in one social studies text at sixth grade, the first time pupils meet the
word *Franks,* that word is defined as ". . . the Franks, the Christian Franks
beyond the Pyranees, . . ." A short phrase (which, incidentally, confuses the
issue with additional words that need explanation) can hardly be called a clarification of the word *Franks.*

Yet, with all of the problems, including those of vocabulary, the task is
not hopeless. In addition to teaching the study skills for better reading in these
areas, there are some other preparatory activities teachers can use to enable
more success in the content areas.

Preliminaries to Reading Content Material

At least three kinds of preparatory activities will enable more effective reading
of the content areas. These include some kind of introduction to the material,
a clarification of strategies to be used, and, in appropriate cases, some pre-
teaching of the vocabulary of the selection. Some of these preliminaries are
involved to the point that they may need to be taught outside the content area,

but students need to be reminded of them prior to the reading of a content selection.

Introduction to the Material

This introduction includes two major tasks: establishing purposes for reading and clarifying or relating the material to previous knowledge.

The importance of establishing a purpose for reading was discussed in connection with teacher questioning techniques. It is even more important here if students are to sift the pertinent information from a myriad of material. If your teachers doubt the importance of purpose setting, you might demonstrate to them in a staff meeting with a little listening test. Tell them you have a paragraph that you will read to them; you want them to listen "carefully" and be prepared to answer a question about it. Also tell them they are not allowed to take notes. Then read the following paragraph, which was adapted from an idea by Hildebrandt (1966, p. 389):

> You're an airline pilot flying a four-engine jet from San Diego to Boston. On board are sixty-eight people, of whom six are crew members, eighteen are married couples, seven are children, and the remainder are an assortment of business people. The plane leaves San Diego at 3:10 PM and arrives in Boston five hours and seventeen minutes later.

Ask if they are ready for the question. Tell them that if they know the answer they are to say nothing but raise their hand. Then ask the question: "What is the pilot's name?" You'll be lucky if one teacher raises a hand. Yet, there would be no problem in answering if you had established a purpose before the reading.

Besides establishing a purpose for the reading, teachers should introduce the material itself. They may do this by giving a brief overview of the content and, if possible, relating that content to what students already know or have just studied. For example, the "Structured Overview" is a fairly elaborate technique for summarizing prior to instruction. It is a summary in the general style and abstractness of the material to be read. Its value seems to be in the repetition and simplification of that material (Hartley and Davies, 1976).

An "Advance Organizer" is the more elaborate method for relating the new material to that already known. It provides a broad framework that ties the new to what is already known. Research on both of these more formal techniques is somewhat mixed in support of their value (Barnes and Clawson, 1975).

Clarification Strategies

Teachers can prepare students to understand content material if they clarify the kind of organization the material represents. Depending on the purpose, a writer presents material in different organizational patterns. If students know the kind of pattern and how to handle it, they will understand that material better.

To do an effective job here, the teacher will need to check in advance to determine the organizational pattern or patterns used in the selection to be read. Then that teacher will review with students how they are to handle that pattern. Following are some suggested strategies, abbreviated and adapted from Robinson (1978):

Organizational Pattern:	*Strategies*
1. Topic Development: topic, followed by main idea and details.	a. Recognize the topic (often the title).
	b. Recognize the organizational format.
	c. Relate supporting ideas to the topic.
2. Cause/Effect: common in the social studies as "effect/cause(s)."	a. Recognize the effect (may be the main idea).
	b. Locate the causes.
3. Enumeration: topic plus facts.	a. Recognize the topic.
	b. Recognize the subtopics.
	c. Organize details related to each subtopic.
4. Generalization: a conclusion with support.	a. Locate the generalization.
	b. Classify it (definition? conclusion?).
	c. Locate supporting information.
5. Sequence: often chronological in the social studies.	a. Recognize the steps.
	b. Recognize the implications of the sequence.
6. Comparison/Contrast: clarification through likenesses/ differences.	a. Recognize key words.
	b. Identify key likenesses and differences.
7. Classification: topic divided, with subtopics under each part.	a. Recognize each topic.
	b. Recognize and assign subtopics.
	c. Understand the classification scheme.
8. Problem Solution: problem/ question, with or without a solution stated.	a. Recognize information about the problem.
	b. Recognize the problem.
	c. Recognize or execute the solution.

Preteaching the Vocabulary

Do your teachers rely on the text to clarify meanings of technical or abstract words? They should do some preteaching of those terms by explaining, using them in other contexts, giving examples, relating them to items known, having students discuss them, and so on. Specifically, a technique demonstrated successful is the Frayer model (Peters, 1975–1976). This approach suggests four different clarifying devices: (1) use of relevant attributes (a *globe* is spherical and represents the earth); (2) use of irrelevant attributes (the size of a *globe* is irrelevant); (3) use of nonexample (a *globe* is not a wall map); and (4) establishment of a hierarchy (solar system, *globe*, map of the United States).

In addition to teaching the specific word or term, teachers have many opportunities in the content areas to develop a generalizable understanding: There are many instances where technical terms are composed of common prefixes, suffixes, or combining forms from Greek or Latin. While not every Latin and Greek root should be taught, we can apply the criteria of frequency of use and consistency in meaning to identify some that are worth teaching.

These affixes should be taught after students are acquainted with a few words that contain them. For example, after meeting the words *hydro-electric* and *hydrometer*, students should examine the meaning of *hydro-* and locate other words with that combining form. A list of the worthwhile items—in terms of frequency of use and consistency in meaning—has been adapted from the work of Deighton (1959) and is provided in Appendix A.

Teaching the Locational Skills

The locational skills include learning to use special aids, learning about parts of a book, and learning to use an index.

Special Aids

Do your teachers familiarize students with the many different kinds of aids available for information? These include the card catalog, at whatever level youngsters are expected to use the library for reference, as well as atlases, time tables, almanacs, biographical dictionaries, encyclopedias, a thesaurus, and even TV schedules.

Primarily, the function of the principal in this area is to be certain the variety of materials are available and used with some instruction. A question might be raised, however, about the use of encyclopedias. Are pupils expected to use them too early? Even fourth graders are often encouraged to use the encyclopedia for a report and to "write it in your own words." Encyclopedic writing is about the most concise writing you will find. In using the encyclopedia too early, youngsters are almost forced to plagiarize. You might consider delaying use of this tool and encouraging all report writing to be done from more detailed reference works. Finally, when students do use the encyclopedia to write a report, suggest the rule that no one takes pencil and paper with them to the encyclopedia. The article should be read, then the student can rethink the information and record whatever is desired.

Parts of a Book

Whenever students receive a new textbook, do your teachers acquaint them with it? Further, do they point out the different parts of the book: title page, table of contents, glossary, appendix, index? Do teachers acquaint pupils with the purpose of each section and how to use it?

Especially important in locating information are the index and the table of contents. Do your teachers clarify the difference in function of the two and give pupils practice in deciding, based on a given question, whether they would look in the table of contents or in the index?

Use of an Index

This is one of the most important reference skills teachers have to teach. Like so many previously mentioned skills, it is usually well taught in basal readers, but it is not applied. Understanding the format of an index is a relatively easy matter. The focus is, and should be, on deciding from a given question what is the key word to be looked up in the index. Usually we begin with a question in which the key word is stated. For example, given a book about agriculture in the United States, youngsters may be asked what would be the key word to look up in the index to find the answer to "Where are oranges grown?"

The next step is to give a question in which the student must decide from two possibilities which is the key word. For example, in the same book, with the question "Where are oranges grown in Florida?" the choices might be *oranges* or *Florida*. Ultimately, the student may be faced with the problem of deciding a key word that is not stated. For example, what if neither *oranges* nor *Florida* can be found in that index? The information might be listed under *citrus fruits*.

In addition to demonstrating and providing practice with the index, teachers might need to be reminded about another point. Too often the tendency is to use the "answer book" to determine if pupils are right or wrong. Especially in the decision about key words for the index, there is no right or wrong—there is only the word that works and the one that does not. Youngsters should not get the impression that there is a right or wrong answer here. Different authors organize an index differently, and the reader must figure out how the one in hand is to be used.

As stated, these skills may be well taught in the basal reader or in the classroom reading class, but often the application is forgotten. It does little good to teach use of an index in reading—no matter how well—if the teacher then directs pupils in the social studies to "open your books to page 74." The index must be used in the content areas.

Teaching the Organizational Skills

These skills usually include note taking, classifying, outlining, and summarizing. Unfortunately, we have very little evidence to demonstrate what is the best way to teach any of these skills. Nevertheless, most authorities are agreed on their importance.

Note Taking

This is a skill that is often delayed until junior high or high school. At the elementary level, whatever note taking is done is a matter of getting notes from reading material for a report; it is not a matter of taking notes from a lecture. Notes may be put individually on separate cards, so youngsters can reorganize the cards for their reports. They should be certain to identify where the note came from. This latter habit is an important one to develop in the event the note-taker needs to return to the source of information to check or to develop a bibliography.

Classifying

This skill of classifying or categorizing began in kindergarten. The purpose and the practice are still the same, although the practice may be a little more sophisticated. The point that youngsters need to understand is that we can sort objects or ideas according to rules that we make up or that someone gives us. This is elaborated on in later grades, where pupils may become involved in science in classifying animals or insects according to certain established "rules" or characteristics. Primarily, the teacher's role seems to be one of demonstrating and providing practice.

Outlining

While research may be lacking on the best way to teach outlining, it does exist to suggest this as one of the most important skills in retaining information. It is more effective than note taking or rereading, and certainly more effective than underlining or highlighting. In fact, both of the latter are of doubtful value as aids in retaining information.

Most often the teaching of outlining begins at fourth or fifth grade. It presumes ability to identify topics and supporting details. It has also been recognized as a very difficult skill for students to master.

There are a few positive suggestions that may be helpful to your teachers in this difficult area. First, they might begin with what the youngsters already know. Instead of asking students to outline a piece of written material, teachers may begin with a writing assignment: "If you were going to write about what you like to do in your free time, how would you organize your ideas? Would you divide the paper into those things you do at school and those you do at home, or things you like to do in good weather and in bad weather? . . ."

After a few examples such as this are placed on the board in a simple outline, youngsters can add details to each of the two main topics. They now have an outline, and can be shown that outlining is a matter of organizing thoughts or, in the case of written material, a matter of finding out how a writer has organized his or her thoughts.

One of the persistent problems in outlining seems to be the practice of teachers who put more emphasis on the format (Roman numerals, letters, and so on) than they do on the idea of what outlining is. It is probably a good idea to begin outlining without the numerals and letters, initially using indentation to separate ideas. Later, the teacher might supply a chart with the format for youngsters to refer to.

After students get the idea of what outlining is about through organizing their own ideas, the teacher may then assign a piece of written material for them to outline. Initial experience in trying to ferret out another writer's organizational plan should be limited to well-organized materials. Usually, science articles lend themselves well to this early experience.

Summarizing

Not much is known about the best way to teach summarizing. We do know that it is a difficult skill and one that teachers need to demonstrate and give pupils practice with.

"Summarizing" lies somewhere between giving the main idea of a selection and retelling or restating the entire selection. Probably one of the reasons summarizing is a difficult skill is that it is also vague. How long is a summary? It may be very brief, including only the major ideas, or it may include major ideas and supporting details. We do know it is particularly difficult for primary children, who tend to "summarize" by retelling in extensive detail the entire selection.

Teachers need to provide practice in summarizing, and they can do this only by taking examples and working with children to demonstrate how we can pull out main ideas in order to give a brief summary. Then they may have pupils practice on a selection and discuss the summaries attempted.

Teaching the Evaluative Skills

If students are to become skilled readers in the content areas and in reading of any kind of "factual" material, they must be able to evaluate the information they have located and organized. There is no need here to repeat a discussion of the critical reading skills presented in Chapter 7, but those skills need to be applied in the content areas.

In order to use these critical reading skills, since students are undoubtedly reading in an area that is outside their own experience and background, they must read on the subject in a variety of sources in order to have some basis for comparison of information. Your teachers also need to be aware that the social studies texts themselves can represent bias. We do not need to go to a British textbook account of the Revolutionary War to see that there are differences in views. Anyone aware of different religious viewpoints can see that the following statement from a sixth-grade text might not be accepted by certain religious groups: [As a result of the defeat of the Moslems by the Franks] . . . "Europe remained free to accept Christianity."

Do your teachers have students compare information on the same topic from a variety of sources in order to use their critical reading skills? Do they also look for the use of slant or bias as they read "factual" material?

Teaching Students to Read for Various Purposes

An important part of teaching in the content areas relates to the kind of teaching we need to do in order to help youngsters learn to read for various purposes and to adjust their manner of reading accordingly. These purposes have to do with rate of reading and with some of the specifics unique to each of the content areas.

Rate of Reading

There is no justification for attempting "speed reading" at the elementary level, the junior high school, or, in most cases, at the high school. It is true that rate can be increased—up to a point—without having comprehension suffer. However, it is also true that, unless the individual is under pressure to maintain the increased rate, as soon as the training program is completed that person drops back again to his or her original, comfortable rate of reading. Few, if any, precollege students are under the necessary pressure that would encourage them to maintain the increased rate that could be achieved through rate training.

We do, however, need to teach elementary students to adjust rate to the purpose for reading. By third or fourth grade, they should learn that they do not read a science or social studies text at the same rate at which they would read a piece of fiction. "Teaching" is mostly a matter of explaining, demonstrating, and giving practice in reading at different rates in different kinds of materials. In fact, evidence suggests that many elementary youngsters pick up this idea on their own, without specific teaching. However, this does not mean that we should leave this skill to chance.

Also related to this adjustment of rate are the skills of skimming and scanning. These, too, need to be explained and practiced. Students should be taught to skim for an idea. When they skim, they do not read the entire selection; they may read a sentence in each paragraph in order to get the general idea of what the selection is about. Practice in this skill is a matter of timed exercise where youngsters know in advance that they have thirty seconds or a minute in which to skim a particular page just to get the general idea of what it is about.

There is no clear "method" that the skilled reader uses in skimming; however, in the beginning stages of development of this skill, students usually need specific direction, such as "Read the first sentence in each paragraph." After some practice, they can discover that they do not necessarily have to read the first sentence, nor do they even have to read a sentence in *every* paragraph.

When we scan, we look for a specific item, such as a date or name. Scanning is somewhat like looking for a four-leaf clover in a clover patch. We do not look at every clover; we have a physical image in mind, and we look for a match to that mental image. If we are scanning for the year in which something occurred, we have a mind set for four numerals. In scanning for a name, the reader has a mind set for a word beginning with a capital letter.

Here again, the teacher needs to explain that no reading is done in scanning. Then youngsters need to practice their scanning for specifics. Incidentally, scanning is most often done in familiar materials. Youngsters will have read the selection and are now scanning it to locate a specific time.

Reading Study-Type Materials

There are certain additional techniques that need to be developed in the content areas. They are basically aimed at retaining or doing something with information read. Unfortunately, many content teachers have too often been told that "every teacher is a teacher of reading." This slogan has alienated many good teachers, especially at the secondary level. A science teacher cannot be blamed for replying: "I'm not a teacher of reading; I'm a teacher of science."

Let's clarify that slogan: It is not that every teacher is—or even should be—a teacher of "reading," but *every teacher* ought to be teaching students how to read in the content area for which that teacher is responsible. To note a specific example, certainly as an elementary principal or consultant you have heard a statement such as I remember hearing from junior high math teachers: "If only those elementary teachers would teach the students how to read, I could teach them the math."

If you have heard this from any source, you might like to try a little experiment. Go into any fifth-, sixth-, or even eighth-grade class and tell the group that you have a math problem you want them to solve. Each student is to do the problem independently and, when finished, to sit quietly until the others are ready. Put a problem such as the following on the overhead projector or on the board:

Mother went to the grocery store. She bought 3 pounds of apples at 85¢ a pound, 2 loaves of bread at 91¢ each, a quart of milk at 79¢ a quart, 1½ dozen eggs at 89¢ a dozen, and 2 heads of lettuce at 79¢ a head. How much was the milk?

If your experience is anything like mine has been, you will be fortunate to have two or three students sit quietly and smile while the others are busy dividing, multiplying, and adding. It's not that those students cannot read and understand the words and sentences in the problem. Their difficulty lies in the fact that apparently no one has taught them how to read a math problem. As a result, when they see more than two sets of figures, they assume they will have to put them all together, and they start right in without ever looking at the final question.

Reading a math problem is much like reading directions. We skim over the entire problem to get a general idea of what it is about and what we are to conclude with, then we go back to pick out the specific facts needed to solve the problem. The point is, each content area has some unique features, and it is the responsibility of the teacher of that area (beginning at the elementary level) to teach children *how* to read in that particular content area.

Another unique feature, for example, is most prevalent in the social studies. Most of these texts include paragraph headings and marginal notes. The evidence is that these "typographical aids" do not help students; they actually confuse them unless those students are taught how to use the aids. Once students are taught how to use them, the aids do become helpful.

Reading to follow directions is another skill that must be taught. Here, the procedure is also different from most reading. Admittedly, many of us as adults do not do too good a job on this one. How often have you written your name on a form before you realize that it says "Please print"? Here again, the primary "teaching" that must take place is a matter of explaining, demonstrating, giving some practice, discussing the practice, and then applying the skill.

In teaching students to read to follow directions, the technique is much like the math problem previously discussed. Students must skim over the material to get a general idea of what the directions are about, what is needed to complete them, and what the conclusion will be. Then they must start over, reading carefully, step by step, to follow the directions. Too often the tendency is to begin with step one, then do step two, and so on, realizing only too late that we have gone astray.

Teachers might even want to demonstrate to upper-grade students the importance of this procedure. For example, in using a recipe, if the reader follows step by step, mixing the eggs, flour, milk, and so on, he or she may discover too late that the wet and dry ingredients were to be mixed separately.

Teachers who want to be a little more dramatic might use an adaptation of an old party game, which should be announced as a timed test and distributed face down. It becomes more effective if a lot of the directions require considerable calling out and jumping up and down, as shown in Figure 8–1.

You will be fortunate, even in an eighth-grade class, if more than one or two students sit quietly while the rest of the group "perform."

CAN YOU FOLLOW DIRECTIONS????
(Time Limit: Three Minutes)

1. Look over all the directions before you begin.
2. Put your name in the upper right corner of this paper.
3. Circle the word paper in the second sentence.
4. Draw three small circles in the upper left corner.
5. Put an X in each circle.
6. Put an square around each circle.
7. Jump up, then sit down and continue working.
8. After the title on this paper, write "yes, yes, yes."
9. On the back of this paper, multiply 703 by 22.
10. Draw a rectangle around the word *three* in sentence number four.
11. Loudly call out your first name when you get this far.
12. Put an X in the lower left corner of this page.
13. If you have followed directions to this point, call out "I have it."
14. On the reverse side of this paper, add 8956 and 9805.
15. Put a circle around your answer.
16. In your normal speaking voice, count from ten to one backwards.
17. Punch three holes in the top of this paper with your pencil.
18. If you are the first person to read this point, loudly call out "I am the leader in following directions."
19. Underline all even numbers on the left side of this page.
20. Now that you have looked over all the directions, do only directions one and two.

Figure 8–1   *Demonstration "test" for Following Directions*

Practice in reading to follow directions can, and usually does, begin in first grade, where it is probably better taught than anywhere else. Pupils can be given simple written exercises on a practice sheet, such as a page of triangles, squares, and circles, with three directions:

1. Make the circles red.
2. Make the triangles blue.
3. Make the squares yellow.

SQ3R is a technique that ought to be taught for reading in the content areas by about fourth grade. This is a technique helpful to the reader who wants to retain information. SQ3R stands for Survey, Question, Read, Recite, Review. It is so effective that it has been copied by many others, under acronyms such as SQ4R, PQRST, OK4R, and SQRQCQ, all of which incorporate the same idea.

In application, the student will first *Survey* or skim the material to get a general idea of what it is about. Then, on the basis of that survey, the reader will establish certain *Questions* that should be answered from the reading. *Reading* takes place, followed by "*Reciting*," which is a matter of thinking back over the answers to the questions originally posed. Finally, the reader will *Review* the material to check on the accuracy of the "answers" and to pick up any additional information desired.

Francis Robinson (1961), who developed this technique, saw its primary benefit in the immediate recall of material read, resulting in a dramatic decrease in forgetting. Probably an additional value of SQ3R lies in the advance setting of purposes for reading, as discussed earlier in this chapter. However, there is no question about the value of immediate recall or review. Evidence from research in outlining and note taking also verifies this particular practice as being most important. In fact, evidence from note taking based on lectures, at the college level, indicates that it is not the note taking itself but the review of notes—whether made by the student or by the instructor—that is the valuable act.

Are your teachers demonstrating to middle-grade students the SQ3R technique, and are they providing practice in assuring its application in appropriate reading materials?

Finally, a heavy load of the information in content or factual reading is carried by graphs, charts, maps, diagrams, tables, and so on. Are your teachers teaching students how to interpret and use graphic materials? That teaching is usually a matter of taking an example, explaining and demonstrating how to interpret it through questions to be answered from that graphic material. Ultimately, additional practice must be gained through use of additional questions that can be answered from the material, and youngsters must then apply their skill in a content area.

In order to accomplish this kind of instruction, teachers must have available to them and their students a variety of materials, not only geographical maps, but typographical, population, rain maps, and so on. They will also need a variety of information available on graphs and tables. *The World Almanac* is a great source of the specific data that students can convert to graphic illustration. In making their own graphs, students often gain a better understanding of how to interpret these informative illustrations.

Comparisons can be made, using the same information, in a variety of kinds of graphs. For example, the relative sizes of the Great Lakes can be found in *The World Almanac*. Then students may make a line graph, bar graph, pie graph, and a table showing this information. In comparing, they can discover the relative advantages and disadvantages of each kind. They should see that a line graph is not appropriate for this kind of comparison becuase it implies a relationship or trend; a table can provide exact figures, whereas a pie graph gives only approximate relative sizes but does this more obviously than a table.

Your sixth-grade teachers may even enjoy using a copy of *How to Lie with Statistics* (New York: W. W. Norton and Company, 1954). They can demonstrate to students different ways of graphing the same information in order to give the reader different impressions. After some of this kind of experience, students can look at different graphs and possibly redraw them to provide different impressions of the same data.

In Conclusion

At the elementary level, every teacher is usually a teacher of reading, as well as a teacher of almost everything else. It is important that those teachers carry over what they know about reading from the "reading" class in order to teach children how to read in whatever content area they are using at the moment. It may be helpful for you to provide your teachers with their own checklist of the major ideas presented in this chapter on content reading. (See Figure 8–2.)

	Yes	Not Clear	No
1. The textbook is at the reading level of those who are expected to use it.			
2. Other reading materials on the subject are available at reading levels *above* and *below* grade level.			
3. The content area objectives are broader than a single text.			
4. Every new text is first introduced and overviewed with pupils.			
5. The teacher preteaches special vocabulary as needed.			
6. The teacher teaches the study skills, including use of appropriate reference and library material.			
7. The teacher introduces the lesson by setting broad purposes and/or using an advance organizer or structured overview.			
8. Follow-up discussion takes place and is a means of checking and reinforcing desired outcomes.			

9. As implied by the instructional procedure, the teacher's major purpose in this lesson seemed to be (check one):
   _____ to teach facts
   _____ to develop understandings/concepts
   _____ to develop study skills

Figure 8–2   *Checklist for Teaching Reading in the Content Areas*

This checklist should enable either you or the teacher personally to evaluate how well that teacher is accomplishing some of the important objectives in the content areas.

SUMMARY

This chapter presented an overview of the important dictionary skills, as well as problems, concerns, and skills related to teaching the content areas.

Three of the basic dictionary skills usually are well taught in basal reading programs and in most classrooms: dictionary readiness with picture dictionaries, locational skills of alphabetical order and guide words, and use of a dictionary for meaning. Use of a dictionary for pronunciation is not well taught, usually because basal reading programs attempt to teach this skill with pencil and paper, yet it is an oral/aural skill. Use of a dictionary for spelling is usually not taught at all. This latter skill must be developed by having students explore the possible spellings of different language sounds, and then by showing them how they can apply this knowledge to use a dictionary for spelling even when they do not know how to spell the word.

The principal's task is to determine if the skills are well taught and to see that appropriate materials are available for that teaching. Not only must regular school dictionaries be available, but the students must also have access to picture dictionaries in kindergarten and first grade, and to advanced dictionaries by fifth and sixth grade. Furthermore, thesauruses must be available at appropriate grades, and their use must be taught.

The unique problems of reading in the content areas were presented. These include the fact that basal readers do not lend themselves well to reading in content, since they are made up almost entirely of fictional material. One of the most difficult problems seems to be lack of clarity of purpose in the content areas of social studies and science: Are teachers to emphasize the facts? concepts? study skills?

Additional problems, especially in the social studies, include the heavy load of concepts, without clarifying detail. Finally, the reading level of content area texts is usually at or above grade level for pupils who are to read for information rather than to strain to their utmost just to read. Included within this problem is the heavy vocabulary load: familiar words with strange meanings, as well as technical words, abstract words, and loaded words.

In order to help students do a better job of reading in the content areas, teachers can prepare them for that reading. Such preparation should include setting purposes, relating the new material to that which is known, and pre-teaching the vocabulary.

A worthy purpose for teaching content areas in the elementary school seems to be that of using those areas as a vehicle for teaching the study skills so that students can become independent in getting whatever information they may need in the future. These study skills include: (1) the ability to locate information from a variety of sources, as well as within one source; (2) the ability to organize information, including note taking, classifying, outlining, and summarizing; (3) the ability to evaluate information, which includes the critical reading skills; and (4) the ability to read for various purposes. The latter includes adjusting rate to purpose, skimming and scanning, and becoming knowledgeable about the organizational patterns of specific content materials.

Finally, a checklist was presented that might be used by the teacher, principal, or consultant in order to evaluate the quality of teaching taking place in the content area.

Suggestions for Action

Here are some more questions and problems to consider. In every case, you may observe to determine status, or you may want to pick a concern for discussion at a staff meeting. You may even let teachers take an item to investigate and report on.

1. Help your teachers become more aware of the differences that exist among dictionaries. You might have them bring to a staff meeting different dictionaries to compare the location of guide words, pronunciation key, accent marks, and the organization of definitions, as well as differences in diacritical marking and the pronunciation of a few example words.

2. What activities promote dictionary readiness in your kindergarten and first grade? What materials do the teachers have, and are they using them? What additional materials or techniques might be needed?

3. At what level do your teachers formally begin dictionary locational skills? How are these skills taught for application? Check some of the practice exercises. Are they realistic, or do youngsters get lost in too many words per list?

4. Observe the teaching of a dictionary for *meaning*. Does the teacher *always* provide the words in context?

5. How do your teachers teach the use of a dictionary for pronunciation? Is the practice oral (as it should be) or pencil and paper? Check the workbooks to determine if they require pupils to put diacritical marks or accent marks over words they know.

6. Are your students being taught how to use a dictionary for spelling? Most are not! When and how do teachers provide the necessary exploration of possible spellings (of vowels and consonants) so that students have the "education" necessary to do the "educated guessing"?

7. What advanced dictionaries and thesauruses are available? Who *teaches* their use? Observe to see if pupils actually use them as tools.

8. Have you and your teachers clearly established your purposes for teaching the social studies and science? Ask some of your upper-grade teachers if their primary purpose is to teach facts, concepts, or study skills? At a staff meeting, you might want to discuss purposes. Then observe, or have teachers report, how materials and methods are used to accomplish the agreed-upon purposes.

9. How do teachers prepare students for special vocabulary in the content areas? Can you find examples of the preteaching of special vocabulary? What important prefixes, suffixes, and combining forms are taught? What important ones are missing from instruction?

10. How do your teachers prepare students to read a selection in a content area? Observe to see if this is done (1) by setting purposes, (2) by relating the new material to that which is familiar, (3) by reviewing the organizational pattern of the material and teaching an appropriate strategy for handling it, or (4) not at all.

11. How well are your teachers teaching the study skills—how to locate information, how to organize it, how to evaluate it, and how to retain it? When and where do students then apply these skills?

12. What kind of instruction and practice do middle-grade students get on how to vary rate of reading? On skimming and scanning?

13. What are the unique features of the content areas taught in your school? How can teachers better prepare students to read in each of the specific content areas? You might want to use the example math problem to check or demonstrate how students read math.

14. At what level do your teachers teach SQ3R or some reasonable alternative? When and how do they teach students to outline effectively?

15. When do your students get instruction and practice on how to read and interpret graphic aids? What types of maps, charts, graphs, and tables are available in classrooms for this purpose?

16. You might use, or have your teachers use, the "Checklist for Teaching Reading in the Content Areas" found at the end of this chapter (Figure 8–2). Each teacher might use it to help identify the area or areas of major concern in teaching content materials.

References

Barnes, B. R., and Clawson, E. V. "Do Advance Organizers Facilitate Learning?" *Review of Educational Research* 45 (1975): 637–659. Analyzes thirty-two studies on advance organizers to conclude that they contribute little to increased success in content reading.

Deighton, Lee C. *Vocabulary Development in the Classroom*. New York: Teachers College, Columbia University, 1959. Identifies the prefixes, suffixes, and combining forms in English that are consistent in meaning and frequently used.

Hartley, James, and Davies, Ivor K. "Preinstructional Strategies: The Role of Pretests, Behavioral Objectives, Overviews and Advance Organizers." *Review of Educational Research* 46 (1976): 239–265. Describes procedures and functions of advance organizers and structured overviews.

Hildebrandt, Herbert W. "Now Hear This . . . " In *Listening: Readings*, ed. Sam Duker. New York: Scarecrow Press, 1966.

Peters, Charles W. "The Effect of Systematic Restructuring of Material upon the Comprehension Process." *Reading Research Quarterly* 11 (1975–1976): 87–111. Describes the Frayer model for developing technical vocabulary and presents research to support it.

Robinson, Francis P. *Effective Study*. New York: Harper, 1961. Presents the SQ3R technique and evidence to support it as an effective aid to retaining information.

Robinson, H. Alan. *Teaching Reading and Study Strategies: The Content Areas*. Boston: Allyn and Bacon, 1978. An excellent text for teaching reading in the content areas. Includes organizational patterns and strategies for the different content areas.

CHAPTER 9

What Are Your Priorities: Adjusting for Individual Differences

Everyone knows that "children differ." Do teachers put this knowledge to practice in the ways they group and teach children? Yes, children differ in development socially, emotionally, physically, intellectually, verbally, and so on. In this chapter we will look at these differences as they apply to our procedures in the teaching of reading.

WHAT ARE THE DIFFERENCES IN READING?

Because youngsters enter school with entirely different backgrounds of experience, as well as with physical and intellectual differences, they begin at different points on the educational continuum. This difference in "placement" was discussed in Chapter 4 in connection with readiness. Also, because of these initial (and possibly inherent) differences, children will progress through the continuum of reading instruction at different rates.

If teachers are to be effective in meeting the individual differences among their pupils, they must take into consideration both the *level* of placement at the time and the *rate* at which each pupil can progress. Let's look at this in terms of a specific class of fifth graders. Table 9–1 shows the distribution of pupils in a typical fifth-grade class of twenty-four students in September. The range of reading levels extends from low Grade 2 through high Grade 7, a range of six years. This typical spread is based on test score distribution for an "average" fifth grade, where 50 percent of pupils will be within one year of grade level (low Grade 4 through high Grade 5), and the entire class will span a range equal to the grade level plus at least one year.

Of course, in better schools, the average will be higher and *the range will be greater*. We might clarify this latter point by considering what would happen in Table 9–1 if all the children were taught and learned 20 percent more than shown on the chart. Then the best reader would be reading at Grade 8 and the poorest would still be reading at Grade 2, an increase in range of one year. The increased range is a direct result of differences in *rate* of learning.

As shown in Table 9–1, the best reader—reading at almost Grade 8—gained an average of two years for every year that child was in school (Grades 1–4). In contrast, the poorest reader gained only about one-fourth of a year per year for the four years that pupil was in school. If both improve by 20 percent, the former gains almost another year while the latter gains only one-twentieth of a year. If teachers are interested in holding the range of achievement steady, the only way they can do that is to keep children from learning anything—and that is difficult to do!

Since these differences exist, it is up to each teacher to adjust instruction and materials to meet them. In order to do this, we must identify for each child where that youngster should be placed on the continuum and what skills that individual needs to be taught.

Table 9–1   Reading Levels for a Class of Twenty-Four Fifth Graders in September

Level of Reading	Number of Students
High Grade 7	2
Low Grade 7	
High Grade 6	4
Low Grade 6	
High Grade 5	6
Low Grade 5	
High Grade 4	6
Low Grade 4	
High Grade 3	4
Low Grade 3	
High Grade 2	2
Low Grade 2	

IDENTIFYING THE DIFFERENCES

One of the most serious diagnostic concerns is the identification of each child's reading level. This is necessary only to enable the teacher to put that youngster into the appropriate level of materials for reading. It tells the teacher little, if anything, about skill needs. While the identification of reading level is imperative, it is also a difficult task to accomplish accurately for several reasons.

Basically, the fact is that we have no accurate test to measure reading level. We can say with certainty that *no* group reading test can be used to identify a given child's instructional level.[1] Most often, group tests overestimate a child's instructional level, but there is no rule of thumb that can be used to adjust the test score to an accurate level.

In addition, every test has a "standard error." In good tests, this tends to be about four months. Hence, if we double the standard error in order to get better predictive odds, this means that when a child scores 3.0 on the test, the odds are nine out of ten that youngster is reading somewhere between 2.0 and 4.0.

Different tests will also provide different "reading levels" on the same individual, as a result of differences in interest appeal—just one of the many factors that affect tested "reading level." Testing the same child on a different day can also result in a different score because that youngster differs in interest and effort or motivation on different days.

Identifying Reading Level

Despite all of these handicaps, we must do our best to get each pupil into the appropriate level of material for reading instruction. When your teachers receive a group of children in September, they should also have some information about their reading ability. They should know that almost 50 percent can read at grade level, so those youngsters can use the books for that grade. However, the remainder must have their reading levels identified so they, too, can be properly placed in materials.

Having ruled out the group tests, we can only turn to individual tests. While there are a number of these available commercially, such as the Gray Oral, the Gilmore Oral, and the Durrell Analysis of Reading Difficulty, I would not use any of these. All of them have their own error. To use them with their error and then to select books at a given reading level, based on a

---

[1]To avoid any misunderstanding here, we should point out that group tests can be used, along with teacher judgment, as an initial screening device. This use is appropriate to tentatively identify pupils to be referred to a remedial reading teacher, who will follow up with more precise testing.

readability formula with its error, is like trying to fit a door by measuring the opening with one rubber yardstick and measuring the door with another.

Since the goal is to match the child with the book at the appropriate reading level, the best way we know to do that is to use a portion of the book as the test. Then, if the child can read it, you know it! The testing procedure is that of an informal reading inventory.

The Informal Reading Inventory (IRI)

The procedure for an IRI is simple: The examiner asks the student to read orally a selection of approximately one hundred words. Then the examiner records the errors in the oral reading and asks four questions to see if the reader understood what was read. If the student makes more than five oral reading errors in the hundred-word selection (95 percent accuracy) or misses more than one of the four questions (75 percent comprehension), then the material is too difficult, and the examiner should try an easier book.

Some schools make up an entire battery of IRIs for use in the school. To do this, you need only take a one-hundred-word selection from each level of the basal reader and construct four questions for each selection. The battery might range from the first reader to fifth or sixth grade. Then, when a new child comes into the school, the teacher can use this to determine proper placement in the reading series in just a few minutes.

If such a battery is to be used, youngsters should be started in a selection that is definitely easy for them. They should then continue through successive levels until they reach the point of frustration—the point where they are below 95 percent word accuracy and 75 percent comprehension. The last previous (successful) level is considered their instructional level.

The following are considered errors in oral reading. Marking procedures are indicated, so that, as teachers become more adept at giving an IRI, they may want to mark the kinds of errors to gain additional information about the child's behavior in a reading situation.

1. Refusal: After a hesitation of more than five seconds, the word is supplied by the examiner. Put two checks over the word.
2. Omission: Any word or punctuation skipped. Put a circle around the item.
3. Insertion, reversal, substitution, mispronunciation: Write in whatever was said.

If a child self-corrects, this is a healthy sign that the child is using context, but it is still counted as an error. Self-corrections are usually marked with a C. Normally, repetitions and hesitations are not counted as errors on an IRI. However, teachers may want to mark them to have the additional insights about a child's reading behavior. Repetitions are usually marked with a line over repeated items; and hesitations of two to five seconds can be signified with a single check. If the latter exceeds five seconds, it is considered a refusal, and is marked with a second check.

There are a number of formalized IRIs available commercially, but they present the same problems as any other reading test. The best method still seems to be to do your own IRI with the material you are considering using with the child.

As you can see from the IRI procedure, this technique can also be used as a quick check on the suitability of the social studies or science text for a given student. Merely open to a selection not yet read and have the student read one hundred words orally while you keep track of the number of errors. Then ask four questions about the selection read.

When your teachers administer an IRI, be certain that they are not "easy" on pupils. Being "easy" in the testing results in being "tough" in the placement, since allowing errors to pass could result in a child being placed in a level that is too difficult. If I had to pick only one major problem in the schools, it would be this one: *Too many children are placed in material that they cannot read!* Anyone can learn from material that is easier than it needs to be, but no one can learn from material that he or she is unable to read.

Of course, there is another reason so many children are placed in material above their reading level. Teachers feel pressured to "complete" so many levels within the year. You can help here by letting them know that it is not a matter of "levels completed"; it is a matter of children learning to read and to enjoy it. This dual goal can be accomplished only if youngsters are in materials they can read.

Even though the IRI must be administered individually, it does not take long. Furthermore, not every child in a class needs to be tested, since teachers usually get enough information to know the reading ability of nearly half the class. For those children reading above grade level, it would be an academic exercise to test them; they can be taught the skills needed from the basal reading program designed for their grade level. This last statement assumes that you do not "accelerate" the bright students in the basal reader. That point will be discussed later. If you do accelerate, then someone had better be checking on the reading ability of all students.

The Cloze Procedure

A group technique that has been used by some in identifying reading level is the cloze procedure. While it has the advantage of group administration, some of us still feel there is not enough research to support it as being as accurate as the IRI procedure. Nevertheless, you and your teachers might be interested in it.

When cloze is used as a test, certain rules must be followed or you will not know how to interpret the results. The selection to be used can be taken from your basal reading materials just as you would do for an IRI, with the following guidelines to be followed:

1. The test selection should be at least 250 words long.
2. Do not mutilate first and last sentences.
3. With the balance, replace every fifth word with a blank line five letter-spaces long.
4. Students are to read the selection silently and fill in the blanks.
5. Exact replacement words are required; synonyms are wrong, although spelling errors are accepted.
6. Approximately 45 to 50 percent accuracy is considered instructional level.

This procedure is suggested as a testing device with some reservations, primarily because of variation in the research on the percent of accuracy to be accepted. Teachers are often concerned by the requirement of *exact* replacement of words, but this is necessary in order to maintain objectivity in the scoring. On the other hand, if cloze is used as a teaching device, such rules may be ignored.

Cloze has been used at various grade levels as a teaching device, where it seems to hold more promise (Jongsma, 1980). It should be helpful in leading students to make better use of context. However, it will not be helpful if teachers merely administer repeated cloze exercises to their pupils. The teacher must follow up with some teaching, which means that teacher will review the exercise with pupils and ask how they knew what word went in the blank. If necessary, the teacher will point out the clues that could have been used to figure out a missing word. When cloze is used in teaching, the selection may be shorter, fewer words may be deleted, and synonyms would be praised as correct.

Identifying Skill Needs

Once reading level has been determined, the teacher knows what materials the youngster can use for instruction. That teacher now needs to know what skills are needed and what ones are mastered. Some of this information can be gained if a record was kept of the kinds of errors made on the IRI.

If the pupil miscalled words by substituting a meaningful word that did not resemble the original, such as "road" for *street*, it is apparent that he or she is using context well but not paying any attention to the phonic clues. On the other hand, that student who reads "string" for *street* is apparently using phonics almost exclusively and ignoring the context.

Group tests cannot be used to determine an individual child's skill needs. Despite all of the "item analysis" provided for in the manual of most group tests, these tests are not helpful in determining skill needs for an individual.

This is not to discourage use of item analysis for groups. Such can be helpful in determining the skill emphases present or needed at a grade level, in a school, or in a school system. The basic point to remember is: Group tests give good information about *groups*; they tell very little about *individuals*.

Most of the diagnosis in terms of skill needs for individuals will be accomplished in a classroom through diagnostic teaching. In other words, in the process of introducing a skill, the observant teacher will note who has the skill and who needs further teaching or reinforcement. There is nothing wrong with this procedure, providing the teacher does not skip any important skills that the children are lacking, and providing he or she does not try to teach pupils what they already know.

Diagnostic teaching is a variation of criterion-referenced testing. The teacher will ask a child to perform a skill and observe if that child can do it. If not, the teacher will teach it. For example, if he or she wants to know whether a child can use a dictionary for meaning, the teacher will present a word in context and ask the child to find its meaning. If the youngster is unable to do this, the teacher may back up to a more basic skill, such as the ability to find a word in alphabetical order in the dictionary.

Management Systems

A current method of providing specific diagnostic tools is the management system. As discussed briefly in Chapter 3, management systems also provide for record keeping of the skill development of pupils. Most modern basal reading programs have their own management systems, and there are separate systems available, such as Wisconsin Design or Fountain Valley.

Any good management system will help teachers become more aware of specific skills, and it will help them avoid trying to teach what their pupils already know. Conversely, any management system has a great number of "skills" that are of questionable value. Using cues from Chapters 4 and 5, you and your teachers might go through your management system and cull out about 50 percent of the items, so that the management system becomes "manageable," and youngsters also have time to really read.

ADJUSTING FOR THE DIFFERENCES

How does one teacher, with a class of twenty-five or thirty, adapt instruction for the differences in reading level and skills that exist? Obviously, the teacher must have different materials for the different reading levels and must teach different skills in order to accommodate those differences. In both cases, there are degrees of individualization to which different teachers go, and the wise principal will recognize that teachers, as well as children, differ in ability.

Materials

Adjustment in terms of reading level usually takes one of two forms: The teacher may adapt the basal reader or may use high-interest, low-vocabulary books as the pupil's reading material.

Modern reading programs are published in levels. While the publisher will provide a guide indicating the approximate grades in which different levels are usually used, a given book is not specifically assigned a grade level. In addition, the stories in pupil books are usually very appealing, so that youngsters will be interested in the content of books typically used a year or more below their grade. Incidentally, because of the levels instead of grade designations, no reading program can be termed too hard or too easy for a school; it is too hard or too easy only if it is mishandled and children are not placed and paced according to their ability.

The "adapted basal" approach is one of placing and pacing pupils at their appropriate levels in the basal reading series. In a fifth-grade group, for example, many students will be in the "fifth-grade" books, some in the "fourth," and a few even in "high third-grade" books.

This adapted basal approach will work in any school unless certain books have been pegged at given grade levels. If books have been identified with fixed grade levels, then no fifth grader wants to be in a fourth grade book. Also, if a student is several years below grade level, the content of the book at that reading level would be too immature to expect the student to tolerate it. In such cases, teachers should use high-interest, low-vocabulary books for instruction.

High-interest, low-vocabulary books are just what the name implies: They are appealing to older students but written at a low reading level. They may be used for instructional purposes, and they may also be used as library books for independent reading. On the latter point, however, it is usually a good idea to keep a closed stock of some series in order to have them fresh for those students who need them for instructional purposes.

Use of such books is not a contradiction of the previously stated concern for consistency of approach with pupils in reading. The consistency comes from the teacher's use of the guide and philosophy of the reading program; it does not matter what the pupil is reading in order to learn the skills.

A list of some of the better high-interest, low-vocabulary books will be found in Appendix B. Reading level is based on the publisher's estimate, which is usually accurate. Nevertheless, your teachers may want to test the book with the IRI technique to be certain that it fits the child.

Determining Readability

As stated earlier, it is usually not necessary for educators to take the time to assess readability of books from major publishers. The publisher will supply you with the readability level, and you can trust that it will be as accurate as the formula used.

For your information, however, readability of school materials is most often determined by one of two formulas: the Spache (current date) or the Dale-Chall (1948). The former can be used only for materials up to and including third-grade reading level; the latter, for fourth through college.

There are many other readability formulas, but none has achieved the acceptance of these two. With the exception of a few efforts to incorporate syntactic complexity, all of the formulas base readability on the same two principles: sentence length and word difficulty. The latter may be measured by counting the number of words of three syllables or more, or by counting the number of words not included on a list of "familiar" words.

These mechanical measures fail to evaluate the entire picture of reading difficulty. For example, "Brown is his hat" and "His hat is brown" would be of equal difficulty according to a formula, yet an inverted sentence is much more difficult for pupils to understand. Hence, we again suggest that the book be used in an IRI situation and measured against the child for greatest accuracy of fit.

Intra-Class Grouping

We have indicated that the range of reading levels increases as one goes up the grades, and that it can be estimated to be about the grade level plus one year. In too many schools there seems to be some sort of "magic" about fourth grade: In classes throughout the primary grades you will usually find at least three reading groups, according to the reading levels of the pupils. Suddenly, at fourth grade, all students are in the fourth-grade reader! Is this true in your school?

Teachers need to group within a class for reading instruction. The traditional method of grouping has been by reading *level*. Table 9–2 is an adaptation of Table 9–1, showing how those fifth-grade students might be grouped by level.[2] The material presented in Table 9–2 is only an approximation, since the exact position of students may vary. It does, however, bring out several points. First, any child who can read at low Grade 5 or above can be in the fifth-grade reader. This grouping accounts for half the class, or twelve of the twenty-four students.

Second, if the same book is to be used in any group below grade level, that book can be no more difficult than the reading level of the lowest pupil in that group. To repeat: Children can learn skills from material that is easier

---

[2] In Table 9–2 and the ensuing discussion, traditional grade-level designations have been used because different basal programs vary so much in their placement of "levels," and in the number of books they assign as "typical" for a given grade.

Table 9–2 Reading Groups for a Class of Twenty-Four Fifth Graders in September

Level of Reading	Number of Students	Reading Group
High Grade 7		
Low Grade 7	2	
High Grade 6		In Grade 5 Book
Low Grade 6	4	(N = 12)
High Grade 5		
Low Grade 5	6	
High Grade 4		
Low Grade 4	6	
High Grade 3		In High Grade 3 Book
		(N = 8)
	4	
Low Grade 3		In mixed books
High Grade 2		(N = 4)
Low Grade 2	2	

than it needs to be, but they cannot learn anything from material they are unable to read.

The middle group in Table 9–2 might vary. Instead of the eight students in a high Grade 3 book, there could be ten in a low Grade 3 book, with only two students in the lowest group. That low group in many classes is most often not a "group," but a collection of individuals who may work together yet are in different books because of the span of reading levels.

If teachers take care that the reading level of the book is no more difficult than the level of the poorest reader in the group, then this traditional kind of grouping is one step toward individualizing—toward recognizing differences among pupils. The accompanying assumption in this kind of grouping-by-level has been that all children at a given level need the same skills—those in the teacher's guide at that level. This is the point where management systems have helped to clarify that there is a difference between reading level and skill needs. Some pupils reading at fifth-grade level have already mastered some of these skills, may also have mastered some "sixth-grade" skills, and may be lacking some "fourth-grade" skills.

This distinction between reading level and skill needs has led to a more sophisticated kind of individualization and a different kind of grouping of children for instruction. While youngsters must still be placed in books at their reading levels, they may be grouped temporarily for instruction in a skill that they need in common, even though they are reading in books at different levels. The groups are flexible and may change from week to week, if not from day to day.

Teachers need the help of a management system in order to do this kind of grouping effectively. Even then, some have difficulty and must not be pushed into it. It is better that they do a good job of placing children in appropriate levels and teaching the skills as they come up than to fail to accomplish anything. The flexible grouping is a plan that you and your staff should have as a goal, even if it is not attainable tomorrow.

Children from Other Language Backgrounds

It is an axiom in the teaching of reading that no one can learn to read in a language that person cannot speak and understand. If you are working with youngsters who come from a different language background, there are only two choices available to you if you want to teach them to read.

The *ideal*, according to the research evidence, is to begin reading instruction in the child's native language while beginning a program in oral English development. Use of this approach has consistently resulted in higher achievement in reading in English within a few years, as compared with similar pupils who *began* their reading instruction in English.

This ideal is usually not practical in most schools, where there is a mix of language backgrounds and where there are not bilingual teachers available. The minimum adjustment must be that children from other language backgrounds will be taught oral English before they are expected to learn to read in that language. Otherwise, the best that child can do is to make noises for print, to say words that have no meaning. For example, look at the following:

Da gap gipped air gopper. Gup nore sum flik.

You can say all the words, but would you call that reading?

In order to develop oral English, teachers need to provide patterns. No one learns a language effectively through experience with words as labels or in isolation. The pupil should not be told "door," "table," and so on. That child should be told, "This is a door. What is this?"

Immersion in oral English is necessary, but most classroom teachers do not have that kind of time to spend with one individual. Here again is where parent volunteers or senior citizens can be most helpful. You can provide guidance for them through the manual from any of several good oral English programs. Two excellent ones are: *English Around the World* by William Marquardt, Jean Miller, and Eleanor Hosman (Scott, Foresman and Company) and *Understanding English* by Louise Lancaster (Houghton Mifflin).

Children from Black Dialect

Black dialect (BD) is not a foreign language; it is a dialect of English, just as Southern, New England, and so on, are dialects. Hence, the principles previously discussed do not apply here.

Black dialect differs from "standard" English (SE) in two major respects:

syntax and pronunciation. Syntax variations might result in a statement such as "She working" or "She be working" for the SE sentence "She is working."

Pronunciation differences include the dropping of medial or final *r* as New Englanders do: *tore* becomes "toe" and *nor* becomes "gnaw." In addition, final /l/, /t/, and /d/ tend to be reduced or dropped. This results in *toll* pronounced as "toe" and past forms of verbs being pronounced as present forms: *past* or *passed* as "pass," *hurried* as "hurry," and so on.

Efforts to copy the evidence from other language teaching and to teach BD children oral SE before teaching them to read have done no more than confuse those youngsters in their own dialect as well. Efforts to print materials in BD seem unfounded, since there is no written form or spelling of BD, anymore than there is a spelling peculiar to Bostonians. Evidence has mounted that the primary difficulty with BD is teachers' negative attitudes toward it, albeit mostly out of a sincere concern that such children "speak right" so they can become successful in our society.

Evidence indicates that this is a misplaced concern. Certainly it is an economic disadvantage not to speak "standard" English, but it is even more of a disadvantage not to be able to read! Let's put first things first. And we have the evidence to do just that.

This evidence is clear on several points. Children who speak BD also comprehend SE. Hence, the stories do not have to be rewritten. In fact, in one study BD speakers preferred the old "Dick and Jane" to materials "relating" more to their own experience.

Second, negative teacher attitude is apparent from several points of view. A walk through most first-grade classrooms will find BD speakers "corrected" by teachers. Further, in a number of studies, teachers considered BD pronunciations and syntax deviations that did not interfere with comprehension as "reading errors." In fact, Black children in one interview were classed as BD speakers when they had fewer characteristics of BD than some of their White counterparts who were not classed as BD speakers.

In order to work effectively with speakers of BD at the elementary level, teachers need to do two things. First, they must accept that child's language and encourage the child to use it. In this way, the oral language will be developed. If the child is "corrected," he or she may quit talking at school. Second, teachers who work with BD speakers must learn to understand the characteristics of that dialect. The youngster who says "pass" for *passed* may be reading quite correctly, and the only way the teacher can find out is to know the dialect and to check on the comprehension. Furthermore, the youngster who reads "She working" for *She is working* may be doing an outstanding job of reading and understanding. That child is reading the idea. The only time the pupil should be corrected here is if the context indicated that she *always or usually* worked. Then the reader made a mistake in comprehension in BD, because he or she should have read "She be working."

While most reading authorities who have investigated BD will agree with everything up to and including the acceptance of the child's BD pronunciation, some may not go to the extent of accepting the syntax difference in reading. Yet, if you believe that reading is a matter of getting meaning from a printed page, what is better "reading" than internalizing the idea represented in print and reproducing it the way you speak? If you work with BD speakers, this is a point you certainly ought to bring up for discussion with your teachers.

Regardless of your position on the last point, it is obvious—even if teachers will only go to the extent of accepting BD pronunciation—that teachers must know the dialect before they can tell if a student is making an error in reading or if that child is merely pronouncing the word differently from the teacher. Or is it too much to expect that teachers should understand the language of the children they work with?

No teacher attempts to change the dialect of the Boston youngster who moves into a midwestern or western school district. Yet, it is an unfortunate fact of life in these times that there are some dialects that are less socially acceptable than others. The economic factor is ultimately a concern for all. The first step in this concern is still acceptance of the child's language. A second step is to develop an awareness of the different ways of speaking so that, ultimately, the individual can become bidialectal.

Title I, Learning Disabilities, and Remedial Reading

Certain students are identified in schools as needing special help in reading. By whatever name that special help is called, the principal must be aware of the program. The principal must also be aware of the selection process and should be instrumental in affecting it within the legal guidelines.

Be certain to *read* your Title I narrative. It is not etched in marble for all time. Within the legal guidelines, and with the help of your state Title I Area Consultant, you may be able to effect some important improvements. Be certain to also include your own Title I teacher in the drafting and in understanding the final product.

Since resources are limited in most schools, the principal should try to provide the extra help in reading where it will do the most good. This is not often what happens in schools in the case of these special programs. Admittedly, probably every child could benefit from some extra help. However, not all children can be seen by the resource people.

There are two kinds of readers that might be identified as needing special help. They are "retarded readers" and "disabled readers." (We will not distinguish between "disabled readers" and "learning disabilities" here, since definitions of the two are essentially the same.)

"Retarded readers" are students who are reading below grade level. They may be slow learners who are reading as well as can be expected, or they may be "disabled readers." In most cases, these "retarded readers" are slow learners who have gotten extra attention in the classroom from the day they began coming to school. Hence, such youngsters will show little additional progress as a result of special help.

"Disabled readers" are those who are reading below their "expectancy" level—the level at which they should be able to read. The assumption here is that, given proper instruction, such students will make progress up to the point of their expectancy or potential. These "disabled readers" may be reading below grade level ("retarded readers"), or they may be reading at or above grade level, but with the potential for even more. A rule of thumb for identifying "disabled readers" is that a student is so classified if, in the primary grades, the reading level is a year below potential; at middle grades, one and a half years below potential.

The distinction between these two types of readers is not merely an academic one. In most cases, children who are selected for special services in reading are predominantly "retarded readers" who are slow learners; they are not "disabled readers." As a result, little progress will be made and the programs themselves will suffer. In this age of accountability, no one will want to keep a program where little additional success is demonstrated.

While you must work within restrictions of federal and state guidelines, there is some leeway for judgment. Use that judgment wherever possible to involve potential as well as low-level achievement.

The "reading potential" of children can be identified in one of two ways. If you have an individual IQ score on the child, that score can be run through a formula to arrive at a reading expectancy. This method, however, is the least satisfactory. Most often there is no individual IQ score available, and different formulas yield different "expectancies."

If, however, you do use a formula, the Horn formula (Harris and Sipay, 1980) seems to be the fairest. For primary level,

$$\text{reading expectancy} = \frac{\text{Chronological Age} + \text{Mental Age}}{2} - 5.0$$

For intermediate level,

$$\text{reading expectancy} = \frac{\text{Chronological Age} + 2\,(\text{Mental Age})}{3} - 5.0$$

The easiest method for determining expectancy of a youngster who is at Grade 2 or above is to measure "listening comprehension." When the teacher administers an IRI and the child reaches frustration level, the teacher will continue through subsequent levels by reading the selections to the youngster and asking the comprehension questions. This will continue until a level is reached at which the child fails to answer three-fourths of the questions based on a selection *read to* him or her. The previous (or successful) level is considered the "reading expectancy" or the level at which that child ought to be able to read, given proper instruction.

"Success" in special programs is measured in a number of ways. It is unfair to the program to measure success as a year's gain in a year, since the students involved *never* made that much gain in one year. Conversely, it would be shortsighted to measure success as being any gain at all, because any youngster, with or without special help, would be expected to show some gain in a year.

The most appropriate measure of success in these programs seems to be a comparison of rate of growth during the treatment period with rate of growth prior to treatment. As an example, consider a fifth grader who was in remedial reading for one year. At the beginning of fifth grade, he was reading at 2.0 and finished the year reading at 2.5, indicating half a year's growth in that year. The rate of growth during the previous four years in school (Grades 1 through 4) was 0.25 per year (1 year of achievement divided by 4 years in school). Hence, the rate of 0.5 during the year of treatment was double the rate of previous years. This procedure is based on the reasonable expectation that previous rate of learning would have continued if intervention had not taken place.

As discussed in Chapter 3, another concern you should have about your special programs has to do with consistency. The children involved need this consistency of approach even more than most. Do your classroom teachers use one approach, only to have it confused with another by the remedial reading, LD, or Title I teacher? This is not to say that the special teachers must become tutors to the classroom program. They may, or even might be required to, use different materials for the youngsters, but their philosophical approach should be the same. Ideally, they will also work in cooperation with the classroom teacher so they are mutually reinforcing the same skills.

Furthermore, how are your Title I teachers selected? Are they merely good primary teachers, or are they adequately trained as reading specialists? The successful primary teacher and the successful special reading teacher may require not only different amounts of training in reading, but they may also need different personality traits.

Finally, do you make the best use of your specialized people? Are LD and Title I teachers working cooperatively with classroom teachers for the benefit of pupils? If you have a remedial reading teacher or consultant, you have greater freedom in their use. Then the ideal is to schedule much of their time for consulting and helping classroom teachers rather than have them entirely scheduled with pupils. If they are scheduled fully with pupils, you have them on a treadmill: There will always be more "customers" waiting in the wings; if you schedule them to help teachers, some of their expertise will carry over into classrooms and benefit more youngsters.

THE WAYS WE SORT CHILDREN

Youngsters do not come to school all cut from the same mold. In our efforts to accommodate their differences, we often get caught up in a variety of bandwagons leading to various ways of classifying and labeling children. Among current slogans, labels, and categories, we find topics such as modalities, learning styles, Piaget's stages, "mainstreaming," "gifted," and the ever-present types of interclass grouping, including promotion/retention.

Modalities

A great deal of attention has been paid to modalities, to the preferred sense used by youngsters in learning. Often considerable time and effort were devoted to identifying whether a given student was an "auditory" or a "visual" learner. Then, of course, the debate had to be resolved as to whether that child should be taught to the strong modality or whether the weaker modality should be strengthened.

The best summary of research on this topic is that by Arter and Jenkins (1979), who reviewed over one hundred investigations. They came to the following conclusions: (1) We do not have a test that will accurately identify a preferred modality; (2) Studies comparing youngsters taught to their "strong modality" show there is no significant difference as compared to youngsters not separately identified; and (3) Studies comparing youngsters taught to their "weak modality" also show there is no significant difference in achievement. Arter and Jenkin's unequivocal conclusion was:

> Unsupported expert opinion and teacher training programs resulting from this opinion appear to have a direct, deleterious, effect on teacher behavior and an indirect effect on children's learning. Not only are teachers adhering to an unvalidated model, but because they have been persuaded that the model is useful, they are less apt to create variations in instructional procedures which will result in improved learning (p. 550).

Learning Styles

A more involved and sophisticated advancement from "modalities" is the current interest in "learning styles." Much of this interest seems to come out of the work of Kolb at M.I.T., furthered by Gregorc, and popularized by the Dunns. Learning styles recognize that individuals differ in their preferences in terms of physical, social/interpersonal, and emotional settings for learning, and learning style advocates see the job of educators as one of matching teaching style to learning style.

While Dunn and Dunn (1979) have learning styles packaged into eighteen elements, Gregorc (1979) is much more cautious. Although this movement may have something to offer educators, more needs to be learned, and a number of questions need to be answered satisfactorily. Some of the most interesting and appropriate questions have been raised by Davidman (1981) and Gregorc (1979). The following are adapted from some of their ideas:

1. Can self-reporting instruments be trusted to give an accurate determination of learning style?
2. Is a learning preference reported today the same as that preference tomorrow?
3. Are these preferences permanent, or can they be changed?
4. In a class of twenty-five or thirty, can teachers realistically adjust to all of the different preferences?
5. Should teachers adjust to professed learning styles of pupils, or are some styles inappropriate behavior?
6. Most important, after giving a "learning-style inventory," will teachers think they know more than they do?

If you and your staff are interested in this area, these are only a few of the questions you should seriously consider. Further, you might also want to take a look at Hunter (1979), who presents a less dogmatic view of learning styles, one that offers guidance for getting information about learning style without presuming that such diagnosis reveals all.

Piaget's Stages

We continue to see an interest in the work of Piaget. While this work is interesting, we must again insert a word of caution. It may be shortsighted to think that children are born into a fixed pattern about which nothing can be done except to wait for them to reach the next "stage." The stages that Piaget has evolved are based on the kinds of experiences children have had up to this point. As educators, we ought to realize that if we change the kinds of experiences, we can have an effect on what a child can learn next.

Donaldson (1978), a former student of Piaget, has further demonstrated that many of the reactions of children to Piaget's tasks can be altered merely by revising the question. She has concluded that children's reasoning was much more advanced than they were given credit for. For example, in the conservation task, when two sticks of equal size were placed evenly and parallel, the child responded correctly that they were the same. When one was moved further out than the other, Piaget found that young children no longer considered them the same. Donaldson's explanation is that, when the examiner does something to change the setting and asks if the objects are still the same, the child reasons that he or she is *supposed* to react differently.

If you and your staff are interested in the work of Piaget, do not let it provide a fatalistic view.

"Mainstreaming"

Public Law 94-142 has established that all handicapped students be placed in the "least restrictive alternative." This has become popularly known as "mainstreaming," although this term is not entirely correct. The goal is to provide the best education possible, with the least degree of segregation necessary.

As you know, the law further provides that children from birth to age two are eligible for diagnosis, that programs for their handicap are optional from ages three to five, and that they are mandated from ages five to twenty-one. Along with this, the school district must follow "due process" and complete an "Individualized Educational Plan" (IEP) on each handicapped child. Contents of the IEP are spelled out in P.L. 94-142 and must be followed by every school.

As an administrator, you probably recognize the positive elements in the emphasis on a "least restrictive alternative." As trends were going in the opposite direction, unfortunately some teachers were spending more time discovering which students they could "get rid of " than they were spending in attempting to reach those students. Now the emphasis is where it belongs: How can I best meet the needs of this student? This brings us full circle to the beginning of this chapter in putting the focus on where the student is and what that student needs.

"Gifted"

"Gifted" children, by whatever definition, are also classified as "exceptional" children, along with the handicapped. In some schools, special "pull-out" programs are developed for these youngsters. How can that be justified right alongside the least restrictive alternative? Or is this a concession to parents who want the distinction of this label?

How do you and your staff, in accord with state guidelines, define "gifted"? While some accept only the limited definition of intellectually gifted, isn't it more appropriate to redefine this as "gifted and talented," recognizing giftedness in science, art, math, music, and so on?

What is a good program for gifted students? Most of the "gifted" programs I have seen have been good programs for *any* student—they were just *good* programs! In other words, we should be providing the best program possible for all students. In addition to whatever special "pull-out" program that may be helpful for certain "gifted" students, your teachers should offer opportunity within the regular class program for students to become involved in special language projects, whether vocabulary ideas or creative writing or dramatics; for them to develop special projects in science to be shared with peers; to engage in special studies in the community, and so on.

One question that comes up in dealing with bright students, whether or not they have been identified as "gifted," is whether or not to accelerate them in the basal program. This question gets us into an unresolved debate between "horizontal" vs. "vertical" enrichment: Should these students be provided a great variety of experiences within the level or should they be moved through subsequent levels?

Part of your answer in reading will relate to your view of the basal reading program. If it is seen as only the skills part of the total program, there is no need to accelerate, since the other half of the program (library reading and use) will enable youngsters to expand their horizons in all directions. However, if the basal is the total program, then about the only alternative is to accelerate the bright.

Acceleration, if carried to its obvious conclusion, can become a blind alley. For example, a bright group of primary pupils, given the opportunity to move through the basal as fast as they can, could be getting into the fourth-grade materials sometime in second grade. They could even do this without a teacher who tried to prove his or her skill by pushing them faster than they could learn. Now those students would be getting into study skills and areas where they can read the materials and learn the skills, but their "life experience" is limited to the extent that much of what they would be expected to read would have little meaning to them. Hence, application of the skills in meaningful material is not there.

Interclass Grouping

Over the years many plans have been proposed for grouping pupils into different classes: heterogenous and cross-age grouping, as well as various kinds of homogenous plans, such as Joplin Plan, achievement grouping, ability grouping, and so on. We might class these kinds of activities as games administrators play.

Teachers often feel that they could do a better job if they did not have quite the range of achievements in their classes. This kind of thinking leads to the idea of some sort of achievement/ability grouping. Yet, the evidence is that teachers fool themselves. Even with three classes at a given grade level and children grouped into the three classes by reading achievement, the range of reading achievements is reduced by no more than 10 percent! Worse, when this kind of grouping takes place, teachers usually then believe they have a "homogenous" group and can teach to the total class.

The most thorough study of the effectiveness of different kinds of grouping plans was reported by Goldberg, Passow, and Justman (1966). Based on all of the different plans, and evaluated in terms of academic success, their research indicated that deliberate "wide range" (heterogenous) grouping was the most successful.

Many years ago, Harold Shane probably said the last word on grouping when he indicated it was not the grouping plan itself but what happened within it that made all the difference. The wise principal will be paying attention to what is happening within the plan and within the classroom, rather than spending too much time rearranging youngsters.

Promotion/Retention

Related to grouping plans is the question of whether or not pupils should be retained, promoted, or double-promoted. Part of the problem here lies in the fact that we call the different years in school "grades." Proponents of the "Non-Graded School" tried to avoid this problem but the idea of grades was too deeply imbedded to be forgotten in most instances.

As you recall from Table 9–1 and its discussion, there is a range of reading levels in any classroom. For someone to tell you that "Johnny is in Grade 5" does not tell you anything about Johnny's academic achievement. Johnny may be reading like a second grader or like an eighth grader. About all you know about Johnny is that he is around ten years old. In other words, a grade level is nothing more than an age grouping.

If we recognize this fact, we have simplified the question of promotion and retention. Academic achievement becomes irrelevant to this decision; children will be placed and will move along with the age group into which they fit best. Of course, this last point opens the door a little, since some children will work better in a younger group.

Teachers often look on retention as a means of putting a child on a more even par academically: A second grader reading at low first grade would seem to fit better with next year's first graders, who will also be at the same level in September. The miscalculation in this line of reasoning lies in the failure to consider *rate of progress*, as discussed at the beginning of this chapter. Yes, the retainee may begin the year at the same level as most of the first graders, but that pupil's slower rate of progress will result in the other first graders quickly surpassing and completing the year at a more advanced level. No matter how often the motorcycle and the bicycle are restarted at the same point, one is soon left behind.

If you prefer to look at the evidence, the research is a little messy. There is no way to both promote aad retain the same child to compare the effectiveness of each. However, the closest research gets to this is to take a group of potential retainees, randomly split it in half, then promote one half and retain the other. In these kinds of studies, consistently those who are promoted gain more.

To look at this another way, there was a time when some schools had a very high retention rate. They were proud to say that they had "high standards," and any child not coming up to standard was retained. Obviously, they were mistaken in their claim for "high standards." They were merely accumulating and saving up their poor students! If you are going to use promotion/retention in order to raise your school's academic standing, you would do just the opposite: You would retain the bright students and double-promote the poor to get them out of the school as quickly as possible!

Seriously, there are a few children who might benefit from retention. Logic and research coincide on who these youngsters might be. Let's stop to consider what a child is given through retention. That youngster is not given more brains—slow learners do not profit from retention; they are not given a solution to an emotional problem—emotionally disturbed youngsters do not profit from retention; the cause of a behavior problem is not removed—such youngsters do not benefit from retention. All that a youngster receives is more time to grow up; he or she is placed with a younger group.

To turn this around, then, the one who might benefit from retention is one who is at least average in ability, has no serious emotional problems, and who is immature. Furthermore, the sooner such a youngster can be identified and placed in a younger group, the more likely that retention will be successful. Hence, kindergarten is the best place for this retention. These pupils are less likely to develop other kinds of problems because they are so egocentric and have not developed close friends at school.

Of course, your problem as principal is a public information one on this point. Until the reasons are made clear to parents in the community, the first reaction you will get is: "What will I tell his grandmother—that he flunked kindergarten?"

Along with this public information, parents need to be brought along very early in their understanding of how their child is doing and what the school is trying to do for that child. Conferences ought to be held in February or March, at the latest, as an initial step toward preparing parents for the possibility of another year in kindergarten. Also, while the school reserves the "right of placement," no school administrator will retain a child against the strong objections of the parent. If you do, everything that ever happens in that child's entire career will be blamed on the school. Nevertheless, when a clear-cut case is at hand, every effort ought to be made to convince the parents— and those efforts ought to be put in writing.

Any points to be made about double promotion would follow in the same vein as those about retention. If there is a child who is bright, unusually large, and socially more mature than that youngster's regular age group, there *might* be some value in considering a double promotion. Here, too, caution is in order.

You and your staff might want to look at your retention policies. Are you kept abreast of potential retention situations? Are conferences initiated early enough? Are children being retained appropriately? If your retention rate is more than about half a percent per year, you might want to take a hard look at that as well.

Perhaps the basic question relating to all of these various kinds of labels and groupings is: Should we be spending valuable time in labeling and pigeon-holing youngsters, or should our efforts be devoted to providing the kind of education each needs within the regular group setting? Admittedly, it would be easier if we could establish a few categories and have youngsters neatly fit into them. However, we ought to know by now that we cannot "homogenize" kids; a much better job is done if we accept their differences and work with those differences.

SUMMARY

This chapter discussed the ways that students differ in reading and what we can do about these differences. In any class, we can expect reading levels to range at least as many years as the grade level plus one year. In addition to this span of years in placement, youngsters also differ in the rate at which they will progress.

The first job of the teacher is to identify the reading level of each student. Group tests are not satisfactory for this purpose. An informal reading inventory (IRI) made from the material the teacher is considering using was suggested. This testing will determine the level of materials to be used for instructional purposes. The cloze technique was also suggested as a possibility for such testing.

Skill needs are usually identified through diagnostic teaching or criterion-referenced tests. Here again, group tests do not provide reliable information about individuals.

Once the individual differences have been identified, they are met by placing youngsters in materials at their appropriate reading levels. Usually this will mean using lower-level books of the basal for poorer readers, or, if they are more than two years below grade level, placing them in high-interest, low-vocabulary books for their reading material.

Traditionally, students have been grouped by reading level (the book they are in) for reading instruction. This is an acceptable first step toward individualization, *if* the level of the book does not exceed the reading level of the poorest reader in the group. The goal in grouping should be to have flexible groups according to skill needs, rather than to assume that every child in the particular level needs a given skill just because it is next in the basal program.

While management systems are criticized as having an excess of busy-work listed as "skills," once skimmed down, these systems are an asset in helping the teacher accomplish the flexible grouping according to skill needs.

Ideally, anyone working with children from other language backgrounds will begin reading instruction in their native language while developing oral English. A minimum adjustment, and usually the practical one, for the different language background must be that such children are taught oral English before they are taught to read in English.

Since Black dialect is not a different language, this principle does not apply. Evidence is clear that Black dialect does not hinder understanding of "standard" English, and that the primary handicap of the Black dialect speaker lies in teachers' negative attitudes toward that dialect. In order to help these youngsters become successful, teachers must not only accept their dialect, they must understand it so they know whether the child is making a mistake in pronunciation and/or syntax, or whether that youngster is reading accurately in his or her dialect. Experience with the other ways of speaking in English should be provided later, by middle grades, so those students have the ability to switch dialects if and when they desire.

To the fullest extent legally permissible, special teachers—LD, Title I, or Remedial Reading—ought to be working with children they can help most, children who have the potential to be reading better. Such youngsters would be the disabled readers rather than merely the retarded readers who are also slow learners. The disabled reader can be identified as one reading below expectancy through a listening comprehension test.

Finally, we discussed various ways of grouping and labeling youngsters, including modalities, learning styles, Piaget's stages, "mainstreaming," gifted, interclass grouping plans, and promotion/retention. In all cases, words of caution—if not impatience—suggested that we ought to spend less time trying to sort and label children and more time identifying and teaching the skills they need in reading.

Suggestions for Action

Following are some questions and topics you and your teachers might choose from as you work together to meet individual differences in your school. A number of these topics can be delegated to individual teachers or resource staff for initial investigation and submission to the group.

1. How well do your teachers recognize and work with the wide range of differences that exist in any class? Should you discuss with them the difference between *present level* and *rate of progress*, using examples from Table 9–1?

2. Review results of your group achievement tests and discuss them with teachers. You might discourage the use of group test results to determine the instructional level or skill needs of individual pupils. Conversely, you ought to use and share with your teachers the diagnostic information—the curricular guidance—about groups that you *can* get from group tests.

3. Are your teachers familiar with and comfortable in using an IRI technique with the materials in class? Perhaps you should ask your Title I or Remedial Reading teacher to give a demonstration in a staff meeting. If your teachers do not already have and use an IRI from the basal series, develop an IRI battery from that series.

4. Determine the basal levels children are placed in. How many in your

school are placed in material that is too difficult for them? A spot check in a few classrooms, using the IRI technique, might be enlightening. What can you do, or have you done, to ease the pressure teachers feel to "cover material" in the basal?

5. If your teachers group by reading level, check some of the poorest readers in each group to determine that the book is not more difficult than the level of that pupil. If your teachers do not group in some classes, you might use some of the facts presented in this chapter to encourage grouping.

6. If teachers group flexibly by skill needs, how effectively are they using the management system for this purpose? If you have not done so, begin now to do that housecleaning job on the excess "skills," as suggested in Chapter 5.

7. What high-interest, low-vocabulary books are available to teachers who have pupils too far below grade level to use the adapted basal approach? Arrange for teachers to have a list, by interest and reading level. Discuss with your staff the need to "protect" these books from becoming labeled as lower-grade books.

8. If your school has children from other language backgrounds, what provisions do you make to assure that they are taught oral English before they are expected to learn to read in that language? What instructional materials are available for this teaching?

9. If you have children with Black dialect, observe to see how well your teachers accept that dialect. How well do they understand it? If you discover a problem here, bring in a consultant to work with teachers in clarifying the nature of Black dialect.

10. What procedures are used by Title I, LD, and Remedial Reading teachers to select their pupils? Discuss with them, and with some classroom teachers, to assess how well they and you are satisfied with these procedures. You might also examine the Title I narrative with that teacher to identify needed changes for the next submission.

11. In what ways do these special teachers work with classroom teachers? Do you have some of their time *scheduled* for this? How consistent is the approach to reading between the classroom and special teachers?

12. How is the effectiveness of these special programs evaluated? Will the procedure suggested in this chapter help in that evaluation?

13. Are you or your teachers involved in any of the popular kinds of approaches or grouping plans discussed? How well has the evidence been checked out before getting into a given plan?

14. What kind of help do your teachers need in adjusting to the "least restrictive alternative" mandate? Is this a place where your special teachers, area consultants, and so on, can be of service in helping the classroom teacher in diagnosis and instructional planning?

15. Where does your school district stand on questions of acceleration vs. horizontal enrichment? How well do your teachers understand the advantages and disadvantages of each?

16. When is the last time you considered and discussed promotion/retention policies? Do teachers understand and follow them? What percentage of pupils were retained last year at your school? at what levels? How successful were the retentions?

References

Arter, Judith A., and Jenkins, Joseph R. "Differential Diagnosis—Prescriptive Teaching: A Critical Appraisal." *Review of Educational Research* 49 (Fall 1979): 517–555. This summary of over one hundred research studies reports negatively on the value of attention to "preferred modalities."

Dale, Edgar, and Chall, Jeanne S. *A Formula for Predicting Readability*. Columbus: Ohio State University, 1948. The Dale-Chall readability formula is used to determine reading level of materials from Grades 4 through college.

Davidman, Leonard. "Learning Style: The Myth, the Panacea, the Wisdom." *Phi Delta Kappan* 62 (May 1981): 641–645. Explores the problems inherent in considering learning styles.

Donaldson, Margaret. *Children's Minds*. New York: W. W. Norton, 1978. An analysis of Piaget's stages and tasks, with the conclusion that many of the stages are based on children's different perceptions of what the examiner is asking.

Dunn, Rita S., and Dunn, Kenneth J. "Learning Styles/Teaching Styles: Should They . . . Can They . . . Be Matched?" *Educational Leadership* 36 (January 1979): 238–244. An explanation of the Dunn view of learning styles and the eighteen categories they have identified.

Goldberg, Miriam; Passow, A. Harry; and Justman, Joseph. *The Effects of Ability Grouping*. New York: Teachers College, Columbia University, 1966. The most thorough study of the effectiveness of various kinds of grouping in schools.

Gregorc, Anthony F. "Learning/Teaching Styles: Potent Forces Behind Them." *Educational Leadership* 36 (January 1979): 234–236. Explores some of the problems associated with identification of learning styles.

Harris, Albert J., and Sipay, Edward R. *How to Increase Reading Ability*. New York: Longman, 1980. A classic text on diagnosis and treatment of reading difficulties. Pages 151–160 contain a discussion of formulas for identifying reading potential. Chapter 8 presents a discussion of IRI and cloze testing.

Hunter, Madeline. "Diagnostic Teaching." *The Elementary School Journal* 80 (September 1979): 41–46. A discussion of the rationale and techniques for matching teaching and learning styles.

Jongsma, Eugene A. *Cloze Instruction Research: A Second Look*. Newark, Del.: International Reading Association, 1980. Summarizes research on the use of cloze for testing and for instruction.

Spache, George D. *Good Reading for Poor Readers*. New Canaan, Conn.: Garrard Press, current edition. Contains the Spache Readability Formula, as well as a listing of books useful with poor readers.

Additional Readings

Dillard, J. L. *Black English*. New York: Random House, 1972. An excellent presentation of the history and characteristics of Black dialect in the United States.

Hillerich, Robert L. *Reading Fundamentals for Preschool and Primary Children*. Columbus, Ohio: Charles Merrill, 1977. Chapter 10 contains a summary of the evidence on individual differences, including teaching children from other language backgrounds and Black dialect.

Smitherman, Geneva. *Talkin and Testifyin*. Boston: Houghton Mifflin, 1977. An outstanding presentation of the nature, background, and culture of Black dialect.

CHAPTER 10

Evaluating a Reading Lesson

If you, as a principal, are to be an educational leader, you must know what is going on in the building, and in order to do that, you must get into classrooms. This chapter deals with the classroom visitation to observe a reading lesson: how to plan, what to look for, and how to follow up.

How many principals have said, "I can tell who are my strong or weak teachers merely by walking down the hall"? This has some truth to it if all you want to do is a summative evaluation of the teacher. But remember what we said about labeling children in the last chapter; is the principal's role one of merely labeling teachers? Your role ought to be one of encouraging and disseminating the good practices and strengthening those that are weak. If this is your goal, you need to have specifics rather than a global judgment from which to work.

This kind of evaluation should not imply to you or to your teachers that you necessarily know more about the specifics of teaching reading than they do. It does imply that you see more than their one classroom and that you can provide ideas from others, as well as for overall direction in the school. Furthermore, you can raise legitimate questions about the instruction you observe for the teacher to clarify.

LAYING SOME GROUND RULES

At the beginning of the school year, you ask for a "Daily Schedule" from each of your teachers. They should understand that this is not just another piece of busywork for them. These schedules serve at least two important functions: They assure that state daily minimums are met, and they provide you with information so you know when to drop into a class if you want to observe a particular kind of lesson.

In preparing their schedules, teachers may need guidance to get more time into the reading classes. As stated in Chapter 1, time is an important factor in achievement, and you need to get as much as possible into reading instruction. Teachers ought to understand, as well, that they have some flexibility in that schedule. One of the advantages of a self-contained classroom is the fact that the teacher usually does not have to interrupt or halt an exciting lesson because a bell rings.

You can also avoid confusion and misunderstanding, if not outright upset, by letting teachers know the kind of behavior they can expect from you and the kind you expect from them in connection with the classroom visitations you will make. Unless you clarify some of the important points, your visit can become a threatening act, even to some of your better teachers. While your own personality and that of different teachers will control your ultimate decision, the following are points to consider.

Purpose

Teachers should understand why you are visiting to observe. If they know this is a routine that you do with all teachers, much of the strain is removed. Further, if they realize the purpose is not to "evaluate" in the sense of giving them a grade for performance, you will also be more welcome.

Purposes for your visit should be shared with the staff. These purposes ought to include the desire to see how pupils are performing, how the reading program is going, and the kinds of instructional activities teachers incorporate into their lessons. The latter can become a wealth of information that can be shared with others who may benefit from the ideas—whether those ideas are shared anonymously or by name will again depend on personalities. All of these, and whatever purposes you care to add, can be summarized in the basic purpose: It is all part of the job of an interested principal.

Notice of Visit

Whether or not you give teachers advance notice of your impending visit is a matter of personal choice. However, your staff should be informed of the procedure, and it should be consistent with everyone. There can be arguments proposed on both sides of this question. On the one hand, you do not want to give advance notice so the teacher can stay up all night preparing an elaborate reading lesson: It is not your purpose to see a "show." On the other hand, you do not want to be seen as an ogre who tries to slip in to "catch" a teacher off guard.

Usually the most comfortable approach is an informal kind of advance notice, beginning with an inquiry: "I'd like to drop in on our reading class sometime in the next few days. What are you doing in reading now?" Such an approach will enable the teacher to suggest an opportune time (so you do not find a test being given or find that today the social studies class has been extended). Such as approach also puts the pressure on you. Now you have a commitment and will have to get it on your calendar! This visit should be scheduled for the entire reading period if possible, but certainly for a minimum of half an hour.

During the Visit

Teachers should also understand that you may or may not participate in any of the class activities. In any event, you do not want to take control of the class from the teacher.

You probably will want to make notes while visiting the class. If you do, be as brief and unobtrusive about it as possible. Most of your energies should be devoted to observing the behaviors of pupils and teacher. Certainly notes should be made immediately after the visit, whether or not some are made during it.

Follow-Up Conference

Teachers should understand in advance that there will be a follow-up of your visit. After all, it would be extremely discourteous to spend a period of time in the classroom and not to make a single comment to your "host" or "hostess."

Again, to avoid any misunderstanding, you should let your staff know whether you will meet with them to schedule a time for the conference, or if they should automatically come to see you whenever they are free after one of your visits.

OBSERVING THE READING LESSON

When you go into a classroom, there are a number of factors you will want to observe. These may be classed as: (1) evidence of teacher preparation and organization; (2) how the reading lesson itself is handled, including pupil placement, participation, and activities; and (3) the interpersonal relationships of teacher and pupils.

Not only is advance preparation necessary in the conduct of a good reading lesson, it is necessary in carrying out a good visitation. You, too, are assumed to make some preparation. This should include a knowledge of the philosophy of your basal reading program, some familiarity with the kinds of skills discussed in previous chapters of this book, and possibly even a look at the lesson in the teacher's guide that your teacher is planning to teach during your visit.

Evidence of Teacher Preparation

You will want to arrive on time for the beginning of the reading lesson. It is at this point that you will observe much about the management of the class. Has the teacher clearly established routines? Do children know what they are to do, or is each movement dependent upon some new direction they must figure out? Nothing can consume time in a classroom faster than a lack of established routine. Furthermore, children are more comfortable if they know what to expect and what is expected of them.

When the teacher brings the reading group together, do the rest of the class know what they are to do? Even more important, is what they are to do worthwhile? Their "seatwork" does not necessarily have to be in "reading," but it should relate in some way to their educational program. In fact, the teacher's established routine may, and sometimes should, allow for some self-selection of activities, but within an established framework.

If this independent work is practice material, is it clear that those doing it have been taught prior to the practice? If not, they are being expected to practice what they have not been taught, and they will either be interrupting the teacher to get help or be creating a disturbance.

Finally, is it clear that a part of the teacher's routine is an expectation of cooperation from pupils? If it is not, every second or third sentence from the teacher will not be instructional; it will be disciplinary. Often this kind of teacher self-interruption is a result of the teacher not learning to ignore unimportant behaviors and/or not following through on those that are important.

As the teacher gets into the reading lesson, you will observe whether or not that teacher has prepared for the lesson by the way he or she handles the material in the teacher's guide. We must assume that the teacher will be using it if your school district uses a basal reader, since that is the primary purpose for purchasing basal programs.

The teacher who uses the guide effectively will usually have some notes or checks in that guide. In fact, it will be just that—a "guide" to the kinds of things that teacher does with the group. If the teacher follows the guide slavishly or blindly, you know it may be the first time she or he has looked at it, and that teacher might be in for a few surprises as the lesson progresses. While you do want your teachers to follow the philosophy and skills sequence in the basal, there is more than anyone can handle in any basal reading program, and they should be making some judgments.

Organization of the Reading Lesson

While the wording and the number of divisions may differ somewhat, most reading professionals would agree that a good reading lesson will incorporate (1) an introduction, (2) reading and discussing, (3) skill instruction, and (4) follow-up activities. What you see in a given classroom on a given day may not incorporate all of these, since many "lessons" extend for more than a day. On the other hand, if you are observing a remedial reading, LD, or Title I teacher, you will most likely see all four sections developed on a specific skill or skills, since they do not usually take such big chunks of material at one time.

Introduction

The introduction to a new lesson should include introducing the new words and introducing the story itself. If you use an extreme phonics program, new words are usually not introduced, but your teachers should remind pupils of what they are to do when they come to a new word. If you use a meaning emphasis series, at the primary level most of these programs introduce new words in context. Does the teacher use context in introducing the new words?

As discussed in Chapter 5, you should also be concerned and concern your teachers with the *purpose* for introducing new words. While most basal readers suggest introducing the new words to *teach the words*, here is a point where you need to discuss a more appropriate purpose with your teachers. Shouldn't they be introducing the new words in order to review with children what they are to do when they come to a word they do not know? If they are merely "teaching words," they are making pupils dependent on them as the "givers of words." If they review the technique to be used, they are helping pupils to apply their skills and to become independent in figuring out new words.

At middle grades, after students have been taught to use the dictionary, the skill that should be reviewed is that of using context and the dictionary. Often, at this level, new words can be introduced in strong context so some preliminary estimates of meaning can be gleaned before the dictionary is opened.

In most cases, the introduction of the story itself is very brief. Its purpose is usually to provide the slight motivating "nudge" to get youngsters into the story. Elaborate backgrounds and purposes do not need to be established. Most often the teacher will have pupils read the title, look at a few pictures and ask them what they think it will be about. Then the basic introduction will be: "Let's read it and find out."

Sometimes by mddle grades, students will be reading a story that includes content beyond their background of experience to understand. Then the introduction of the story should include the kind of background information they will need in order to fully understand that story. Even here, as in the case of introducing new words, if the goal is independence for youngsters, the teacher will not spoonfeed the background information. Better, the teacher will have a short, factual selection that provides the information and will have students read and discuss it in order to get their own background.

Reading and Discussing

The initial reading of any selection will *always* be silent. No matter how few words on the page and no matter what the grade level, youngsters should *always* have an opportunity to read the material to themselves before being asked to read it orally.

With longer stories, teachers sometimes ask if they should break the story into sections for discussion rather than expect pupils to read the entire selection at one time. The answer here will depend on the group. Publishers at upper levels will often have a long selection and suggest breaking points. These are only estimates that may fit the plot of the story but might not fit with a group of children. The only answer to this question is that teachers must judge their group and decide accordingly. Some groups can read extremely long stories, while others cannot handle more than a page at a time. The teacher should break the story as much as necessary to avoid losing the group.

As pupils read silently, observe what they do and what the teacher does if they come to a word they do not know. If they raise their hands to ask for help, does the teacher remind them of what they can do to figure out the word, or does that teacher merely tell them the word?

If any single pupil asks for help very often on words, you might also suspect that child is in material that is too difficult. A follow-up discussion with the teacher is in order to see if the teacher is aware of the situation and what is planned to check on that pupil's placement.

The silent reading should be followed by discussion. This discussion should be just that; it is not to be a quiz in order to see if children read every word or even every sentence in the story. The perfect statement on this point was once made by Paul McKee, who said, "We ought to discuss a story with children in the same way we'd discuss a book we read with a friend—*that we wanted to keep!*"

Why do teachers so often want to make a quiz out of the "discussion"? Basically, the reason seems to be an insecurity on their part. If they have done a good diagnostic job with the skills, they know whether or not children have them; if they have placed youngsters properly in the reading material, they know those children can read that material; and if they are motivating enough to make the discussion fun, those youngsters will not want to be left out.

The purpose of the discussion is not to check such items, nor is it to be certain to share the content of the story with those who cannot read it—as some teachers might use the discussion in the social studies. The primary purpose of the discussion ought to be to increase children's enjoyment of the story. Just as you or I can enjoy a story more if we talk about it with someone, so too with youngsters.

A secondary purpose for the discussion can be to range through some of the comprehension skills in order to provide practice in them. If this questioning is handled as suggested in Chapter 7, it too will avoid the quiz stage, since it will focus on interpretation, creative, and critical reading.

You ought to be concerned about more than whether or not there *is* a discussion. It ought to be a *good* discussion, involving youngsters in give and take among themselves. A teacher-pupil question and answer session is *not* a discussion. At its best, a discussion by upper graders will involve the pupils raising questions as well.

Following the discussion, there *may* be purposeful oral reading. Purposes for oral reading were discussed in Chapter 3, and they do *not* include taking turns reading orally. There is no excuse for this "round-robin" reading, which results in slow, plodding readers and in a loss of interest in reading independently. If this exists in your school, the sooner you stamp it out, the sooner you will improve the reading program and the achievement of your students.

Skill Instruction

At this point you would expect the teacher to teach some skill or skills from the basal guide. These may be new skills or old skills retaught. As discussed extensively in this book, all basals include considerable padding. You certainly do not want your teachers trying to teach children skills they already have, nor do you want them to teach worthless items. On the other hand, you do not want them to skip important skills that youngsters lack.

Just as there are many instances where we ought to look at what we present to children through their eyes, there are also many cases where we should listen to what we say to them through their ears. It is not being picayune to ask teachers to "watch their language" and to say what they mean, whether in this or in any other part of a lesson.

How often are teenagers accused of using lazy, sloppy, and imprecise language? Did they learn to do this at the feet of a kindergarten teacher who asked them if "fish" and "fan" *sound* alike, when she meant "do they begin alike" or "do they begin with the same sound"? Or did they learn this from the first-grade teacher who asked them "What sound does *b* make?" as if letters *made* sounds? What that teacher meant was "What sound does *b* represent (or stand for)?" or, in shortened form, "What is the sound for *b*?"

As you visit classes, you might pick up some points for discussion along the lines of instructional language. Do your teachers say what they mean and are they clear in their use of instructional language?

The teaching of the skills is one of the primary reasons any school purchases a basal reading program. Yet, you may find some upper-grade teachers who introduce the story, read and discuss it, and then assign workbook pages. Such a procedure is not teaching anything; it is providing practice in reading, followed by practice on skills that have not been taught.

Along this same line, is the teacher actually teaching or merely assigning? "Teaching" is a matter of explaining, demonstrating, or otherwise clarifying a task. "Assigning" is a matter of telling pupils to do something. Durkin (1978–1979) reported on observations of comprehension instruction in fourth-grade classes. She found only *1 percent* of the time devoted to actual instruction. The balance was spent in assigning, helping in assignments, assessment, and so on. How will students learn effectively, except through instruction?

Your follow-up conference with the teacher on this point will depend on where you and your staff stand regarding the various specifics about skills discussed previously in this book. In fact, that follow-up discussion is a good starting point if you and your staff want to get into a cooperative venture in cleaning up some of the skills.

Follow-Up Activities

These activities may include additional practice of certain skills on workbook pages or duplicated exercises, as well as suggested further reading and application of skills. Does the teacher automatically distribute for independent work all of the workbook pages and duplicated exercises related to the lesson? Or does that teacher use some judgment, not only on *what* is assigned, but *how* it is to be done?

First of all, it is assumed that any such practice material will be for skills that have been taught. Second, you and your teachers ought to establish some criteria for the selection of such material to be used, since some of it is a waste of time. In fact, the limited research on the effectiveness of workbooks— beyond the skill type in kindergarten—suggests that they contribute little, if anything, to increased reading achievement.

Some criteria for the selection of practice exercises that you might share with your teachers should include:

1. Do my pupils need more practice in this skill?
2. Does this exercise provide practice in the skill it claims, and is this the best kind of practice for this skill?
3. Is this a worthwhile skill for success in reading?
4. Are the mechanics of doing the page more difficult than the skill itself?

You and your teachers might be amazed at how many worksheets can be faulted on any of these simple questions. If you want only one criterion that usually works, it is this: Look at the exercise from the eyes of the child and ask yourself, "What will I learn if I do this?"

When the teacher does use a worthwhile practice exercise, does he or she use it effectively? For example, there are some that are completely inappropriate as independent activities, but they can be helpful if done orally as a group. Distinctions can often be made by deciding if the skill is a visual one or an oral one.

Finally, how well does the teacher follow up on the practice? Let's hope that teacher does not collect the workbooks and take them home to "grade." The exercise should be reviewed as soon as possible after pupils complete it, and it should be reviewed with them—orally. It should be a learning experience, not a testing experience. Hence, the emphasis in the review is not to be on how many are right and how many are wrong. It should be on *what* the pupils' responses were and *why* they answered as they did. With this approach, the teacher may find some children's answers better than the ones suggested in the guide.

One technique that helps put the proper emphasis on use of practice exercises is the pairing of students, two to an exercise. Together they must decide on the "answer" to each item. Then, in the shared "correction," they have an opportunity to present any discussion of items they may have had. Of course, this buddy system raises the noise level in a classroom, but it is a positive noise.

Additional reading is often suggested in the teacher's guide. There is nothing sacred about the specific items listed, but there should be additional reading. This can be the other half of the reading program—the reading and using of library reading that was suggested in Chapter 6.

Interpersonal Relationships

Equally important with the skills is the atmosphere, the affective learnings that take place in a classroom. It is here that children's self-concepts are enhanced or eroded. It is also here that children's attitudes toward reading are established.

To begin with, we might summarize this entire section with one question: "In this classroom, do you get the feeling that children are important?" If you can answer positively, be certain to let that teacher know in the conference. More specifically, is there positive reinforcement? Are students being told what they are doing right, rather than what they are doing wrong? No child is so inept that he or she cannot do something worth acknowledging. Further, do children see that they are getting somewhere? Do they have individual or (noncompetitive) group records of their progress? Examples of work, with a comment on some positive attribute, ought to be displayed.

In contrast, little can be more destructive than a whispered comment about a child in front of him or her or others. The classroom is not the place to talk about a child, unless it is with that child.

We have discussed classroom organization briefly, but you should also notice the groupings of students. First of all, do they appear to be properly assigned in reading groups, so they can all read at the level in which they are placed? In addition, there should be some flexibility in the groupings, in terms of skill instruction and in terms of interest groups.

Not only should the instructional language of the teacher be clear, the directions given by that teacher ought also to be understandable. Directions that are poorly stated—and, as a result, must be repeated—can do much to consume valuable instructional time. If an efficient routine has been established, much direction-giving is avoided. Further, youngsters will be more task-oriented if they have a clearly established routine. If they lack routine, discipline will be the order of the day.

Finally, if you have a management system in your school, is the teacher using it—and using it intelligently? The teacher should find it a valuable aid in diagnosing and keeping a record of the skills of pupils. If it gets out of hand, that teacher can become the servant, so busy keeping records that no teaching can take place.

FOLLOWING UP THE OBSERVATION

The follow-up conference should be held as soon as possible after the visit. You, as principal, will set the tone, and it is best if these conferences can be kept out of the frame of reference of "evaluative" conferences. This conference is part of your job of working *with* teachers, as a team, to improve instruction in the school. You must assume that your teacher is just as interested in improving instructions as you are. Just as with youngsters, teachers will perform better with positive reinforcement. Just as with youngsters, there is no teacher so poor that you cannot find something good to say.

While you may want to make up your own checklist of points to be discussed with each teacher, it is not necessary. However, the basic points from this chapter could serve as your topics in such a checklist. Often, the conference is better if it is less structured, with only a few notes prepared after the visit, to guide you. Basically, it will be a sharing of what you observed in the organizational pattern of the class, the teaching of the lesson, and the general atmosphere, as well as some comments about specific pupils.

One essential point: Do not jump to conclusions about something you saw! If you observed what you considered strange or inappropriate behavior, instructional or directional, on the part of the teacher, do not be ready to criticize. The best thing you can do is ask why it was done. You would be surprised (or maybe you wouldn't) at the reasonableness of some apparently ridic-ulous behaviors when they are put into proper context.

In conferences with many of your teachers, you may have nothing but a few questions and praise. You may also ask about disseminating some idea within the building or having the teacher present that idea at a staff meeting. This is a time, too, to discuss some of the directions you have in mind for the reading program and to get reactions on a one-to-one basis.

In the case of a few teachers, you may feel that the reading lesson was less than perfect. In such cases, remember you still cannot do everything at once. Pick out a few of the positive actions you observed and the one item you feel most needs improving. Discuss that item and how you can help, whether through discussion with the teacher, demonstration, visitation by that teacher, help from a consultant, or some other means. The conference should con-clude with a clear agreement on how this weakness can be overcome, or at least worked on.

If you are dealing with a teacher who is being considered for dismissal, extreme care must be taken to follow due process. In such cases, you will want complete and dated records of every visit and every conference, including all of the positive suggestions and assistance provided for that teacher.

HAVE YOU DONE YOUR PART?

Getting into the classrooms to observe the teaching of reading is a very impor-tant part of the job of an effective principal. While it is probably the most neg-lected part, there are some other factors that must be considered if improved reading instruction is to continue.

"Time" has been stressed in a number of instances. As principal, you have some control over time. You can help teachers get the most scheduled time for reading instruction. Further, you can then assure the maximum "time on task" by establishing procedures that will keep scheduled time from being eroded by external influences, such as the public address system and visitors, as well as by inordinate amounts of time devoted to "practicing" for some performance.

In terms of materials, do you assure that teachers have the books, exer-cises, manuals, and ancillary materials necessary for the proper conduct of the basal program? Another administrative responsibility is the guarantee of appro-priate materials for pupils who do not "fit" in the basal. There should also be materials, such as high-interest, low-vocabulary books, properly housed and scheduled, for teachers who need them.

The library portion of the reading program also needs looking after. You may prefer scheduling classes to the library, but that library also needs to be open for individuals at all times, and books need to be available to be taken to the classrooms.

Among other schedules and procedures, do you have a clearly understood procedure for referral of children to the remedial reading, LD, and/or Title I teacher? Have your staff and those teachers had a chance to give some input into the making of such procedures? Your established routines are as important to the smooth functioning of the building as are the teacher's to the classroom. These special teachers should also be available to aid a classroom teacher in decisions on diagnosing or working with a given child.

What happens when a new student transfers to your school? We all know that in most cases months will pass before you see any records from the previous school. Every school ought to have a routine for smoothly inducting a new student into the reading class. It might be through use of an IRI by the classroom teacher or by another member of the staff. If at all possible, the teacher who will work with the child is the one who should give the IRI, so additional subjective information is available to that person.

If you have been using some of the ideas presented in previous chapters as part of your regular staff meetings, you are probably providing the best kind of inservice for your staff—the kind where they become personally involved with you in improving the reading program. However, there are times when some outside help is also advisable. Are there provisions in your school or district for such outside help from the area or county agency, a local university, or another school district? Further, do you make use of the consulting help that should be available from the publisher of your basal program?

Most often, the kind of help you will want will be specific to your own building needs, rather than a general "speaker." Most often, too, the best help is not the "hit and run" kind, but a professional who fits your needs and can return for follow-up visits to the school.

If you believe in the continuous progress of youngsters, you must also have an established procedure for end-of-year transition to the next teacher. Since most pupils do not fit our neat, preconceived packages, not too many children will conveniently arrive at the end of a book or workbook at the end of the year. Procedures need to be established for the books to move along with the children to the next teacher, so they can pick up next year where they left off.

Another important part of the job of the effective principal is interpreting the reading program to the school community, as discussed in Chapter 1. This is an opportunity to take the offensive and to avoid future unrest about the teaching of reading in your school. While outside speakers can also be helpful, I believe parents really want to "hear it" from you and your staff or local consultants. They do not really care so much how well reading is taught in the United States; they want to know how well their own child is being taught to read. Also, in addition to the regular parent meetings, you may find it helpful to get interested parents involved in study groups, where you can go into more detail about how reading is taught in your school.

Finally, you have the responsibility for leadership in the continuous evaluation of the reading program. Such evaluation should include both input and outcomes.

Outcomes are often evaluated through standardized tests. This is one aspect of success: How well does our school do in terms of national norms in reading and in comparison with our results from previous years? You will also want to look at outcomes in terms of the affective domain: How interested are our children in reading? While this element is more difficult to measure accurately, it can be estimated by the amount of library reading done, or through inventories of interest in reading.

As you evaluate standardized tests, you will want to consider some of the points made previously in this book about such tests: know the standard error of the test, so you know whether or not any differences are significant; and use the item analysis for groups, but do not let the test dictate your curriculum.

In terms of input, you should be evaluating continuously with your staff their instructional procedures in reading. Your direct responsibility also includes assurance that the teachers have the necessary materials in sufficient quantity, both basal and supportive, in order to teach the reading program effectively.

In addition to the ongoing continuous evaluation of the program, a more intensive evaluation usually takes place every four or five years. This is when you and the staff look at the total picture, see what else is new in the teaching of reading, and make a decision about what basal reading program you will use in the next four or five years. This kind of evaluation is the subject of the next chapter.

SUMMARY

In this chapter we have suggested that one important function of the principal is that of evaluating reading classes. This evaluation is intended to be a formative evaluation, one aimed at helping rather than labeling teachers. To do this kind of evaluation smoothly, you need to inform your teachers of some of your expectations, such as whether or not you will notify them of a visit in advance and how you will handle the follow-up conference.

In observing a reading lesson, you will want to note classroom routines, kinds of "seatwork" used, grouping plans, and use of the teacher's guide from the basal. The reading lesson itself will be evaluated in terms of the teacher's handling of the introduction, the reading and discussing, skill instruction, and follow-up activities. Most important of the points brought out here were the method of introducing new words, consistent provision for silent reading before oral, judgment in the selection of skills taught, and proper use of the workbook and other practice materials.

The follow-up conference after the class visitation is essential and should be a positive review of what you observed, with whatever questions you may have about certain behaviors. If the conference is with a teacher who needs to show considerable improvement, one major point of concentration ought to be selected and clearly defined for the teacher.

Getting back to more administrative responsibilities, the principal plays an important part by controlling *time* through avoidance of interruptions; by providing for adequate materials, both basal and library; by taking care that appropriate schedules are made and understood for referrals to any special teachers available in the building, as well as those for inducting new pupils and moving all pupils in a continuous progress plan into the next school year; by providing for inservice of staff and for community understanding of the reading program; and by assuming leadership in continuous evaluation of the input and outcomes of the reading program itself.

Suggestions for Action

Most likely the best "suggestions for action" are those that occurred to you as you were reading this chapter. However, the following points may revive some of the highlights.

1. If you have not done so, clarify the ground rules for your class visitations—what teachers can expect in terms of purposes, advance notice, and follow-up conferences.

2. From your visits, is classroom management or advance planning a pervasive problem to be discussed at a staff meeting, or is it one that might require inservice?

3. Judging from your visits, you may find that portions of a reading lesson should be discussed at a staff meeting. They may even require services of the publisher's consultant. Specifically, consider problems relating to: (1) word introduction, (2) oral vs. silent reading, (3) discussion of stories and questioning techniques, (4) decisions on skill instruction, and/or (5) use of workbooks and other practice materials.

4. How do your teachers use the basal guide: with preplanned judgment? ignore it? follow it blindly? Is this an area for inservice?

5. If you still have not checked, observe to see that all pupils are properly placed in reading groups and materials.

6. Briefly visit some classes for the singular purpose of determining if the classroom atmosphere is such that *you* would like to be in that class. Make a list in two columns of the examples you see of positive and negative reinforcement. When you have a composite, do you want to generalize it (to avoid identifying individuals) and share it with your teachers? Perhaps you would just like to share the positive examples.

7. Examine your notes to evaluate how well you have handled the last several follow-up conferences. Should you do more advance planning? Do you need to make a checklist or revise your old one?

8. How well have you kept up on your administrative responsibilities in the reading program, including teacher understanding of procedures? Which of the following might be slipping?

a. *Schedules:* time for reading, referral procedures, library use, induction of new students, end-of-year movement of students.

b. *Support:* basal and library materials, appropriate inservice, community information about reading.

c. *Evaluation:* achievement and diagnostic evaluation of pupils, continuous cooperative evaluation of instructional procedures and materials.

Reference

Durkin, Dolores. "What Classroom Observations Reveal about Reading Comprehension Instruction." *Reading Research Quarterly* 14 (1978–1979): 481–533. Reports an evaluation of classroom instruction in reading and concludes: "Practically no comprehension instruction was seen."

Additional Readings

Gudridge, Beatrice M. *Teacher Competency: Problems and Solutions.* Arlington, Va.: American Association of School Administrators, 1980. One of the AASA "Critical Issues" reports, this is an excellent presentation of research and ideas for using teacher evaluation to improve instruction. It is only 79 pages, and written in a concise, summary style.

Sergiovanni, Thomas J., ed. *Supervision of Teaching.* Alexandria, Va.: Association for Supervision and Curriculum Development, 1982. An excellent presentation of the "science and art of supervision," including discussion of strategies, models, and future prospects.

CHAPTER 11

Evaluating Reading Programs for Adoption

Usually about every four or five years a school district evaluates reading for a possible new adoption. Most often this is, and should be, a system-wide endeavor. Nevertheless, any principal who has some ideas is certainly going to have an opportunity to contribute—as if you needed a few more things to do!

Considering the impact of any adoption, there are few endeavors more important for your attention. A good procedure for evaluation can pay off for the next five years, not only in terms of a good reading program, but also in terms of staff harmony. A poor procedure may arrive at the same program, but dissention can continue for the entire period of the adoption. In fact, I would say that the *process* of evaluating programs can be a more important influence than the ultimate *product* or program you arrive at.

A basic principle, going back to the need for and importance of consistency, is that any adoption ought to be for a single basal. This position is stated for more than its obvious financial benefit in controlling inventory. While some districts do use co-basals (and even tri-basals), such adoptions weaken the teachers' view of what a basal is for; they lead to seeing a basal as a collection of stories that pupils are to be gotten through. Second, putting different levels of youngsters in different "basals" tends to lock them into that reading group or series. Different series vary considerably in terms of their vocabulary load at the primary and in terms of the point of introduction of skills—not to mention the differences in inclusion of skills—at intermediate levels, so it is not a simple matter to move a child from one series to another.

Nevertheless, for school districts that insist on more than one "basal," the principles outlined in this chapter will still apply. Furthermore, they will also apply if the consideration is for a locally developed curriculum guide or for adoption of a management system to be used with a language experience approach or any other noncommercial approach to reading instruction.

Before getting into an outline and description of procedures that have been followed successfully in a number of school districts, let's remove from consideration a few of the booby traps—the practices that can lead to difficulty in any consideration for adoption.

PROCEDURES TO AVOID

Not many school districts make an adoption through the once popular "Superintendent's Decision." At least the procedure here was simple: The books were getting old, so the superintendent had lunch with a favorite book representative and bought a new reading program. While administrators may (and should) have input into the philosophy and direction of the reading program, decisions must be cooperative ones.

In most school districts these days, committees are formed. Unfortunately, that committee is often given the responsibility for deciding on the reading program. When this happens, the decision base, as compared with the "Superintendent's Decision," is widened very little. Not only is the base too narrow, but the procedures often followed by these committees leave much to be desired.

Hearings

A common procedure is to decide on the programs to be considered and then to invite the publishers' representatives to hearings by the committee. From these presentations, the committee supposedly will make its decision. Such a procedure has a number of weaknesses.

First, it is usually not the reading program that is being evaluated in each case; it is the personality and presentation of the representative. Besides, doesn't every publisher's representative think that program is the best ever published? When have you had a representative tell you what was wrong with his or her program?

Second, this procedure is symptomatic of another problem: The committee members do not want to do their homework. They want someone to come in and tell them which is the best program. Incidentally, on this point,

I do not want to go so far as to rule out a reasonable possibility: If, *after* the committee and staff have done a thorough job, they want some clarification of philosophy or approach, then there is nothing wrong with inviting in a publisher's *consultant* or *author* to explain the items in question, or the entire program.

Finally, on this point of hearing from the representatives, I recall a school district that was following this procedure. I asked a committee member about one of the programs that had been presented early in the year and was told that she did not really remember much about that one; they would probably adopt reading program X that they had more recently heard about. They had been listening to about a dozen representatives on a schedule of one every other week! Is it any wonder the earlier presentations had faded from memory?

Piloting

Another common fallacy among adoption procedures is that of piloting programs under consideration. Usually this is done with the excuse that the strengths and weaknesses of a program cannot be determined until the program is used with children. If this is true, it is a terrible condemnation of teachers. It should also mean that an engineer cannot tell how good the bridge is until he or she tries it with trucks. Experienced teachers certainly ought to be able to look at materials through the eyes of youngsters and to envision how their pupils would react.

Besides, piloting can prove nothing! We all recall the National First Grade Studies, with all of their sophisticated researchers and designs. If they could not identify the better programs through a research comparison, what school district can?

To recall a specific example, one school district had a carefully planned design, complete with random selections of schools, to pilot four reading series at the first-grade level and to test the effectiveness of these programs at the end of first grade. Knowing these four programs, I made some mental predictions that youngsters in program A would score highest and those in program Z would be lowest. When the testing was completed, results indicated just the opposite findings from my predictions. However, in the final report, the "limitations" revealed the reasons for this surprise: Program A was in a new school that did not open in September; in fact, it was nearly January when those first graders got their books. Therefore program A was the lowest in results. Program Z was in a school where the principal did not really approve of it, so he grudgingly cooperated but insisted that any pupil who had difficulty would be put into the old program and not tested. Naturally, at the end of the year—with all low-achieving pupils removed—program Z produced the highest test scores of all four programs!

Not only does piloting prove nothing, it is counterproductive. One of the important outcomes of any reading adoption ought to be its clarifying and unifying effect on the staff. Piloting is a divisive influence, since the teacher who already favors a program volunteers to pilot it. Each pilot teacher becomes further entrenched in a favorite program. What better evidence of this entrapment effect than those representatives who "sell" their programs by offering a free pilot to the schools. My own feeling was always expressed in the reply, "If your program is so poor you have to give it away, we aren't interested."

Related to piloting is the desire of some teachers to see a series in use in another school district. The fact that the program is or is not successful there has little, if any, relation to how well it will be handled in your district. Differences in teachers, philosophies, acceptance, and implementation—not to mention differences in pupils—can make a world of difference.

Reviews of Programs

Reviews of reading programs may be found at times in professional journals. While such reviews might provide an interesting supplement to the district's evaluation, they really offer little help. For one thing, they are more like summaries than critical reviews, tending to provide an overview of the positive features of the program. An examination of the contents of these reviews will reveal also that their focus is most often on the content of the pupil books rather than on the approach and skills content in the manuals.

Part of the problem with these reviews is not with the reviewers themselves. Since they attempt to keep their own philosophies from entering into the review, they offer little help in making a decision. Any decision about a reading program ought to be made in terms of its match with the philosophy of reading instruction of the school staff.

While not a major fallacy, another typical action to be avoided in an adoption is the removal from consideration of the basal reading program currently in use. Admittedly, teachers get tired of the same program, no matter how good it is. They forget that it is new to youngsters, no matter how many years it has been in the school.

Let's also remember that any basal reading program goes through revisions, usually fairly major ones every five years. If the staff are still in agreement with the philosophy of the old program, they ought to consider that program's revised edition among the other programs under examination.

A POSITIVE APPROACH TO EVALUATION

Research has been unable to identify what is "the best" reading program. Nevertheless, the goal of any evaluation for adoption is to find the *best* reading program available today for your youngsters—"best" in terms of coming closest to meeting your philosophy of reading and your goals for instruction. Further-

more, the process of evaluation ought to be a unifying force and one that results in growth among the staff in terms of their understanding of the reading
process.

This latter point might suggest that you will begin with some inservice of
the staff. While this may not be necessary—and the "inservice" may come
about as a result of the process—if there is any indication that the staff needs
help in understanding its view of reading, this is the point at which inservice
should be introduced. Do not wait until teachers get into difficulty and then
try to get someone to bail them out.

Initial planning ought to include some kind of time schedule. While a
reading adoption is not something you do over night, neither is it a process
that should drag out for two years or more. Usually, if the plan calls for an
adoption, with materials to be ordered in May, basic details should be taken
care of in the previous Spring, so a committee is already organized and ready
to go to work in September.

Establish a Committee

Most reading adoptions are K–6, although a number might be for K–8. In the
latter case, we should recognize that the Grade 7 and 8 materials, while they
may carry over an author or so, are usually not integrally related to the previous levels.

The committee should be representative of the staff. It should include a
teacher from each grade level concerned, as well as a principal and/or consultant, and a special teacher of reading—whether remedial, LD, or Title I. It
should also be representative of the buildings in the district if they do not exceed ten or twelve. In other words, all of these people identified could each
come from a different building in the case of a K–6 adoption in a district with
ten elementary schools.

Your committee might also include a parent representative or two. Some
school districts find it necessary to have a "Parent Review Board," a committee
of parents who review the content of all books. The danger here is that such
boards may begin to see their job as one of censorship, a view certainly not to
be encouraged.

Finally, the committee should not be so large as to become unwieldy.
About a dozen is maximum if you are to get anything done. This means that,
in larger districts, some compromise will have to be made between building
representation and size of the committee.

State Your Philosophy of Reading

Once a committee has been established, their first step is to clarify and evolve
a statement of the philosophy of reading in the school district. The committee
should understand that such a "philosophy" is not one of those magnificently

abstract pieces of grandiloquent prose so often developed to be filed with the board of education. This "philosophy" should be a specific statement of what the staff believes is the proper approach to beginning reading and the proper emphasis in reading at higher levels. This step is a time-consuming one, but it is probably the most important phase in the whole process. Properly done, it will result in the smooth completion of the balance of the evaluation and will save time in the long run.

This step is also often a most difficult one. It may help the committee to get started in their thinking if you use an instrument such as "Clarifying a Philosophy of Reading" in Appendix C. While there is nothing unique about the instrument or the items in it, such a device may help the committee to think more specifically about elements that can go into their statement of philosophy. Of course, another alternative is to bring in a consultant who can help the total staff by clarifying the different approaches and emphases in reading instruction.

Once the committee has hammered out their tentative statement of philosophy, they have really only begun. That statement represents what *they* have agreed upon, but it does not include the rest of the teachers, who must also work with any reading program that is adopted. Hence, now the tentative statement must go back to the total staff for debate and possible alteration. It may even be helpful to use the instrument in Appendix C with the total staff, either before the committee has evolved the tentative philosophy, or at this point.

This involvement of total staff is crucial and again provides for unifying and clarifying their views on reading. If every building is represented on the committee, each committee member can return to the home building and lead a discussion of the philosophy in that building. Sometimes it is also helpful to establish system-wide grade-level meetings, where the tentative statement can be discussed under the direction of the grade-level representative on the committee.

When the committee reconvenes, they may be satisfied that they have a consensus on philosophy and can produce the final draft. If not, another round of building and/or grade-level meetings may be in order.

Develop Criteria for Evaluation

What should teachers look for as they evaluate reading programs? Most often they do not know unless they have some guidance. In fact, I have found that most teachers do not even know what a reading *program* is. Once, as teachers were criticizing a basal reading program, I asked them what they would look for if they had unlimited freedom and resources. They began mentioning items such as "interesting stories," "attractive illustrations," "language patterns that were similar to what children used," and so on. They had not mentioned one element of a reading program; they had merely been describing anthologies.

Do your teachers know that the pupil books are *not* the reading program? They are nothing more than anthologies—albeit most often of excellent children's literature—and they do not teach any skills. They are the vehicle a teacher uses to teach and to give practice on the skills outlined in the teacher's guide. It is the teacher's guide or manual that contains the reading program.

If your teachers are conscious of this point, they are unusual. A survey of 121 experienced teachers asked them to list the items they would look for in evaluating reading programs. From their list of first priority items, 61 percent of those items related to the stories in the pupil books; only 13 percent of the items related to the teacher's guide and skills. Is it any wonder that so many textbook adoptions are made on the basis of the "pretty pupil pages"?

Many of the publishers of basal programs do a better job of recognizing where the program is. As much as three-fourths of the items in publishers' criteria for evaluation related to the skills and the teacher's guides. Nevertheless, no school district would dare use any one publisher's criteria for evaluating reading programs. Those criteria are specific and do deal with philosophy or emphasis. However, as a result, if you used a publisher's criteria for evaluation—and used it honestly—you would most certainly adopt that reading program.

This is not a criticism of publishers or their criteria. Any good list of criteria will be specific to a reading philosophy. Therefore, the criteria developed by your committee should be specific and reflect the philosophy they have evolved. If this job is done well, the criteria listed will almost point to a reading program.

The committee may decide on separate criteria for primary and for middle grades, since the elements they will look for at these different levels vary so. At primary, they are more concerned about the approach to reading, readiness, the role of phonics, word attack methods, and so on. By middle grades, no program contains every possible skill with equal emphasis. Hence, upper-level programs differ in their skill content and emphasis more than in basic approach or philosophy of reading. Some may emphasize inferential comprehension to the neglect of study skills, or vice versa. Therefore, at this level, decisions will be made more on the basis of emphasis: Which programs include the skills consistent with our needs?

This is a point, also, where information from your standardized testing may be used. Results by grade level and item analysis by skill areas may point up some strengths and weaknesses of the past and may lead to items that should be included in the criteria.

The break between "primary" and "middle grades" may also differ. Traditionally, the break came between third and fourth grade. Beginning in the 1970s, a more appropriate break was between second and third grade, since the assumption in those programs was that the average pupil would master the decoding skills by the end of second grade.

Figures 11–1 and 11–2 are guidelines or criteria developed by one school

		Name of Program				
Evaluating Teacher:_____Grade:_____ 3=Very Good; 2=Good; 1=Poor; 0=Omitted in program						
Teacher edition	Philosophy clear (Introduction)					
	Specific direction for skill teaching					
	Ease of use					
	Provision for individual differences					
Content	Interest appeal to children					
	Variety of types of reading					
Format	Physically clear and attractive					
Illustrations	Aesthetic appeal					
ADEQUACY OF SKILL DEVELOPMENT						
Readiness deals with letters and sounds in words, not just with general language development.						
Skills are learned through use, not just through memorizing rules.						
Child is shown how the skill is used in reading.						
Reading includes use of context, emphasis on reading for meaning.						
Suggested questions for discussion cover the inferential and critical as well as literal levels.						
Readiness for comprehension and study skills begins with these skills at the listening level.						
The child is taught a definite system for attacking an unknown word (Mark *Yes* or *No* in each column.)						
What is the system? (Put a check in proper columns.)						
Guess from context only.						
Remember the word from the introduction.						
Apply a rule or rules.						
Sound out the word.						
Use context and consonant-sound associations.						

Figure 11–1. *Evaluation of Reading Program: Kindergarten–Grade 2*

Evaluating Teacher:_____Grade:_____

3 = Very Good; 2 = Good; 1 = Poor; 0 = Omitted in program

Name of Program

Teacher edition	Philosophy clear (Introduction)					
	Specific direction for skill teaching					
	Ease of use					
	Provision for individual differences					
Content	Interest appeal to children					
	Variety of types of reading					
Format	Physically clear and attractive					
Illustrations	Aesthetic appeal					

ADEQUACY OF SKILL DEVELOPMENT
(Provisions for Teaching, Practicing, Applying)

Literal comprehension	Dictionary skills					
	Reading for detail Reading for topic of paragraph Reading for main idea of selection Reading to recall sequence Reading to determine cause/effect					
Inferential comprehension	Drawing conclusions Making judgments Predicting outcomes Interpreting figurative language					
Critical reading	Distinguishing fact and opinion Determining adequacy/completeness Determining relevance: evidence—conclusions					
	Determining slant/bias—propaganda Determining author's viewpoint/purpose Determining author's competence/datedness					
Study skills	Notetaking Classifying Outlining Summarizing					
	Use of index					
	Reading to follow directions Adjusting rate to purpose Reading content material Reading graphs, charts, etc.					
Literary appreciation	Personal reactions Identification with character/events					
	Reactions to language Imagery					

Figure 11–2. *Evaluation of Reading Program: Grades 3–6*

Reprinted from "So You're Evaluating Reading Programs!" Elementary School Journal 75 *(December 1974): 172–182 by Robert L. Hillerich by permission of The University of Chicago Press.* © *1974 by the University of Chicago. All rights reserved.*

district for evaluation of reading programs. Figure 11–1 was developed for Grades K–2, while Figure 11–2 was used by Grades 3–6. These guidelines are not included here to provide anyone with ready-made criteria. They are offered as an example of the specificity that is needed, and they may suggest a format. As you see in Figure 11–1, at the primary level these teachers were concerned with the particular approach to word identification. Figure 11–2 shows a special concern for study skills, with use of an index singled out for a separate evaluation.

The philosophy developed by your staff, if it is appropriately specific, will provide a sound basis from which to develop the criteria for evaluation. The format suggested in Figures 11–1 and 11–2 may be helpful in indicating that the list of criteria should be brief—limited to one page if at all possible. Teachers cannot be expected to complete a long, involved checklist on a number of different reading programs.

Many guidelines for evaluation are four or five pages long. There should be no need to list items that are important but that every program includes. For example, why indicate whether or not a reading series has "good literature," "attractive illustrations," "evaluative materials," "provision for adjustment to individual differences," "stated objectives," "known authorship," or even "freedom from sex or racial bias," when you are hard pressed to find a program—at least from any major publisher—that could be faulted on any of these counts?

On the other hand, in addition to some thoughts about criteria such as suggested in Figures 11–1 and 11–2, your committee may want to use a different breakdown and certainly will decide to include some different items. They may use guidelines from *several* publishers as sources of ideas for specific points to be included in the criteria they are developing. Major headings from which they might develop additional specific criteria could include: Format, Reader Content, Readiness, Vocabulary, Word Attack, Comprehension, Study Skills, Method, Workbooks, Tests, Other Aids.

Since decisions ought to be made on a reasoned basis, your committee may also find it helpful to add two open-ended points to their guidelines for the evaluation of each series under consideration:

1. What is the outstanding strength of this program?
2. What is the outstanding weakness of this program?

While committees do not often think of it, another important factor in a decision about a text series of any kind should be the availability of consultant help from the publisher. Most major publishers do have consultants, but your service from them may vary. This is a point that ought to be included in deliberations.

You will note in Figures 11–1 and 11–2 that there is provision in the right-hand columns for writing in the names of the programs under consideration. It is helpful to have them all together on the guide. If the philosophy has been specific, your staff will not have to evaluate a dozen or more reading programs. There is no need to look at programs that do not come within the philosophy of the district. Further, some programs that fit the philosophy may be of no interest to anyone in the district. It is wise to try to keep the number of programs to be examined down to a reasonable quantity, such as four to six. Otherwise, there is danger of a superficial examination when the number becomes overwhelming.

Also, as shown in Figures 11-1 and 11-2, the evaluation of items should be qualitative. Teachers need to evaluate with more than a "yes/no" response, since it is unlikely that important items are completely omitted from any program. The evaluation should be an indication of adequacy.

Once the committee has developed their criteria for evaluation, they must again go back to total staff with the tentative draft. If not, those criteria will not be understood or appreciated by other teachers. Once more, the readjustment may be done through building and/or grade-level meetings.

While the development of the criteria is taking place, sample reading programs that fit the philosophy already developed may be ordered. With this kind of preliminary effort on the part of your teachers—and knowing that they are serious contenders—publishers selected should be willing to provide a sample set of their programs for each building. The texts need to be easily accessible if teachers are to do a thorough job of evaluating.

Apply the Criteria

Once the criteria for evaluation have been established, copies should go to all teachers in the district. Each teacher should be expected to use the criteria to evaluate each program at his or her grade level. Further, each teacher should be asked at least to look at the levels immediately above and below that grade level. Examination will focus almost entirely on the teacher's guides if the criteria have been developed with an emphasis on "program" rather than on pupil books. In fact, it is often helpful to remove some of the clutter by storing the pupil books away from the guides that are to be evaluated.

Such a system-wide approach will provide a good horizontal evaluation of the programs under consideration. There also needs to be some vertical evaluation, since there are, unfortunately, some published programs that simply do not hang together. There are some that are very poorly articulated from level to level.

The vertical evaluation can be a good job for members of the committee. Each member may pick a skill at random, or they may each be assigned a skill, and can follow it through each of the programs. This tracing of skills must be done with the teacher's guide, not with the "Scope and Sequence" that usually accompanies programs. Too often you will find a "Scope and Sequence" that has a lot of window dressing in it (a lot of nonexistent skills), at least as far as that program is concerned.

This vertical evaluation must also be qualitative. The evaluator should see *how well* the given skill is taught, reinforced, practiced, and applied. In one examination, for example, a given series provided practice in a skill at the level *before* that skill was taught. In another, there were gaps of a year between teaching and the practice of a skill.

Arrive at a Consensus

When the committee collects the evaluations from the entire staff, it will be most unusual to find that the teachers have agreed on a single program. However, most often two programs will stand out as the most preferred ones.

A tendency at this point is to count the "votes" and determine a "winner." To do this would be most unfortunate, since the committee would be giving equal voice to two kinds of teachers: There was the teacher who spent hours thoughtfully examining each series, and there was also the teacher who took a perfunctory glance at each and put down an evaluation. These two kinds of teachers do not deserve an equal voice in the selection.

Usually the best way to handle a split or close decision is to go back to the staff with the criteria and have the criteria applied again to the two programs. Along with the evaluation this time, the committee might ask for an explanation of *why* this program is so good and *why* you cannot live with the other one. With reasons to accompany this final survey of staff, the committee can usually make the hard decision on what reading program to recommend for adoption. Sometimes, however, there are additional factors to consider.

There are cases when the primary staff are clearly in favor of program A, while the intermediate staff are clearly in favor of program B. Can there be a successful split adoption? Yes, there have been a number of them. While it is not the most desirable approach, it can be workable if the programs represent some compatability. There needs to be a careful examination of the point of juncture of the two series—another job for the committee members, possibly working with teachers of the grades where the split will take place. For example, if the change is to be between Grades 2 and 3, you would not want a primary program introducing dictionary skills at Grade 3 when the intermediate series that will be used in Grade 3 presumes those skills were introduced in Grade 2. While this would present a gap in skill instruction, the reverse kinds of programs would provide a duplication.

This is not the place to ask an outside consultant to come in to resolve the dilemma. No consultant is going to make the decision for you. Ultimately it is up to the committee to make a final recommendation, and it is the function of the board of education to make the formal adoption.

IMPLEMENTATION OF THE NEW PROGRAM

Usually it is the administrator's role to place the order for text materials. With the variety of levels and ancillary materials, such ordering is often best done with the help of the publisher's local representative.

Equally important as having the apppropriate materials in sufficient quantity for the opening of school is the plan for inservice of the new program. Arrangements should be made in the Spring for such inservice. While some inservice can be conducted by local staff, it is usually wise to have a consultant from the publisher to do an initial presentation in order to further clarify the philosophy and approach of the program. These people know their programs and usually have had the experience with other staffs that enables them to pinpoint possible difficult spots.

Adoption of a new reading program also necessitates more community information. You may want to plan an early parent meeting for the next year in order to highlight some of the outstanding features of the new program. This is an excellent place to make use of your committee members in order to clarify the care with which a new adoption takes place in your school.

SUMMARY

This chapter has suggested procedures for evaluating reading programs for adoption. Among those not recommended but sometimes followed are procedures such as the unilateral decision of the superintendent, presentations from publishers' representatives, piloting programs, or relying on published reviews of programs.

A good procedure for evaluating reading programs will be headed by a representative committee, but will involve the total staff in the following steps:

1. Establish a committee that is representative of the entire school district.
2. State the philosophy of reading in clear and specific terms.
3. Develop criteria for evaluation that reflect the agreed-upon philosophy of the staff.
4. Apply the criteria, and this application must be by the entire staff.
5. Arrive at a consensus rather than regard the application of the criteria as a "vote."
6. Implement the new program through advance planning of inservice and use of the publisher's consultant or author.

This kind of evaluation process is probably more important than the ultimate product. A good process will be a unifying factor for the entire staff and will involve the following general principles:

1. Total Involvement.   The whole staff, not just the committee, must be part of the total process.
2. Clear Philosophy.   The total staff must evolve a clear and specific statement of their philosophy of reading instruction.
3. Criteria for Evaluation.   Specific criteria, based on the stated philosophy, must be developed and used in the evaluation of all series under consideration.
4. Keep It Moving.   The process of evaluation should be completed within a school year.
5. Reasoned Decision.   The final decision on a series to be recommended for adoption should not be based on a raw vote; it should be based on reasoned justification.
6. Planned Implementation.   The program is not just bought; it is inserviced.

Suggestions for Action

If your school district plans to evaluate reading programs for possible adoption, you may want to use the summary of principles to judge your overall plan for evaluation. Then you might chart a timetable, using the summary of steps as your entries.

References

Aukerman, Robert C. *The Basal Reader Approach to Reading.* New York: John Wiley and Sons, 1981. An excellent objective description of fifteen major reading programs. The evaluations of the programs, however, should be accepted with caution.

Hillerich, Robert L. "So You're Evaluating Reading Programs!" *Elementary School Journal* 75 (December 1974): 172–182. The original article from which this chapter was adapted and updated.

CHAPTER *12*

Parting Shots

This book has attempted to provide guidance to educational leaders in their role of improving reading instruction. Some of the ideas are based on my own mistakes as a principal; others come from observation of the good practices of many competent principals around the country.

The foundation of this book rests on a firm belief in three essential and research-based tenets:

1. The principal is important in improving reading instruction.
2. The principal must establish priorities for instruction.
3. The principal can lead in "bootstrap" inservice.

To fulfill the expectation of these tenets, the principal must, first of all, have some knowledge of what reading is all about and, second, must assume a leadership role. These are essentially the major headings under which all points in this book can be subsumed.

KNOWLEDGE OF READING

As stated in the introduction, the principal does not need to become a reading specialist, but that principal must know something about the teaching of reading. We have presented an overview of what the skills are and how they might be taught effectively.

Basically, the viewpoint expressed here is a simple one: Reading instruction is not as complicated a process as some would have us believe. There is a place for common sense in the teaching of reading. In greatly oversimplified terms, the main concerns expressed about the teaching of reading have been:

1. Eliminate the irrelevant "skills" that clutter up the instructional scene.
2. Be certain to teach the important skills effectively and efficiently.
3. Be certain that pupils are placed properly in materials at their reading level.
4. Be certain that children also have time to "really read."

In terms of specific items of knowledge about the reading process, you may want to go back to the "Suggestions for Action" in individual chapters in order to pick out your area or areas of concern. The following major topics were discussed in detail:

1. Kindergarten Diagnosis
2. Reading Readiness
3. The Approach to Beginning Reading
4. Basic Decoding Skills (including phonics, word recognition, use of context, structural analysis)
5. Independent Reading
6. Comprehension Skills (including literal, inferential, and critical reading)
7. Dictionary and Study Skills

These are the areas of knowledge that the principal must be familiar enough with to at least be able to ask the right questions. With some background in these areas, you can provide the leadership and assistance needed to continue improving the reading program.

LEADERSHIP ROLE

Other topics included in this book dealt with the leadership role of the principal and those organizational and management tasks related to the reading program. They included:

1. The importance of the principal
2. The importance of *time* for instruction

3. The need for consistency with an individual pupil
4. The need to support and justify the reading achievement in your school
5. The need to identify reading levels and skills of pupils
6. The need to group children appropriately for instruction
7. The need to adjust for differences in language or dialect
8. The use of management systems
9. How to evaluate a reading lesson
10. Procedures for evaluating reading programs for adoption

Throughout, the premise has been that the principal is working on these items *with* staff. The "leader" who gets too far out in front will not be leading anyone. This working-with-staff may be on a one-to-one, may be through inservice, and may be in staff meetings.

The inservice will also vary with the needs and available talent. You may use your own teachers for some, but do not forget to make use of whatever area or local reading consultants you have. There are also times when the publisher's consultant for the reading program is a good choice. In other words, you do not need to do it all.

Your role of leadership is shown, however, through your direct interest in reading instruction. In addition to your visits to observe, you do need to devote time at staff meetings specifically for discussion of reading. Further, your teachers should have access to the professional journals suggested in Chapter 1. You may also want a small "library" of professional books for reference by you and your teachers. You will find what I consider a sound nucleus of references at the end of this chapter.

IN CONCLUSION

This book has included literally a lifetime of work for any principal in any school. And that's fine—any professional book ought to be a little out in front of good practice; it ought to hold up goals to be strived for. This book has attempted to do just that.

HOWEVER . . .

IF you are visiting reading classes and talking with teachers about the reading program;

IF your teachers are enjoying reading and the discussing of stories with children;

IF your pupils are really reading—at whatever level—and enjoying it;

THEN you have a good reading program going! Any additional ideas you can implement from this book will be icing on the cake.

A Beginning Professional "Library"

While there are many good books on the teaching of reading, the following are suggested as a beginning. They provide a balance among the topics of concern in reading, from beginning reading to diagnosis.

Aulls, Mark W. *Developmental and Remedial Reading in the Middle Grades.* Boston: Allyn and Bacon, 1978. This is an excellent presentation of the study skills and questioning techniques. It makes a good companion text to Hillerich's primary book.

Bond, Guy L.; Tinker, Miles A.; and Wasson, Barbara B. *Reading Difficulties: Their Diagnosis and Treatment.* Englewood Cliffs, N.J.: Prentice Hall, 1979. A classic on this subject. Especially good on reading disability and its "causes." (However, if you purchase only one book in this area, Harris and Sipay is better.)

Friedman, Myles I., and Rowls, Michael D. *Teaching Reading and Thinking Skills.* New York: Longman, 1980. An excellent presentation of comprehension instruction.

Harris, Albert J., and Sipay, Edward R. *How to Increase Reading Ability.* New York: Longman, 1980. The classic work on identification and treatment of reading problems.

Hillerich, Robert L. *Reading Fundamentals for Preschool and Primary Children.* Columbus, Ohio: Charles Merrill, 1977. A thorough treatment of primary reading instruction, including detailed research justification as well as methods of instruction. A good companion to Aulls.

Smith, Frank. *Understanding Reading.* New York: Holt, Rinehart and Winston, 1978. An excellent presentation of what the process of reading is all about from a psycholinguistic view.

Wilson, Robert M. *Diagnostic and Remedial Reading for Classroom and Clinic.* Columbus, Ohio: Charles Merrill, 1981. A broad-coverage text, less technical than the Bond or Harris books.

APPENDIX A

Prefixes, Suffixes, and Combining Forms

The following items are frequently used and consistent enough in meaning to be worth teaching. They have been adapted from Lee C. Deighton, *Vocabulary Development in the Classroom*. New York: Teachers College, Columbia, 1959.

Prefixes. Of 68 common prefixes, only these are useful:

apo-	from, detached, formed from
circum-	around, about
equi-	equal, equally
inter-	between
extra-	beyond, on the outside
intra-	within, during, between layers of
intro-	in, inward, within
mal-	bad, abnormal, inadequate
mis-	bad, wrong, opposite of, not
non-	not, absence of
over-	so as to exceed or surpass, excessive
pre-	before (in time or space)
re-	again/anew: *retell*; back/backward: *recall*
syn-, sym-	with, at the same time

Two additional prefixes are so common, but with variant meanings, that they may be taught with caution:

in- (il-, im-, ir-)	not, in, into, or as an intensifier
un-	not, the opposite of

Suffixes. Most suffixes indicate the part of speech, rather than meaning.

Noun endings indicating agent: *-eer, -ess, -grapher, -ier, -ster,*
                                   -ist, -stress, -trix.
Noun endings used as diminutives: *-ule, -cle, -cule, -ock, -kin, -let.*

-ana	collected items concerning: *Americana*
-archy	rule, government: *monarchy*
-ard, -art	one associated with a characteristic: *dullard, braggart.*
-aster	inferior or not genuine: *criticaster*
-chrome	colored thing or matter: *heterochrome*
-cide	killer, killing: *pesticide*
-ee	recipient, performer: *grantee, escapee*
-fer	one that bears: *conifer*
-fication	making, production: *electrification*
-gram	drawing, writing, record: *telegram*
-graph	something written or instrument for: *telegraph*
-graphy	writing in a manner or on a subject: *oceanography*
-ics	study, knowledge, skill, practice: *electronics*
-itis	malady from or proneness: *televisionitis*
-latry	worship: *idolatry*
-meter	instrument or means for measurement: *barometer*
-metry	art, process, or science of measuring: *chronometry*
-logy	doctrine, theory, science: *sociology*
-phore	carrier: *gametophore*
-phobia	exaggerated/illogical fear: *claustrophobia*
-scope	means for viewing or observing: *microscope*
-scopy	viewing, observation: *radioscopy*

Adjective Endings.

-est	superlative form: *biggest*
-ferous	bearing, producing: *coniferous*
-fic	making, causing: *horrific*
-fold	multiplied by, times, having so many parts: *threefold*
-form	in the form/shape of: *cuniform*
-genous	producing, yielding, originating from: *homogenous*
-wards	in the direction of: *backwards*
-wise	in the manner/direction of: *slantwise*
-less	without, unable to act or be acted upon: *dauntless*

-able, -ible, -ble	capable of, liable to: *perishable, collectible*
-most	most toward: *headmost*
-like	resembling or characteristic of: *ladylike*
-ous	full of or having the qualities of: *poisonous*

Combining Forms. Most commonly used in technical terms.

anthropo-	human being: *anthropology*
auto-	self, self acting: *automatic*
biblio-	book: *bibliography*
bio-	study of life: *biology*
centro-, centri-	relating to the center: *centrifugal*
cosmo-	relating to the universe: *cosmopolitan*
heter-	other, different: *heterogenous*
homo-	same, similar: *homogenous*
hydro-	water, liquid: *hydroelectric*
iso-	equal or uniform: *isodose*
lith-	stone: *lithology*
micro-	small: *microbiology*
mono-	one: *monorail*
neuro-	nerve: *neurology*
omni-	all, universally: *omnibus*
pan-	all, every: *Pan-American*
penta-	five: *pentagon*
phil-	loving or having an affinity for: *philhelene*
phono-	sound, voice: *phonograph*
photo-	light: *photograph*
pneumo-	air, gas: *pneumatic*
poly-	many, several, much: *polychrome*
proto-	first: *prototype*
pseudo-	false, spurious: *pseudo-psychology*
tele-	distant: *telephone*
uni-	one, single: *unicycle*

APPENDIX B

High-Interest, Low-Vocabulary Books

This appendix contains some suggested high-interest, low-vocabulary materials, classified by appropriate grade level for use. No attempt has been made to exhaust the possibilities, but the items listed have proven interesting to students at the levels indicated.

Skill Materials

"Specific Skills Series" (Barnell Loft, Ltd.)
>This series contains booklets on the following skills: Following Directions, Using the Context, Locating the Answer, Getting the Facts, Getting the Main Idea, Drawing Conclusions, and Detecting the Sequence. For each skill, booklets are available at levels A–L. These levels are about a grade below the reading level, so Level A ought to be considered Grade 2; Level B, Grade 3; and so on.

"Individualized Reading Skills Program" (Houghton Mifflin)
>This series of three kits contains pre- and post-tests and instructional booklets for thirty skill lessons at each of Grades 4–6. It is designed for poor readers at those grades, with emphasis on comprehension and study skills. Reading level is below grade.

High-Interest, Low-Vocabulary Stories

"Reader's Digest Skill Builders" (Reader's Digest, Educational Division)
   A series of four to six books per grade level, for grades 1–8. Interesting stories in an adult format. While the "skill building" is questionable, the reading material is excellent for developing any skill the teacher wants to teach.

Primary Grade Interest: High-Interest, Low-Vocabulary Books[1]

Series Title	Preprimer Level	Primer Level	Grade 1 Level	Grade 2 Level
The Buttons . . .	at the Zoo Bucky Buttons	Take a Boat Ride & the Pet Parade	at the Farm	and the Boy Scouts & Little League (Grade 3) & Soap Box Derby (Grade 3)
Alley Alligator	Alley Alligator	& the Fire	& the Hurricane	& the Big Race & the Hunters (Grade 3)
Sailor Jack . . .	& Homer Pots Sailor Jack	& Bluebell's Dive & Bluebell & the Jet Plane		& the Target Ship
Cowboy Sam . . .	& Big Bill & Freckles & Dandy	& Miss Lily & Porky Cowboy Sam	& Flop & Shorty & Freddy	& Sally & the Fair & the Rodeo
Butternut Bill . . .	Butternut Bill & the Bee Tree & Big Catfish	& the Bear & Little River & Big Pumpkin	& His Friends & the Train	
(Animal Adventure)	Becky Rabbit Squeaky Squirrel Doc the Dog Pat the Parakeet Kate the Cat	Skippy Skunk Sandy Swallow Gomar the Gosling	Sally Screech Owl Pudgy Beaver Hamilton Hamster Horace Horse	
Peter . . .			Rocket Sitter & Rocket Fishing	& the Rocket Team & Big Balloon & Rocket Ship (Grade 3) & Two-Hour Moon (Grade 3)

Primary Guide Interest: High-Interest, Low-Vocabulary Books¹ (Continued)

Series Title	Preprimer Level	Primer Level	Grade 1 Level	Grade 2 Level
Moonbeam . . .	is Caught Moonbeam & the Captain	is Lost at Rocket Port & the Big Jump	& Rocket Ride & Dan Starr	Finds a Moon Stone & Sunny (Grade 3)
(Tom Logan)	Pony Rider Talking Wire	Track Boss Cattle Drive	Secret Tunnel Gold Train	
Treat Truck . . .	& Fire Mike & . . .	& Dog Show & Big Rain	& Parade & Lucky Lion	& Storm & Bank Robbery (Grade 3)

¹From Benefic Press, 10300 W. Roosevelt Road, Westchester, IL 60153.

Intermediate Grade Interest: High-Interest, Low-Vocabulary Books[1]

Series Title	Grade 1 Level	Grade 2 Level	Grade 3 Level	Grade 4 Level
(Checkered Flag)		Wheels 2.4 Riddler 2.5 Bearcat 2.5 Smashup 2.6	Scramble 3.0 Flea 3.5	Grand Prix 4.0 500 4.5
(Deep Sea Adventure)	Sea Hunt 1.8 Storm Island 1.8	Treasure Under Sea 2.1 Submarine Rescue 2.4 Sea Gold 2.2 Enemy Agents 2.5 Castaways 2.6 Pearl Divers 2.8	Frogmen in Action 3.1	Danger Below 4.4 Whale Hunt 4.7 Rocket Divers 5.0
Jim Forest . . .	& Ranger Don 1.7 & the Trapper 1.7 & the Ghost Town 1.8 & the Bandits 1.9 & Lightning 1.9	& Phantom Crater 2.0 & Mystery Hunter 2.2 & the Plane Crash 2.4 & Dead Man's Peak 2.6 & the Flood 2.8	& Lone Wolf Gulch 3.1 & Woodman's Ridge 3.2	
Mystery of . . . (Morgan Bay Mysteries)		Morgan Castle 2.3 Marble Angel 2.6	Midnight Visitor 3.2 Missing Marlin 3.5 Musical Ghost 3.5 Monk's Island 3.7 Marauder's Gold 3.9	Myrmidon's Journey 4.1
(Wildlife Adventure)		Gatie Alligator 2.6 Sleeky Otter 2.8	Skipper Dolphin 3.0 Tawny Mountain Lion 3.2 Bounder Jackrabbit 3.5 Thor Moose 3.6 Ruff Wolf 3.7	Arctos Grizzly 4.4

[1]From Addison-Wesley, 2725 Sand Hill Road, Menlo Park, CA 94025.

Intermediate Grade Interest: High-Interest, Low-Vocabulary Books[1]

Series Title	Grades 1 & 2 Level	Grade 3 Level	Grade 4 Level	Grades 5 & 6 Level
(Horses and Heroines)	Saddle Up 2 Junior Rodeo 2	High Jumper Harness Race	Ride the Winner Steeplechase	
Chopper Malone . . .	& New Pilot P & Susie P & Big Snow 1 & Trouble at Sea 1 & Mountain Rescue 2	& Skylarks		
Dan Frontier . . .	Dan Frontier PP & the New House PP & the Big Cat P Goes Hunting P Trapper 1 with Indians 1 & the Wagon Train 2 Scouts with the Army 2	Sheriff Goes Exploring	Goes to Congress	
(Inner City)	Beat the Gang 2	Tough Guy Runaway	New Boy in School No Drop Out	

(Cowboys of Many Races)	Cowboy w/out Horse PP
	Cowboy on Mountain P
	Cowboy Matt &
	  Belleza 1
	Adam Bradford,
	  Cowboy 2
		Cowboy on the Trail	Cowboy Soldier	Cowboy Marshall 5

(Space Science Fiction)	Space Pirate 2 Milky Way 2	Bone People	Planet of Whistlers	Inviso Man 5 Ice Men of Rime 6

250

(Sports Mystery)	Ten Feet Tall 2 No Turning Back 2 Luck of the Runner 2	Gymnast Girl Fairway Danger Tip Off Pitcher's Choice Ski Mountain Mystery	Scuba Diving Face Off Swimmer's Mark Tennis Champ
Mystery Adventure of . . .	Talking Statues 2 the Jeweled Bell 2	At Cave	Indian Burial Ground	Long Cliff Inn 5 Smuggled Treasure 6
(World of Adventure)	Lost Uranium Mine 2 Flight to South Pole 2	Hunt Grizzly Bears Fire on the Mountain	City Beneath the Sea Search for Piranha	Sacred Well Sacrifice 5 Viking Treasure 6
(Racing Wheels)	Hot Rod 2 Motorcycle Scramble 2 Motorcycle Racer Destruction Derby	Drag Race Baja 500 Stock Car Race Safari Rally	Road Race Grand Prix Races Indy 500 LeMans Race

¹From Benefic Press, 10300 W. Roosevelt Road, Westchester, IL 60153.

251

APPENDIX C

Clarifying a Philosophy of Reading[1]

Use the separate answer sheet to indicate your responses to the following items. For each row of four items, select the *one* that most closely identifies your view. Please answer every item, even though some may be far removed from your teaching level or may not exactly coincide with your views.

What is Reading?

1a. Reading is a process of translating printed symbols into sounds they represent.	1b. Reading is a process of saying words in print.	1c. Reading is a matter of understanding what an author has said in print.	1d. Reading is a process of approximating and reacting to ideas expressed in print.
2a. The most significant structures in reading are individual letters and sounds.	2b. The most significant structures in reading are syllables.	2c. The most significant structures in reading are words.	2d. The most significant structures in reading are sentences.
3a. Reading is a collection of skills to be learned.	3b. Reading is a collection of rules to be verbalized.	3c. Reading is a collection of words to be learned.	3d. Reading is a collection of skills to be applied.
4a. Good readers will know the sounds of individual letters.	4b. Good readers will be able to state rules about sounds and syllables.	4c. Good readers will be able to say all the words on a list at their level.	4d. Good readers will be able to interpret the meaning of a selection at their level.

5a. Good readers will never miscall a word.

5b. Good readers will rarely miscall a word.

5c. Good readers will sometimes miscall a word and seldom correct themselves.

5d. Good readers will sometimes miscall a word but will self-correct if the error does not make sense.

What is Readiness?

6a. A level of physical development.

6b. A level of social maturity based on age.

6c. A level of skill development resulting from experience and instruction.

6d. A level of cognitive and emotional development resulting from experience and instruction.

7a. Readiness involves checking for age, IQ, physical development, and many other items.

7b. Readiness focuses on social experiences.

7c. Readiness is a matter of drill on phonics.

7d. Readiness is a matter of involvement in all aspects of language development.

8a. Readiness cannot be "taught."

8b. Readiness instruction includes listening for differences in sounds, looking for differences in shapes, . . .

8c. Readiness instruction focuses on letter names and sounds.

8d. Readiness instruction is a continuum from basic oral language through actual reading instruction.

9a. Structured drill is the best method for having children learn to read.

9b. Study of word lists, along with use of flash cards, is the best way to teach children to read.

9c. A combination of skill instruction and library reading is the best way to teach children to read.

9d. Extensive library reading and discussion is the best way to teach children to read.

10a. New words do not need to be introduced prior to reading.

10b. Rules or patterns need to be reviewed prior to reading.

10c. New words need to be taught prior to reading.

10d. New words are used to review word identification skills prior to reading.

11a. When they come to a word they do not know, pupils should sound it out.

11b. When they come to a word they do not know, pupils should use the rule.

11c. When they come to a word they do not know, pupils should try to remember the word.

11d. When they come to a word they do not know, pupils should use context and phonics.

21a. It is immaterial whether students drill on sounds.

12b. The teacher's role is to tell, provide practice, and correct errors.

12c. The teacher's role is to listen to children's reading and reinforce or correct.

12d. The teacher's role is to interact with pupils in investigating the language.

13a. Oral reading is one method of checking on the accuracy of pronunciation.

13b. Oral reading is one method of checking on the understanding of ideas.

13c. Oral reading is one method of determining if pupils recognize all the words.

13d. Oral reading is one method of sharing information or ideas in print.

14a. The teacher seldom needs to ask questions about a selection read.

14b. The teacher should usually ask questions about a selection read.

14c. The teacher should always ask questions about a selection read.

14d. The teacher and students should raise questions and discuss the selection read.

15a. Knowledge of the sounds for vowel letters is essential.

15b. Knowledge of rules about vowels is essential.

15c. Vowel rules probably ought to be taught.

15d. Vowel rules are of questionable value.

16a. Rules for dividing words into syllables are essential.

16b. Pupils need extensive practice in dividing words into syllables.

16c. Rules for dividing words into syllables probably ought to be taught.

16d. Rules for dividing words into syllables are of questionable value.

17a. Pupils must learn how to put accent marks over the proper syllable.

17b. Pupils need much practice in putting accent marks over the proper syllable.

17c. Pupils probably should have some experience in putting accent marks over syllables.

17d. Pupils do not need to learn to put accent marks over syllables in words.

18a. Questions about a selection should be kept to a minimum.

18b. Questions about a selection should be mainly factual to check on understanding.

18c. Questions about a selection should be about 50/50 between factual and inferential.

18d. Questions about a selection should be primarily inferential and evaluative.

Consider each of the following items as beginning: "From intermediate level through secondary . . ."

19a. Use of a dictionary for pronunciation is of vital importance.

19b. Dictionary skills are of minor importance.

19c. All dictionary skills are of equal value.

19d. Use of context + dictionary is essential.

20a. Instruction in phonic and structural analysis should continue through these grades.

20b. Emphasis should be on comprehension skills at the expense of the study skills.

20c. Emphasis should be on the study skills at the expense of the comprehension skills.

20d. Skill instruction should be equally balanced between comprehension and study skills.

21a. It is immaterial whether students' books contain fact or fiction.

21b. Students' books should contain mostly factual selections.

21c. Students' books should contain mostly fictional selections.

21d. Students' books should contain a balance of fact and fiction.

22a. The instructional emphasis in the content areas isn't important.

22b. Instructional emphasis in content areas should be on learning the facts.

22c. Instructional emphasis in content areas should be on learning concepts.

22d. Instructional emphasis in content areas should be on learning the study skills.

23a. The primary purpose for teaching literature is to develop good taste in reading.

23b. The primary purpose for teaching literature is to have students learn a body of information.

23c. The primary purpose for teaching literature is to acquaint students with literary allusions.

23d. The primary purpose for teaching literature is to develop inferential and critical reading skills.

24a. By secondary level, all "normal" students should be reading at grade level.

24b. By secondary level, no student should be reading more than two years below grade.

24c. By secondary level, no student should be reading below junior high level.

24d. By secondary level, some students will be reading as low as fourth grade level.

25a. Poor readers will have to use the grade level text.

25b. Poor readers will have to get basic information on their own.

25c. Poor readers will use taped recordings of the text and will benefit from the discussions.

25d. Poor readers will be provided material to read at their reading level.

CLARIFYING A PHILOSOPHY OF READING—ANSWER SHEET[1]

Grade Level: _____ Put "X" on your preferred answer.

What is Reading?

1a	1b	1c	1d
2a	2b	2c	2d
3a	3b	3c	3d
4a	4b	4c	4d
5a	5b	5c	5d

What is Readiness?

6a	6b	6c	6d
7a	7b	7c	7d
8a	8b	8c	8d

Content and Method

9a	9b	9c	9d
10a	10b	10c	10d
11a	11b	11c	11d
12a	12b	12c	12d
13a	13b	13c	13d
14a	14b	14c	14d
15a	15b	15c	15d
16a	16b	16c	16d
17a	17b	17c	17d
18a	18b	18c	18d
19a	19b	19c	19d
10a	20b	20c	20d
21a	21b	21c	21d
22a	22b	22c	22d
23a	23b	23c	23d
24a	24b	24c	24d
25a	25b	25c	25d

SUGGESTIONS FOR INTERPRETING "CLARIFYING A PHILOSOPHY OF READING"

Probably the most important function of this instrument is that it gets teachers to think in terms of specifics as they attempt to clarify their philosophies. It gives them a place to start.

As you and/or a committee attempt to evaluate the results, the most helpful discoveries will be your own analysis in terms of your philosophical inclinations. However, you might also be interested in certain patterns that might reveal themselves.

For items 1–5: the continuum (a–d) on each numbered item ranges from extremes of decoding to meaning, with the left side (a) being the decoding emphasis.

For items 6–8: the left side is the traditional informal view of readiness; the right, more cognitive oriented.

For items 9–18:   the left side tends toward a drill emphasis; the right, to application or understanding.

For items 19–25:   the left-hand columns tend to a factual/inflexible view; the right, more toward adaptation, balance, and an emphasis on understanding.

For item 20:   *b*, *c*, and *d* ought to be seen as fairly open choices for emphasis in any school.

In conclusion, your direction for action may be to take the results and respond in one of three ways:

1. "Well, that's just the way it is."
2. "Boy! Do we need some inservice!"
3. "Wow! Do I have a good staff!"

APPENDIX D

List of
Publishers' Addresses

Following is a select listing of major publishers. While many produce a variety of materials, specialties of particular interest to the principal are identified as follows:

    B = Basal reading series, including management systems
    D = Dictionaries
    H = High-interest, Low-vocabulary materials, including remedial skills booklets.
    L = Library selection references
    M = Management systems
    P = Professional organizations
    T = Test materials

H Addison-Wesley Publishing Company, Jacob Way, Reading, MA 01867.
B Allyn & Bacon, 470 Atlantic Avenue, Boston, MA 02210.
B American Book Company, 135 West 50th Street, New York, NY 10020.
T American College Testing Program, P.O. Box 168, Iowa City, IA 52240.
T American Guidance Service, Publishers Building, Circle Pine, MN 55014.

L   American Library Association, 50 East Huron Street, Chicago, IL 60611.

P   Association for Childhood Education International, 3615 Wisconsin Avenue, N.W., Washington, D.C. 20016.

H   Barnell Loft, 958 Church Street, Baldwin, NY 11510.

H   Benefic Press, 1900 North Naragansett, Chicago, IL 60639.

L   R. R. Bowker Company, 1180 Avenue of the Americas, New York, NY 10036.

H   Bowmar/Noble Publishers, 4563 Colorado Boulevard, Los Angeles, CA 90039.

T   California Test Bureau (McGraw Hill), Del Monte Research Park, Monterey, CA 93940.

L   Children's Book Council, 67 Irving Place, New York, NY 10003.

P   Council for Exceptional Children, 1920 Association Drive, Reston, VA 22091.

H   Developmental Learning Materials, 7440 Natchez Avenue, Niles, IL 60648.

H   Dexter & Westbrook. *See* Barnell Loft.

B   The Economy Company, Box 25308, 1901 North Walnut Street, Oklahoma City, OK 73125.

P   Education Commission of the States, 1860 Lincoln Street, Suite 300, Denver, CO 80203.

T   Educational Testing Service, Princeton, NJ 08540.

P   ERIC Clearinghouse on Reading and Communication Skills, 1111 Kenyon Road, Urbana, IL 61801.

H   Fearon Pitman Publishers. *See* Pitman Learning, Inc.

H   Field Educational Publications. *See* Addison-Wesley.

H   Follett Publishing Company, 1010 West Washington Boulevard, Chicago, IL 60607.

M   Fountain Valley. *See* Zweig Associates.

H   Garrard Publishing Company, 107 Cherry Street, New Canaan, CT 06840.

B   Ginn & Company, 191 Spring Street, Lexington, MA 02173.

H   Globe Book Company, 50 West 23rd Street, New York, NY 10010.

L   Great Books Foundation, 307 North Michigan Avenue, Chicago, IL 60601.

D   Grosset & Dunlap, 51 Madison Avenue, New York, NY 10010.

T   Gryphon Press, 220 Montgomery Street, Highland Park, NJ 08904.

B   Harcourt Brace Jovanovich, 757 Third Avenue, New York, NY 10017.

B   Harper & Row, 10 East 53rd Street, New York, NY 10022. *See* Lippincott.

H   Harr Wagner. *See* Addison-Wesley.

B   Holt, Rinehart & Winston, 383 Madison Avenue, New York, NY 10017.

L   Horn Book, Park Square Building, 30 St. James Avenue, Boston, MA 02116.

B   Houghton Mifflin, 2 Park Street, Boston, MA 02107.

P   Instructional Objectives Exchange, 10884 Santa Monica Boulevard, Los Angeles, CA 90025.

P   International Reading Association, 800 Barksdale Road, Newark, DE 19711.

H   Jamestown Publishers, Box 6743, Providence, RI 02904.

B   Laidlaw Brothers, Thatcher & Madison, River Forest, IL 60305.

B   J. B. Lippincott, 521 Fifth Avenue, New York, NY 10017.

B   Lyons and Carnahan. *See* Riverside Publishing Company.

B   Macmillan Publishing Company, 866 Third Avenue, New York, NY 10022.

H   McGraw-Hill Book Company, 1221 Avenue of the Americas, New York, NY 10020.

D   G. & C. Merriam Company, Springfield, MA 01101.

B   Charles E. Merrill Publishing Company, 1300 Alum Creek Road, Columbus, OH 43216.

P   National Association of the Deaf, 814 Thayer Avenue, Silver Springs, MD 20910.

P   National Association for the Education of Young Children, 1834 Connecticut Avenue, Washington, DC 20009.

P   National Council of Teachers of English, 1111 Kenyon Road, Urbana, IL 61801.

B   Open Court Publishing Company, Box 599, La Salle, IL 61301.

T   Personnel Press, 191 Spring Street, Lexington, MA 02173.

H   Pitman Learning, 6 Davis Drive, Belmont, CA 94002.

T   Psychological Corporation, 757 Third Avenue, New York, NY 10017.

B   Rand McNally. *See* Riverside Publishing Company.

B   Random House, 201 East 50th Street, New York, NY 10022.

H   Reader's Digest, Educational Division, Pleasantville, NY 10570.

P   Reading is Fun-Damental, L'Enfant 2500, Smithsonian Institute, Washington, DC 20560.

T   Riverside Publishing Company, 1919 Highland Avenue, Lombard, IL 60148.

H   Scholastic Magazine, 50 West 44th Street, New York, NY 10036.

H   Science Research Associates, N. Wacker Drive, Chicago, IL 60606

B   Scott, Foresman, 1900 East Lake Avenue, Glenview, IL 60025.

T   Slosson Educational Publications, 140 Pine Street, East Aurora, NY 14052.

P   Teachers College Press, 1234 Amsterdam Avenue, New York, NY 10027.

P   Charles C. Thomas, 301 East Lawrence Avenue, Springfield, IL 62717.

P   U.S. Government Printing Office, Superintendent of Documents, Washington, DC 20402.

H   Webster. *See* McGraw-Hill.

H   Weekly Reader, 245 Longhill Road, Middletown, CT 06457.

T   Western Psychological Services, 12031 Wilshire Boulevard, Los Angeles, CA 90025.

L   H. W. Wilson, 950 University Avenue, Bronx, NY 10452.

B   Winston. *See* Holt, Rinehart & Winston.

M   Wisconsin Design for Reading Skill Development, National Computer Systems, 4401 West 76th Street, Minneapolis, MN 55435.

H   Xerox Education Publications, 245 Longhill Road, Middletown, CT 06457.

M   Zweig Associates (Fountain Valley), 20800 Beach Boulevard, Huntington Beach, CA 92648.

Glossary
of Reading Terms

Abbreviation: a shortened form of a word, ending in a period *(Mr., Mrs.)*.
Contrast: **Acronym; Clipped Form; Portmanteau**

Abstraction, Levels of: *See:* **Levels of Abstraction**

Accent: *See:* **Stress**

Acronym: a coined word formed from the first letter(s) of each word in a compound term (NATO from North Atlantic Treaty Organization).

Affix: a bound morpheme attached either before (prefix) or after (suffix) a base word in English. *See:* **Prefix; Suffix**

Alexia: loss of previously acquired reading ability, usually a result of brain injury.

Alliteration: a literary device making use of repeated initial sounds ("seven silly snakes"). *See:* **Onomatopoetic Word**

Analytic Method: an approach to teaching beginning reading in which whole words are taught first. These words are then "analyzed" to develop phonic generalizations. Often referred to as "meaning emphasis" or "sight" approach. *Contrast:* **Synthetic Method**

Anomaly: a negative deviation—physical, emotional, intellectual—from the norm or typical; an abnormality.

antonym: a word that has the opposite meaning of another word (hot/cold).
Contrast: **Synonym**

263

Aphasia: loss of the ability to use language as a result of defect or injury of the brain. May be congenital or acquired and may be expressive and/or receptive.

Auditory: experienced through the sense of hearing; an auditory approach to reading refers to one that emphasizes hearing.

Auditory Acuity: sharpness of hearing.

Auditory Discrimination: the ability to distinguish between sounds; in reading, this ability requires distinguishing between sounds in spoken words: "hat/bat," "tone/ten."

Basal Reading Program: a series of graded texts, manuals, and ancillary materials designed to provide for sequential, consistent development of reading skills, usually encompassing grades K or 1 through 6 or 8.

Base: a free morpheme(s), unencumbered by affixes; the base of *runs* and *running* is *run*. Distinguished from **Root** or **Stem** only in the case of compounds, where *lighthouse* is a **Base** composed of two **Roots** or **Stems**.

Behavioral Objective: Specific instructional goals stated in observable, measurable terms.

Bibliotherapy: the use of reading material on topics related to the reader's personal concerns or problems in an effort to help solve those problems.

Blend: *See:* **Portmanteau.** (Often used inappropriately to refer to a **Consonant Cluster.**)

Borrowing: the practice of adding words from another language, with spelling and/or pronunciation sometimes changed.

Bound Morpheme: *See:* Morpheme

Checked Vowel: *See:* Vowel, Simple

Chronological Age: the number of years and months an individual has lived. *Contrast:* **Mental Age (MA)**

Clipped Form: a shortened version of a word *(gas* for *gasoline). Contrast:* **Abbreviation; Acronym; Portmanteau**

Closed Syllable: *See:* Syllable, Closed

Cloze: a procedure in which every *n*th word (usually every 5th or 10th) is deleted from a selection. Readers are to supply the missing words. Used to test for reading level of individuals, reading difficulty of materials, and also for instructional purposes.

Cluster: *See:* Consonant Cluster

Coined Word: an invented word, often from a trade name *(ditto* for any brand of duplicating paper; *kleenex* for any tissue).

Colloquialism: a word or expression characteristic of a regional dialect and considered too informal for use in "standard" English. *See:* **Dialect; Jargon; Slang**

Combining Form: a Greek or Latin root used to form English words *(uni-, -ology)*.

Combining Sentences: *See:* Sentence Combining

Complex Vowel: *See:* Vowel, Complex

Compound: A single unit formed by combining two or more free morphemes as "closed compounds" *(rowboat)*, "hyphenated compounds" *(law-abiding)*, or "open compounds" *(lead pencil)*. *See:* **Morpheme**

Configuration Clues: the general shape of a word, used as an aid in word recognition. While awareness of configuration adds speed to recognition, instruction in its use is of questionable value at beginning levels of reading.

Connotation: the emotional impact of words that goes beyond the denotation or dictionary meaning; *hamburger* and *ground beef* denote the same substance but have different connotations. *See:* **Denotation; Semantics**

Consonant: a sound, or letter representing a sound, produced by constriction of outgoing breath at a point or points between throat and lips. American English contains 21 consonant letters and 25 consonant phonemes. *Contrast:* **Vowel**

Consonant Cluster: a combination of two or more consonant letters, representing a "blending" of sounds they usually represent *(bl* in *blue, str* in *street)*. *Contrast:* **Digraph, Consonant**

Context: surrounding words in printed or spoken statements that aid in determining the meaning of a word in question.

Contraction: a word formed by shortening, through omission of phonemes (in speech) or letters replaced by an apostrophe (in writing) *(he will* = *he'll)*. *Contrast:* **Abbreviation; Acronym**

Controlled Vocabulary: a plan in basal readers, especially at primary levels, for fixing the rate and variety of words introduced in the selections to be read. *See:* **Vocabulary Load**

Corrective Reading: instruction in reading, within the classroom setting for individuals having a moderate deficiency in reading. *Compare:* **Developmental Reading; Remedial Reading**

Creative Reading: a process whereby the reader goes beyond ideas in print, using them as "jumping off points" to new or innovative ideas.

Criterion-Referenced Tests: tests used to determine if an individual can or cannot perform a certain act, with no concern for comparing that performance against the achievement of others. *Contrast:* **Norm-Referenced Tests**

Critical Reading: a thought process applied to printed material that results in justified action of conclusions on the part of the reader. It involves determination and evaluation of an author's stated or implied conclusions, based on objective evaluation of that author's supporting statements, as well as on analysis of the means—the logic and language—used to arrive at those conclusions. *Compare:* **Inferential Comprehension; Literal Comprehension**

Crossed Dominance: the preferred or consistent use of opposite hand and eye; for example, right hand and left eye, or left hand and right eye. Of doubtful significance in learning to read. *See:* **Lateral Dominance; Mixed Dominance**

Decoding: the basic reading process of converting the printed "code" into its speech forms or directly into the meaning units conveyed by the speech forms. *Contrast:* **Encoding**

Denotation: the lexical or dictionary meaning of a word (*house* and *home* both denote abodes). *Contrast:* **Connotation**

Derivation: a process whereby the grammatical function of a base is changed by the addition of a prefix or suffix. *See:* **Derivational Affix** *Contrast:* **Inflectional Affix**

Derivational Affix: a prefix or suffix that changes the grammatical function of a word (from the noun *friend* is derived *friendly, befriend*). *Contrast:* **Inflectional Affix**

Derivative: a word formed by adding a derivational affix to a base. *See:* **Derivational Affix**

Determiner: a member of a group of structure words in English, serving to "mark" or signal a noun (*the, a, many, some*). *See:* **Structure Word**

Developmental Reading: sequential instruction in reading skill development for individuals who are progressing typically for their age. *Contrast:* **Corrective Reading, Remedial Reading**

Diacritic or **Diacritical Mark:** a mark or symbol used with a letter in order to represent a sound as opposed to either a spelling or a letter name (ä represents the vowel sound in *father*; ā, the vowel sound in *make*).

Dialect: form of a language as spoken by a social or geographic group within the language community. Dialect may vary from the "standard" in pronunciation, vocabulary, or syntax, but not sufficiently to distinguish it as a separate language. *See:* **Colloquialism; Jargon; Slang**

Diagraph, Consonant: a combination of two consonant letters representing a single phoneme different from the phonemes usually represented by the letters (*sh, ch, th*). *Contrast:* **Consonant Cluster**

Digraph, Vowel: in traditional terminology, two vowel letters representing a single sound (*ea* in *meat, ie* in *grief*). *Contrast:* **Diphthong**

Diphthong: in traditional phonics, a blending of vowel sounds in a single syllable (*/oi/* in *boy*). A confusing classification sometimes reserved for /oi/ and /ou/ and sometimes including various complex vowel sounds. *See:* **Vowel, Complex** *Contrast:* **Digraph**

Disabled Reader: an individual whose reading ability is below potential or expectancy. The degree is often considered to be one year below at primary and 1½ years below potential at intermediate grades. *See:* **Reading Expectancy Level** *Contrast:* **Retarded Reader**

Dominance: *See:* **Lateral Dominance**

Due Process: the legally-required safeguards to which a person is entitled for self-protection; includes conferences, explanations, and appropriate waiting time before decisions are made.

Dyslexia: a term often synonymous with disabled reader or learning disability, used for an individual who is not reading up to expectancy level and the cause cannot be identified.

Eclectic Method: an approach to reading instruction that combines what the user considers strengths of a variety of approaches. *Compare:* **Analytic Method; Synthetic Method**

Encoding: the process of representing the spoken language with visual symbols; in English, the process of writing/spelling. *Contrast:* **Decoding**

Entry Word: the word in the alphabetical listing in a dictionary.

Eponym: a person's name used to designate the thing named after that person. (*sandwich* for Earl of Sandwich, *macadam* for John Macadam).

Etymologist: one who specializes in tracing the origin of words.

Etymology: the linguistic specialty dealing with the history or origins of words. *See:* **Etymologist; Linguistics**

Exceptional Child: a child who deviates significantly from the norm—above or below—in any attribute: intellectual, physical, academic.

Figurative Language: words or expressions used metaphorically or nonliterally for emotional or stylistic effect. *See:* **Idiom; Metaphor; Simile; Slang**

Fixation: the pause, during which actual reading takes place, as the eye moves across a line of print.

Flash Cards: individual cards with a word printed on each, used to provide practice in rapid recognition of words.

Flexible Reading Rate: the ability to adjust rate of reading according to the reader's purpose and the type of material being read.

Form Class Words: set of words that take certain affixes. There are four form classes: nouns, verbs, adjectives, and adverbs. *Contrast:* **Structure Words**

Formative Tests: achievement tests used to measure student accomplishment of particular portions or specific skills in an instructional program. Such tests are often criterion-referenced. *See:* **Criterion-Referenced Tests** *Contrast:* **Summative Tests**

Free Morpheme: *See:* **Morpheme**

Frustration Reading Level: the level of reading achievement at which an individual is unable to handle certain material. Usually defined as a level where the reader is below 95 percent word accuracy and below 75 percent comprehension. May also refer to the material used in this situation. *Compare:* **Independent Reading Level; Instructional Reading Level**

Function Word: *See:* **Structure Word**

Geminate Consonants: consonant letters that are doubled to represent a single phoneme in a word (*bb* in *rabbit, ll* in *yellow*).

Glided Vowel: *See:* **Vowel, Complex**

Grade Equivalent: a norm-referenced means of reporting achievement scores in terms of years and months. A score of 3.5 implies "third grade, fifth month" and is often *mis*interpreted as meaning that.

Grammar: the study of word classes, inflections, and syntax. *See:* **Form Class Words; Inflections; Structure Words; Syntax**

Grapheme: the minimal unit in writing, a letter or letters, used to represent a phoneme (sound) (*b* in *bat, th* in *thumb*). *See:* **Encoding; Morpheme; Phoneme**

Grapheme-Phoneme Correspondence: a decoding skill establishing the relationship between letter (grapheme) and the sound (phoneme) it usually represents (*b* usually represents the sound at the beginning of *bat*). Also referred to as "letter-sound association." *See:* **Decoding; Grapheme; Phoneme** *Contrast:* **Encoding; Phoneme-Grapheme Correspondence**

Guide Words: prominent pair of words in a dictionary, usually in boldface at the top of the page or facing pages, indicating the first and last entry word on the page. *See:* **Entry Word**

Homograph: one of two or more words with the same spelling, which may differ in pronunciation and/or meaning and/or origin (*pool*—table and *pool*—for swimming; *read* pronounced /rēd/ or /red/). "Homonym" is a confusing term sometimes applied to homographs, to homophones, or to words with multiple meanings. *Contrast:* **Homophone; Multiple Meanings**

Homonym: *See:* **Homograph; Homophone**

Homophone: one of two or more words with the same pronunciation, which may differ in spelling and/or meaning and/or origin (*pair, pare, pear*). *See:* **Homograph; Multiple Meanings**

Idiom: in any language, an expression whose meaning cannot be determined from the literal meaning of the individual words (*hit the ceiling, lose your head*). Idioms may be peculiar to a specific dialect or common to the entire language community. *See:* **Dialect**

Independent Reading Level: the level of reading achievement at which an individual can work without assistance. Usually defined as a level where the reader can function with at least 98% word accuracy and 90% comprehension. May also refer to the material used in this situation. *Compare:* **Frustration Reading Level; Instructional Reading Level**

Individualized Educational Plan (IEP): a specific written plan for each handicapped child that includes present level of development, specific goals to be achieved, and specific educational services to be provided.

Inferential Comprehension: the kind of understanding of a printed selection that is required to draw conclusions or to interpret what an author *means* by what was said in print. *Compare:* **Critical Reading; Literal Comprehension**

Inflected Count: a method used in tabulating the number of different words in material, whereby each different inflected form of a word is counted as a separate word (*play, plays, played* would be counted as three different words). *Contrast:* **Lexical Count**

Inflection: (1) a change in the pitch or volume of the voice; (2) a change in a base word to reflect number or tense, but with no change in that word's grammatical function. *See:* **Inflectional Affix**

Inflectional Affix: those prefixes or suffixes that change the tense or number of a base but do not change its grammatical function *(-s, -ed, -ing)*. Con-*trast*: **Derivational Affix**

Informal Reading Inventory (IRI): a device consisting of a graded series of reading selections and follow-up questions, used as an oral reading test to identify an individual's reading level.

Instructional Reading Level: the level of reading achievement at which an individual can work with guidance in certain material. Usually defined as a level where the reader can function with 95–98% word accuracy and 75–90% comprehension. May also refer to the material used in this situation. *Compare:* **Frustration Reading Level; Independent Reading Level**

Intonation: *See:* **Inflection**, definition #1

Jargon: the vocabulary—technical or idiomatic—peculiar to a specific group (educational jargon, medical jargon, and so on).

Juncture: the degree of pause in speech. Linguists identify four degrees: "plus" (I + scream vs. ice + cream); "single bar" (Our dog/Blackie/ . . .); "double bar" (associated with rising pitch, as in counting—one/ /two/ /three); and "double cross" (as at the end of a statement #). *See:* **Phoneme, Suprasegmental; Pitch; Stress**

Language: a system of communication, never clearly defined by linguists, consisting of common elements and mutually intelligible to its users; a broader category than dialect. *See:* **Dialect**

Language Experience Approach (LEA): an approach to reading instruction that uses the pupil's own dictated stories as vehicles for instruction.

Lateral Dominance: the preferred and consistent use of one side of the body over the other in terms of eye, hand, and foot. *See:* **Crossed Dominance; Mixed Dominance**

Lax Vowel: *See:* **Simple Vowel**

Learning Disability: a term often synonymous with disabled reader, used for an individual who is not reading up to potential and the cause cannot be identified. *See:* **Disabled Reader**

Learning Style: an individual's preferred way of learning, considering not only modalities but environmental factors such as heat/cold, bright or dim light, individual/group, self- or other-directed, and so on. *See:* **Modalities**

Least Restrictive Alternative: placement of handicapped pupils that assures that student's removal from regular classes will be no more than necessary to maximize his or her chances for the full educational program. *See:* **Mainstreaming**

Levels of Abstraction: semanticists' term for the varying degrees of specificity in communication, from the particular to the general. A concern in critical reading, where one may not jump from the specific—"Tabby scratches"—to the general—"Cats scratch."

Levels of Usage: degrees of formality or informality used in speaking or writing; for instructional purposes, the distinction of three levels should be adequate: extreme formal, standard, and informal. *See:* **Dialect; Jargon; Slang**

Lexical Count: a method used in tabulating the number of different words used in material whereby all "regular" inflected forms are considered repetitions of the same word (*play, plays, played* are counted as three occurrences of *play*). *See:* **Base Word; Inflection** *Contrast:* **Inflected Count**

Lexical Meaning: the "dictionary" or semantic meaning of a word as distinguished from its structural meaning as part of a sentence. *See:* **Structural Meaning**

Lexicon: the collection of words in a language. The English lexicon is divided into two groups of words, structure words and form class words. *See:* **Form Class Words; Structure Words**

Linguist: one whose discipline is the study of human languages.

Linguistics: the scientific study of languages dealing with phonology (sounds), morphology (structure/meaning), syntax (grammar), and etymology (origins). Subareas include psycholinguistics (the psychology of language), historical linguistics (language and word history), paralinguistics (nonverbal communication), and so on.

Listening Comprehension: the level of difficulty at which an individual can understand material read to him or her. A means of determining reading expectancy level. *See:* **Reading Expectancy Level**

Literal Comprehension: the process of understanding only directly stated facts in print, without drawing conclusions or evaluating. *Compare:* **Critical Reading; Inferential Comprehension**

"Long" Vowel: a phonics term often used by reading teachers to refer to the vowel sounds in *raid, reed, ride, rode,* and *few.* The term has nothing to do with the length of the vowel sound and is not synonymous with "complex." *See:* **Vowel, Complex; Vowel, Simple**

Mainstreaming: a less preferred term for "least restrictive alternative," meaning that handicapped pupils will be included in regular classes to the greatest extent possible to assure opportunity for a full educational program. *See:* **Least Restrictive Alternative**

Malaprop: a confused usage of words ("neon shirt" for "nylon shirt"). *See:* **Spoonerism**

Mental Age (MA): an intellectual ability score usually found by multiplying chronological age times IQ.

Metaphor: figurative language in which a comparison is implied between normally unlike things or actions. (The game was a circus.) *See:* **Figurative Language** *Contrast:* **Simile**

Minimal Pair: any two utterances containing only one significant difference in phonemes (*toy/boy, bat/bet*). *See:* **Phoneme, Segmental**

Minimal Terminal Unit: *See:* **T-Unit**

Miscue: a term referring to the miscalling of a word or words in oral reading.

Mixed Dominance: the inconsistent use or preference for a given hand and/

or eye, such as ambidexterity or ambieyedness. Of doubtful significance in reading achievement. *See:* Crossed Dominance; Lateral Dominance

Modality: the preferred sense used in learning: auditory, visual, or kinesthetic.

Morpheme: the smallest unit of meaning in a language. "Free" morphemes stand alone (*boy, play*), while "bound" morphemes must be attached to other morphemes (*-s, -ed*). Hence, *boys* and *played* are two-morpheme words.

Morphophonemic Alternations: shifts in pronunciation—with no change in spelling of the base—that often accompany derivational changes in words (*angel/angelic, athlete/athletic*). This fact of English makes reading-for-meaning easier and spelling-by-sound more difficult.

Multiple Meanings: most English words have more than one meaning. This feature is not to be confused with homographs, which have the same spelling but are listed as separate entry words. *See:* Homograph

Neologism: a newly coined word, developed by invention or by using an existing word with a new meaning. *See:* Coined Words

Nonstandard English: variations in the use of English—in vocabulary, pronunciation, or syntax—that differ from the "norm" or standard. *See:* Colloquialisms; Dialect; Jargon; Slang

Normal Curve Equivalent (NCE): a method of reporting scores that is similar to percentile except that the distance between any two NCEs is the same: a gain from NCE of 3 to 4 represents the same amount of growth as that from NCE of 49 to 50, whereas the distance between the 3rd and 4th percentile is much greater than that between the 49th and 50th.

Norm-Referenced Tests: standardized tests that measure performance in relation to others. *Contrast:* Criterion-Referenced Tests

Onomatopoetic Word: a word that sounds like the noise it refers to (*hiss, splash, whee*).

Open Syllable: *See:* Syllable, Open

Phoneme: the smallest significant unit of sound in a language. English contains about 46 phonemes: 25 consonant phonemes, 9 vowel phonemes, and 12 suprasegmental phonemes. *See:* Phoneme, Segmental; Phoneme, Suprasegmental; Vowel, Simple

Phoneme-Grapheme Correspondence: an encoding (spelling) skill establishing the relationship between a sound (phoneme) and the letter (grapheme) usually used to represent it. (*Laugh* is composed of three phonemes: /l/ represented by *l*, /a/ by *au*, and /f/ by *gh*.) Also called "sound-letter association." *See:* Encoding; Grapheme; Phoneme

Phoneme, Segmental: the smallest significant unit of sound in a language. (*Laugh* is made up of three phonemes: /l/, /a/, and /f/, and differs from *calf* by only one phoneme, the initial phoneme.) *See:* Minimal Pairs; Phoneme, Suprasegmental

Phoneme, Suprasegmental: the elements of pitch, stress, and juncture (pause) imposed on the segmental phonemes (sounds) of the language.

Linguists identify four levels of pitch, four of stress, and four of juncture in English. *See:* **Juncture; Phoneme, Segmental; Pitch; Stress**

Phonemics: a specialty within the linguistic area of phonology that deals with the study of phonemes. *Contrast:* **Phonetics; Phonics**

Phonetics: the study of the speech process: the production, transmission, and reception of speech sounds. *Contrast:* **Phonemics; Phonics**

Phonics: a method used in teaching beginning reading to establish letter-sound relationships. *See:* **Grapheme-Phoneme Correspondence**

Phonogram: a pronounceable unit or syllable of language, whether or not meaning is attached *(-at, -ick, -et)*; used to provide practice in word patterns by adding initial consonants. *See:* **Syllable**

Phonology: study of the sound structure of language, including phonemics and phonetics. *See:* **Phonemics; Phonetics**

Pitch: tonal quality in English speech that signals meanings. Linguists define four levels: 4 = very high, 3 = high, 2 = normal, 1 = low.

　　2　3　3　　　　　　　　　　　　2　2　3

"Is she home?" differs in meaning from "Is she home?"

See: **Juncture; Phoneme, Suprasegmental; Stress**

Portmanteau Word: a word created by the combination of existing words or word parts *(motel* from *motor hotel)*.

Prefix: an affix (bound morpheme) added to the front of a base and altering the meaning of that base *(un-* reverses the meaning of *lock)*. *See:* **Affix; Base Word; Morpheme, Bound**

Psycholinguistics: the study of the interrelationships between linguistics and psychological factors in human behavior.

Readability: a measure of the difficulty of printed matter, usually by use of a formula involving sentence length and word difficulty.

Reading: a process, vocal or subvocal, of approximating and reacting to ideas or information presented in visual form; most often restricted to printed form. *See:* **Decoding**

Reading Disability: *See:* **Disabled Reader**

Reading Expectancy Level (REL): the level at which an individual, given proper instruction, ought to be able to read. Usually determined through IQ or listening comprehension tests.

Reading Readiness: a multifaceted continuum of physical, cognitive, and affective elements, developed from birth to that stage (not a "go/no-go" point) when an individual has the skills, understandings, and attitudes necessary for beginning reading.

Rebus: a written statement using pictures for some or all of the words: "The (picture of a ball) is on the (picture of a table)."

Recognition Vocabulary: the collection of words an individual can read instantaneously and without aid of context, phonics, or structural analysis. Sometimes called "sight vocabulary."

Regression: a reverse eye movement performed in order to reread words already passed over in printed text.

Reliability: the extent to which a test yields consistent results over time and over items. Checked through test-retest or by comparison of results on items within the test. *Contrast:* **Validity**

Remedial Reading: instruction in reading, outside the regular classroom and individually or in small groups, for students severely disabled in reading. *Compare:* **Corrective Reading; Developmental Reading**

Retarded Reader: any individual reading below grade or age norms, regardless of potential. May include slow learners and/or disabled readers. *Compare:* **Disabled Reader**

Reversals: letters, words, or sentences read backwards ("b" for *d,* "was" for *saw*). Most often a result of lack of familiarity with print.

Root: *See:* **Base Word**

Running Words: in a word count, every word and every repetition of every word; all the words in a sample of speech or print ("The big boy rode the big bike" contains 7 running words but only 5 different words).

Scanning: rapid examination of print in order to find a specific item of information: a name, date, and so on. *Compare:* **Skimming**

Schema: a cognitive unit of knowledge and information on how to use that knowledge.

Schemata: plural of **Schema**

Schwa: the symbol ə or the sound it represents. It is the sound heard at the beginning of *abut* according to traditional dictionaries. According to G & C Merriam dictionaries, it is also the second vowel sound in that word, since they make no distinction whether that sound occurs in accented or unaccented syllables. The schwa is the most frequently used vowel sound in English.

Segmental Phoneme: *See:* **Phoneme, Segmental**

Semantics: the study of human communication as it influences human interaction, usually going beyond the denotation (lexican meaning) of words to consider their connotations (emotional effects). *See:* **Connotation: Denotation, Lexical Meaning**

Sentence Combining: a technique for developing sentence flexibility through experience in various ways of combining related ideas from simple sentences into complex sentences.

"Short" Vowel: reading teacher's term for the vowel sounds in *pat, pet, pit, pot,* and *putt*; not synonymous with "simple" vowel. *See:* **Vowel; Vowel, Simple**

Sight Vocabulary: *See:* **Recognition Vocabulary**

Simile: figurative language wherein a comparison is literally stated between unlike things or events: "The game was as funny as a circus." *Contrast:* **Metaphor**

Simple Vowel: *See:* Vowel, Simple

Skimming: rapid examination of print in order to get the gist or general idea of what it is about. *Compare:* **Scanning**

Slang: informal, nonstandard vocabulary used by a particular age or social group; usually consisting of coined or changed words, meanings, or figures of speech; similar to jargon but usually less lasting. *See:* **Colloquialism; Dialect; Jargon**

Slanting: a writing technique whereby an author deliberately selects emotionally loaded words to achieve a desired effect on the reader.

Slash Marks: the marks "/ /" used in writing by linguists to indicate that symbols so enclosed refer to the phoneme (sound) as opposed to the grapheme (letter) (/e/ refers to the vowel sound in *head* or *bed*, while *e* would be called by the letter name). Technically called "virgules."

Sound-Letter Association: *See:* **Phoneme-Grapheme Correspondence**

Spoonerism: a confused juxtaposition of sounds in words ("It's kisstomary to cuss the bride."). *See:* **Malaprop**

SQ3R (Survey, Question, Read, Recite, Review): a technique useful as an aid to recall or memory in reading study-type or factual material. Variations of this original include SQ4R, SQROCQ, PQRST, OK4R.

Standard English: the broad "norm" of English as spoken or written by most native English speakers; includes some agreement on vocabulary, pronunciation, and syntax. *See:* **Colloquialism; Dialect; Jargon; Slang**

Standardized Reading Test: *See:* **Norm-Referenced Tests**

Stem: *See:* **Base Word**

Stress: the degree of force or emphasis with which a sound or word is pronounced. Linguists identify four levels of stress: primary (′), secondary (^), tertiary (`), and weak (˘); often combined with pitch to signal meanings; important too in pronouncing homographs such as *re cord′* and *rec′ ord*. *See:* **Juncture; Phoneme, Segmental; Pitch**

Structural Analysis: the process of examining a word for its component parts, either morphemes or syllables. *See:* **Morpheme; Syllable**

Structural Meaning: knowledge of the function of a word, based on understanding of the syntax of the language. The English speaker has structural meaning for *gleap* and *glipped* in "The gleap glipped," even though these words have no lexical meaning. Also called "syntactic meaning." *Contrast:* **Lexical Meaning**

Structure Word: any word not a member of the four form classes. Structure words (determiners, prepositions, connectives, and so on) have little or no lexical meaning; they serve to tie together the form classes into meaningful syntactic patterns, thereby providing structural meaning. Also called "function words." *See:* **Lexical Meaning; Structural Meaning**

Subvocal Reading: the practice of some readers of saying the words to themselves while supposedly reading silently. Subvocalization may range from actual lip movement and whispering to a nearly immeasurable vibration of the throat. The latter is "normal"; the former is expected only at the beginning stages of reading and becomes a handicap if continued at higher levels.

Suffix: an affix (bound morpheme) added to the end of a base word to alter meaning or form class. Suffixes may be inflectional *(-s, -ed)* or derivational *(-ful, -able)*.

Summative Tests: achievement tests used to measure achievement of ultimate goals or to "summarize" achievement. Such tests are usually norm-referenced. *See:* **Norm-Referenced Tests** *Contrast:* **Formative Tests**

Suprasegmental Phoneme: *See:* **Phoneme, Suprasegmental**

Syllabic Consonant: a final consonant phoneme that comprises the entire final syllable of a word (in *certain* and *battle*—contrast *captain* and *capital*—/n/ and /l/ are the final syllables). Some dictionaries show this final syllable with a vestige of a schwa—a superscript schwa preceding the consonant sound.

Syllabication: the process of determining the point of division between syllables in a word. There are at least three different standards for such division: visual or entry word *(yel-low)*, which is the writing convention; speech syllabication (/yel-ō/); and morphemic or meaning syllabication *(bomb-ard* vs. *bom-bard)*. *See:* **Syllable; Syllable, Closed; Syllable, Open**

Syllable: the next larger unit of sound beyond a phoneme, consisting of at least a vowel sound or syllabic consonant and usually one or more consonant sounds; *syllable* contains three syllables: *syl-la-ble* or /sil-ə-bəl/. *See:* **Syllabication; Syllable, Closed; Syllable, Open**

Syllable, Closed: any syllable ending in a consonant sound; the first syllable in *babble* vs. that in *baby*.

Syllable, Open: any syllable ending in a vowel sound; the first syllable in *baby* vs. that in *babble*.

Synonym: a word whose denotation (lexical meaning) is similar to that of another word *(sour* and *tart* are synonyms). *See:* **Denotation; Lexical Meaning**

Syntactic Meaning: *See:* **Structural Meaning**

Syntax: that portion of grammar that deals with the way words are strung together to form meaningful phrases, clauses, and sentences. *See:* **Grammar**

Synthetic Method: an approach to teaching beginning reading in which a sound is taught for each letter. Then the sounds are blended or "synthesized" in order to sound out words. Often referred to as a "phonics-first" approach. *Contrast:* **Analytic Method**

Tachistoscope: a device used to flash print at a rapid rate as part of instruction in word recognition or speed reading.

Tense Vowel: *See:* **Complex Vowel**

Token: in a word count, each appearance and repetition of a word or pattern in the lexicon (in counting the representations of /ā/, *pain, raid,* and *take* are three tokens but only two types—*ai* and *a-e*). *Contrast:* **Types**

Trade Books: library books or nontext books; those books used for recreational reading as opposed to text or reference materials.

T-Unit (Minimal Terminal Unit): any independent clause with all its subordinate clauses and modifiers. The number of words used, per T-unit, is a good measure of sophistication in expressive language, oral or written.

Types: the distinct varieties of words or patterns found in a lexicon (*ai* and *a-e* are the two **Types** found in the four **Tokens** *rain, sake, brake, lake*). *Contrast:* **Tokens**

VAKT (Visual, Auditory, Kinesthetic, Tactile): a technique for learning words; usually reserved for severely disabled readers.

Validity: the extent to which a test measures what it claims to measure. *Compare:* **Reliability**

Virgules: *See:* **Slash Marks**

Visual Acuity: sharpness of vision.

Visual Discrimination: the ability to distinguish similarities and differences. In reading, awareness of the fine differences in shape or direction that distinguish one letter from another.

Vocabulary Load: the variety and difficulty of words at a given level. The more difficult and different the words, the higher the readability of the selection. *See:* **Controlled Vocabulary**

Vowel: a sound, or letter representing a sound, produced by vibration of the vocal chords without blockage of air between throat and lips. There are seven to nine vowel phonemes in English, which combine with each other or with the semi-vowels /y/ and /w/ to form an additional eight complex vowels, resulting in the approximately fifteen vowel sounds represented in a dictionary key. *See:* **Vowel, Simple; Vowel, Complex** *Contrast:* **Consonant**

Vowel, Complex: a vowel "sound" made up of more than one phoneme, usually beginning with a simple vowel followed by /y/ or /w/ glide. The complex vowel sounds usually identified are those in *bait, beet, bite, boat, butte, bout, boot, boy*; sometimes called "glided" or "tense" vowels, but not synonymous with "long" vowel. *Contrast:* **Vowel, Simple**

Vowel Digraph: a term from phonics referring to a combination of vowel letters representing a vowel sound (*ea* in *head*). More simply referred to as an alternate spelling of that sound.

Vowel, Simple: the vowel sounds consisting of one phoneme, without glides. Only seven exist in most dialects: the vowel sounds in *pit, pet, pat, putt, pot, put, paw*. Sometimes called "checked" or "lax" but not synonymous with "short" vowel. *Contrast:* **Vowel, Complex**

Word Analysis: the use of phonic and/or structural elements in a word in order to figure out or "read" that word. *Contrast:* **Word Recognition** *Compare:* **Word Identification**

Word Attack: *See:* **Word Identification**

Word Identification: the use of any or all decoding skills to figure out or "read" a strange word. *Contrast:* **Word Recognition** *Compare:* **Word Analysis**

Word Recognition: the process of reading or calling a printed word instantaneously, without aid of context, phonics, or structural analysis. *Contrast:* **Word Analysis; Word Identification**

Name Index

279

Subject Index